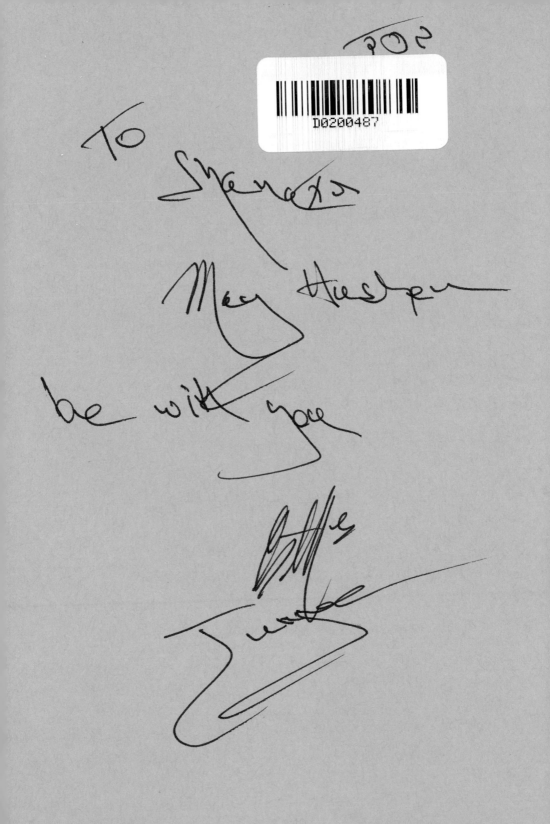

THE SHAAR PRESS

THE JUDAICA IMPRINT
FOR THOUGHTFUL PEOPLE

LIFE IS

IS

A
SHAAR
PRESS
PUBLICATION

REBBETZIN ESTHER JUNGREIS

A TEST

How to meet life's challenges successfully

Published by **SHAAR PRESS**
Distributed by MESORAH PUBLICATIONS, LTD.
4401 Second Avenue / Brooklyn, N.Y 11232 / (718) 921-9000 / www.artscroll.com

Distributed in Israel by SIFRIATI / A. GITLER
6 Hayarkon Street / Bnei Brak 51127

Distributed in Europe by LEHMANNS
Unit E, Viking Business Park, Rolling Mill Road / Jarrow, Tyne and Wear, NE32 3DP/ England

Distributed in Australia and New Zealand by GOLDS WORLD OF JUDAICA
3-13 William Street / Balaclava, Melbourne 3183 / Victoria Australia

Distributed in South Africa by KOLLEL BOOKSHOP
Ivy Common / 105 William Road / Norwood 2192, Johannesburg, South Africa

ISBN 10: 1-4226-0196-X
ISBN 13: 978-1-4226-0196-9

Printed in the United States of America by Noble Book Press
Custom bound by Sefercraft, Inc. / 4401 Second Avenue / Brooklyn N.Y. 11232

Table of Contents

Dedication *v*

Acknowledgments *vii*

Book I: Tests of Learning Who You Really Are 9
    Chapter One: Life Is a Test 11
    Chapter Two: Recognize Your Potential 25
    Chapter Three: Who Are You? 39
    Chapter Four: Hearing Your Inner Voice 55
    Chapter Five: To Be a Jew 73
    Chapter Six: But I'm Not Religious! 91

Book II: Tests of Relationships 113
    Chapter Seven: Finding your Soul Mate 115
    Chapter Eight: When Love Spells Disaster 139
    Chapter Nine: Who Wins 161
    Chapter Ten: Not the Horse I Wanted 177
    Chapter Eleven: As Smart as a Rooster 193
    Chapter Twelve: Why? 207

Book III: When Tests Are Wake-Up Calls 221
    Chapter Thirteen: Wake-Up Calls 223
    Chapter Fourteen: He Has Not Forgotten Us 243
    Chapter Fifteen: When the Tests Are Miracles 259

Epilogue 277

Dedication

I have been very blessed in life, for I have lived among great human beings who knew how to pass the many difficult tests of life with faith, courage, and fortitude — my saintly, revered parents, HaRav HaGaon, HaTzaddik, Avraham HaLevi Jungreis, *zt"l*, my mother, Rebbetzin Miriam Jungreis, *o"h*, and my beloved husband, HaRav Meshulem HaLevi Jungreis, *zt"l*. Their Torah, their shining examples, their wise words, their acts of kindness, are forever with me and help me pass my own life tests.

I continue to be very blessed, for G-d has granted me children — Rabbi Shlomo and Chaya Sora Gertzulin,

Rabbi Yisroel and Rivkie Jungreis, Mendy and Slovie Wolff, and Rabbi Osher and Yaffa Jungreis — and precious grandchildren and great-grandchildren who lend joy and meaning to my every day. I dedicate this book to them.

My dearest children — words cannot express my love for you. You are everything a mother, a grandmother, could wish for. You have filled the painful vacuum, the terrible emptiness left in my life when Zeide, Mama, and Abba were called on High. I pray that *HaShem* bless you, watch over you, and grant you *much naches*. May you see children, grandchildren, and great grandchildren follow the path of Torah and *mitzvos*. May *HaShem* always bless you with His choicest blessings, for you are a blessing.

Your mother, who loves you with all her heart and soul
V'nafshi k'shurah b'nafsham.

Acknowledgments

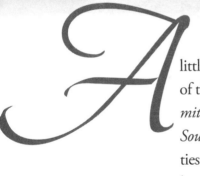A little less than a year ago, I undertook the writing of this book. In the past, when I wrote *The Committed Life*, *The Committed Marriage*, and *Jewish Soul on Fire*, I curtailed many of my other activities. With this book, however, I did not have that luxury. Not only did I not reduce my work load, but as things turned out, additional responsibilities were added to my already heavy schedule here in the United States, as well as worldwide.

The title of my book, *Life Is a Test*, has always been a reality of my own life. As I wrote each chapter, I often smiled to myself and found strength in the words, "Life is a test and *HaShem* has and will continue to help me pass." So first and foremost, I must express my gratitude to *HaShem*, Who enabled me to write this book, deliver it on schedule, and helped me pass my tests. I ask only that He allow me to serve Him with honor and a joyous heart, and it is to that service that I dedicate my life.

And now it's time to express gratitude to all the special people who have helped me along the way.

Firstly, my deepest of thanks to Barbara Janov, Executive Director of Hineni, who is always at my side, who patiently fed the computer night after night after we returned from Hineni Torah classes in Manhattan, and who brought the laptop along on all my programs in the United States and abroad.

A heartfelt *yasher koach* to the publishers and editorial staff of ArtScroll Mesorah Publications — to Rabbi Nosson Scherman, who carefully reviewed every chapter and whose input was invaluable; to Rabbi Meir Zlotowitz, who, with great enthusiasm, packaged the project; to Eli Kroen, for his creative cover design; to Yosef Wartelsky, for the cover concept; to project coordinator Gavriel Aryeh Sanders, to whom this work is a labor of love; to my patient editor, Mrs. Judi Dick; to the conscientious team of proofreaders and typesetters, including Felice Eisner, Yehudit Sanders, Esty Lebovits, and Shevy Grossman, who all gave the manuscript priority treatment.

I would also like to thank my son-in-law, Rabbi Shlomo Gertzulin, Executive Director of *Agudas Yisroel*, and Rabbi Moshe Kolodny, Chief Archivist of *Agudas Yisroel* for their research, and Tania Cohen, our Hineni secretary, for e-mailing all the chapters to the publisher, and my wonderful extended family of Hineni, my students and friends throughout the world. Your friendship and love mean so much to me. Finally, I would once again like to thank my children and grandchildren. Please know that wherever I go, wherever I am, you are always with me.

Book I

Tests of Learning Who You Really Are

"All that befalls us in this world, the good as well as the bad, are tests..."

Rabbi Moshe Chaim Luzzatto
Mesillas Yesharim — The Path of the Just

1

Life Is a Test

I was born at a turbulent time in history. The Nazi Party had gained ascendancy in Germany, the winds of war were blowing throughout Europe, and we felt the fury of the impending storm in Hungary, the country of my birth. There had always been anti-Semitism in Hungary, but we had managed to live with it, even as one endures inclement weather. But now, the powerful Nazi influence transformed anti-Semitism into a politically correct ideology. Overnight, the world became a hunting ground — we Jews became the *hunted* and the remainder of the world, the *hunters*.

My father was the Chief Rabbi of our city, Szeged, the second largest city in Hungary and the hub to which all young Jewish men were gathered by the Hungarian authorities for deportation to slave-labor camps. Our home became a haven for them and their families. Day and night, people knocked at our door, seeking lodging, guidance, and blessings. With infinite patience and kindness, my father attended to all their needs, while my mother lovingly served them hot meals and provided them with care packages for the road.

With the Nazi occupation, our little apartment became the center of the ghetto. Jews were brought in from the provinces and countless people moved in with us. My mother's cooking was now very limited since supplies were simply not available. We survived on meager starvation rations, but when we were deported to the concentration camps, even that came to an end. Day and night, the message was driven home to me — *the world is divided into two — the hunters and the hunted, and we were the hunted.* As young as I was, the reality of death never left me.

My paternal grandparents, my aunts, uncles, and cousins, were all killed in the gas chambers and crematoria of Auschwitz. Through the grace of G-d, my parents, siblings, and I survived and made our way to these blessed shores. With the passage of time, my life returned to normal, and we, who only yesterday were *the hunted*, became *builders.* Yes, we were committed to build a better, kinder, more peaceful world. The years passed quickly and I soon became a bride. I married a magnificent man, a spiritual giant, a third cousin (with the same family name), also a survivor of the Holocaust, and together, we continued to build. We built synagogues, schools, and communities, and most important, we built lives. The struggle was no longer one of mere survival, but rather, for more meaning and more purpose.

Then suddenly, without warning, the Angel of Death came calling once again, albeit this time it was obvious that he was sent from the One Above Who measures our days and decides when it is time to return home. He was calling my husband — that gentle, wise soul. Cancer had overtaken his life and in six short weeks it was over. Now I had to wrestle with a new challenge — not how to survive in a world of hunters, nor how to live a meaningful life, but how to continue after G-d called my beloved home.

My husband and I were a team. Together we built, together we taught, planned, and dreamed. Our vision was quite simple, and yet awesome: to share the wisdom of our faith with our people. Now my partner, my Rabbi, was gone. How could I carry on alone? It was he who would raise my spirits when the going was rough; it was he who would erase the furrows of worry from my brow with his warm, loving smile. Even now I can hear his voice. "When there is no reason to smile, put a smile on your face and G-d will give you every reason to smile. Wipe out all negative thoughts — just wipe them out! Everything will be good" — and with *him*, it was good. We shared so much together, there was so much that had to be done. We were blessed with what our sages call "*shalom bayis*" — a tranquil, peaceful home.

Admittedly, we did have one source of conflict. My husband was a compulsive collector. If he read something that he liked, he would clip it and put it away. He also compiled copious notes on his speeches, and over the years these papers piled up. Time and again I would tell him that I was drowning in a sea of papers, that he should discard some of them, but my words went unheeded.

As our children grew up, married, and moved into their own homes, he filled the dresser drawers in their rooms with the overflow of his papers. In vain did I complain, but today, I thank G-d that he did not take my complaints to heart, for it was among those papers that I found a message that has kept me going. It took me a while after his passing to go through his many folders. I couldn't bear to touch them — it was too painful, but then, my children, who were always at my side, came to help and together, we found a note written in his bold, beautiful hand, "A long life is not good enough, but a good life is long enough. Thank you." The words kept repeating themselves in my mind. It was as if my husband was sending me a message, telling me that he was grateful for the *good years* that G-d had granted him and urging me to continue to strive to make the years that remained to me "good."

This goodness cannot be measured by the length of our years, but by *how* we live those years. This goodness is not about what we amass, but what we *give*; it is not *having more*, but *being more*, for in the end, our lives are judged not by the businesses, houses, and portfolios that we built, but by the lives we touched and made better. Once this realization becomes part of our psyches, our entire attitude towards life will be altered. Instead of being consumed by competitiveness, serenity will set in, a serenity that will enable us to say "thank you" for the life that G-d has given us.

Instead of feelings of entitlement, we will be overcome by feelings of indebtedness, a need to give back, to make a difference in the world. Ten years have gone by since my husband was called on High, but to this day, I meet people who, with tears in their eyes and a loving smile, remember their Rabbi who touched their hearts. So, yes, my husband lived a "good life."

But you may argue that not everyone can build a synagogue, not everyone is a wise gentle Rabbi, and not everyone can *live that good life*, so how can *you* make a difference in the world?

Every person has been created to make a difference — every person has been shaped and molded by G-d for a special mission that only he or she can fulfill, and if we have lost sight of that mission, it is only because we no longer know how to identify it.

"What is life all about?" At one time or another, all of us wrestle with that challenge. Having no clear answer we tend to dismiss this question and continue our humdrum existence or attempt to define our lives through metaphors such as "Life is a deck of cards, and you have to play the hand you are dealt" or "Life is a marathon — not only do you have to run, but you have to come in first" or "Life is a game and you have to know how to play it", and more, "Life is a stage, and you have to act your part 'til the curtain falls." We embrace these metaphors because, as facile as they may be, in essence, they represent our reality. They reflect our 21st century mores, culture and life-style.

If we believe that life is a deck of cards, then it follows that we are just pawns in a world that lacks rhyme or reason, for the hand we are dealt is mere chance and beyond our control. Unable to shape our destiny, it is easy to become cynical, fatalistic, and bitter, especially if we are dissatisfied with our lot. We throw up our hands and conclude "It is what it is — there's nothing we can do about it." So, we either succumb to hopelessness and despondency, or we go to the other extreme and "live it up" in an orgy of self-indulgence. Neither option is terribly attractive.

For those who believe that life is a marathon, the only thing that really counts is coming in first. They keep running — they cannot stop, and if in the process they crush those who stand in their way or neglect those who need them most, so be it — it's justified. After all, life is a marathon.

Some years ago, I read a brief news item in *The New York Times* about an Olympics for Special Children in Seattle, Washington. It was a small blurb, innocuously placed, and I would probably have missed it had my daughter not pointed it out to me. The story was about disabled children who competed in a race. When the whistle sounded, they started to run. Suddenly, one of the young boys fell, skinned his knee, and began to cry. When the others heard his cry, they stopped in their tracks, turned around, and went to his aid. One little girl, who had Down Syndrome, bent down, kissed his knee and said, "Here, this will make it feel better." The children helped the boy to his feet, linked hands, and ever so slowly, they all walked as one to the finish line.

Could it be that these children know something that those who are running have lost sight of? A world-renowned Torah sage in the holy city of B'nei Brak, Israel and a revered Rosh Yeshivah, the Dean of a Rabbinic academy in New York, would both stand up for Down Syndrome children, for they believed that these souls are pure and holy and possess wisdom that our sophisticated world has yet to grasp.

One must wonder, who is disabled?

During my high school years, I read a short story that was so powerful that it has remained with me all this time. It was about a king who issued a proclamation calling for a national marathon. The winner would be awarded all the land that he covered, declared the king. There was great excitement in the kingdom. Among his subjects was a poor peasant, who saw this race as the opportunity of a lifetime — his one chance to become rich. He practiced day and night — he was determined to win. His wife called out to him. "Not now," he said, "wait until I win!" His sons and daughters tried to catch his attention, and to them too, he gave the same response. His friends and neighbors called for his help, but he was so focused on his running that he never even heard them. His ailing old father cried out in pain, but he never heard his plea. "When the race is won and the land is mine," he told himself, "I will attend to everyone." He was determined to win and become rich — and win he did! He was led to the king to collect his reward. His life dream would now be fulfilled. But no sooner did he arrive at the palace than he collapsed and died.

It's just a story, but it could be the story of any one of us. We run, we run, and never see those who are near and dear to us. We delude ourselves into believing that we are doing it all for their sake, but in the process, it is *they* who are sacrificed. Too late do we discover that although we may have won the race, we have lost our families, our friends, our very lives.

Then there are those who view life as a game, and to them, the end goal is *fun*. The main thing is to have a good time. They seek one form of entertainment after another — entire industries have been created to indulge them in their quest. From movies to sports, to the latest in computer games, there are myriad distractions guaranteed to numb and anesthetize their hearts and minds. There was a time, in the not-too-distant past, when people took walks to clear their heads, to contemplate and reflect upon their lives, but such introspective moments are relics of the past. Today, when people walk and jog, cell phones and iPods accompany them — all filtering out reality. One cannot help but wonder what would happen if all theaters, movie houses, television stations, sports stadiums, computers and iPods were shut down for one day. How would these people fare? Would they fall apart? For those to whom life is a game, distractions become necessities — tools through which they can escape the challenge of their reality.

Finally, for those to whom the metaphor that rings truest is "Life is just a stage," they will go through the motions, but it's all an act. They live their lives without ever discovering who they really are. From time to time, they may have moments of clarity, moments when they hear the still, small voice of their conscience prodding them, calling them — but not knowing how to respond, they bury their angst with all sorts of diversions. They indulge in shopping sprees, an extravagance that was once limited to the rich, but which credit cards have now made accessible to almost everyone. The media and Madison Avenue all conspire to seduce people into believing that they need more, that if they have the "newest" and the "latest," they will find the happiness they crave — so they discard the old and obsessively continue to shop. But the high of acquisition quickly palls, and as much as they try, they cannot escape the purposelessness of their lives. Long ago, the Torah admonished us "Not by bread alone does man live, but by everything that emanates from the mouth of G-d..." (*Deuteronomy* 8:3). Having no comprehension of that which emanates from G-d, they find solace in artificial stimuli, be it shopping, a pill, a drink or drugs.

In the end, it doesn't matter with which metaphor we chose to identify — they all short-change us and rob us of the essence of our lives.

So what is life?

"*Hafoch bah, hafoch bah, d'kulah bah,*" — "Turn the pages, turn the pages, everything is [to be found] therein" is the wise counsel of our sages. Turn the pages of G-d's Book, the Torah, the Bible, and therein find your answers. When people consult me seeking guidance for their problems, I never express my own opinion, for I might be wrong, and people's lives are too precious to play with. Consider the "magic" panaceas that only yesterday were regarded as sacrosanct, but that today have been discredited. Not only were they of no avail, but worse, they wrought havoc in people's lives. The advice these new-age gurus offered encompassed a wide range of subjects, from raising children to the feminist movement, to diet, medication, and so on. Alas, I have seen the casualties, the people who suffered by following the proponents of these different life styles and philosophies; as well intentioned as some of them may have been, they misled an entire

Life Is a Test

generation and caused untold damage. The teachings that I proffer are based on eternal truths that have passed the test of time — truths that were authored by the One Who created us and I substantiate everything with chapter and verse from our Creator's instruction manual — the Torah.

Even as every reputable manufacturer knows that, along with his product, he must provide an instruction manual, so our Heavenly Father Who created us, would not have launched us onto this planet without first providing us with guidance and direction. The Torah is that instruction manual. Within its pages, the purpose of our lives, our sojourn on this planet, are defined. We need only study it and it will all become clear to us.

But to which page should we turn? Which chapter? Which verse will provide us with the answers that we seek? Our sages advise us to search for the very first time that a subject is mentioned in the Torah, for that is always definitive. Another key is to probe the inner meaning of the Hebrew in which it was written, for therein are to be found untold treasures. Hebrew is unlike any other language. It is the Holy Tongue, the language in which G-d Himself spoke, and no translation can do it justice. It is by probing these two avenues – the Torah and the Hebrew language — that we will try to understand the true metaphor for life.

From the Torah we learn that the definitive metaphor for life is a *test*. It is written that G-d *tested* the patriarch Abraham (*Genesis* 21:22), to which Abraham responded "Hineni, here I am," ready to do Your bidding, to fulfill the purpose for which You created me." On ten different occasions, Abraham was tested and he passed each time. G-d continues to test each and every one of us. These tests are custom-made, designed with our unique needs in mind, so that we might discover and fulfill the higher purpose for which He created us.

From the moment we are born, to the day that G-d calls us, we are *tested*. In essence, everything is a test, and once we absorb this, it will become easier to bear the many challenges and trials of life. These tests come in many shapes and forms — the way we relate to G-d, to our parents, our teachers, our peers, our neighbors, our co-workers, our colleagues, even to a clerk in a store, the waiter in a restaurant, or a fellow driver on the road, are all tests. These tests reflect the genuineness of our commitment, the depth of our faith and the measure of our character, and at the end of the day, we are marked "pass" or "fail." In the "University on High," even little things — things that we would normally consider innocuous and insignificant — count, and therefore, are tests. For example, we wake up in the morning and have a mental tug of war over whether we should get up and pray or be kind to ourselves and linger in bed just a little bit longer. After all, we reason, our little prayer won't make a difference; it won't really matter to G-d whether we pray or not. In any event, G-d would certainly want us to take care of ourselves and protect our health. We need our sleep. But how much sleep do we really need? Six hours? Eight hours? How much?

The *Yetzer Hara* — the evil inclination, that little voice inside us that seeks to entice and divert us from passing our test and fulfilling our higher purpose — will cunningly persuade us that we need *"just a few minutes — never a few hours,* more." "*A few more hours*" we would reject out of hand, but *a few minutes more* seems reasonable enough, so we succumb. We allow ourselves to be seduced and shut our eyes for those *few minutes more,* but those few minutes turn into many minutes and sometimes even a lifetime. We failed that little test, and now we find ourselves in a downward spiral, for one little failure will lead to another and we never realize that we are being tested and are failing. To be sure, every once in a while, we sense a void in our lives — something is missing, but we don't quite know what. We feel restless, lonely, and depressed. With renewed zeal, we immerse ourselves in our chosen metaphors, hoping that they will provide us with the relief we so desperately seek, as life passes us by.

But, you may argue, if there is such a force as the *Yetzer Hara* that exists for the sole purpose of misleading and diverting us, how can we possibly hope to pass the test? Aren't the cards stacked against us?

"I have created the *Yetzer Hara*," G-d proclaimed, "but fear not, I created the Torah as an antidote to it…" (Talmud). "You need only anchor yourself to Torah and you will not only pass every test, but you will grow and thrive."

But more significantly, why does G-d have to test us? A physician has to test his patients to determine the nature of their illness, a teacher has to test his students to evaluate their progress, but why does an all-knowing G-d Who sees everything, Who is familiar with even the most secret machinations of our hearts — why does He have to test us?

Undoubtedly, our Creator knows us. He knows every fiber of our being. He knows our strengths as well as our weaknesses, but the problem is that *we do not know our own selves*, our own potential. We have no understanding of the energy that G-d planted within our souls — therefore, G-d has to test us to bring forth those treasures that are buried deep within ourselves and make us unique.

In the Holy Tongue, the word for "tested" is "*neesa.*" "*V'HaElokim neesa es Avraham*" — "And G-d tested Abraham" (*Genesis* 22:1). There are three additional meanings to be found in the word "*neesa,*" and if we find the connecting link between them, we will come to appreciate the deeper meaning of the tests that G-d sends our way:

1) "*Neesa*" — tested

2) "*Neesayon*" — trial or challenge

3) "*Nes*" — flag or banner — something that you raise on high

4) "*Nes*" — miracle

So once again, what is the connecting link between these four words?

G-d, our Heavenly Father Who created us, loves us with great intensity. Each and every one of us is precious to Him. Like a good parent, He wants us to achieve and attain our potential, to walk on the right path, so He sends us wake-up calls — *tests,* in the form of *trials* and tribulations.

But we protest — why do we have to undergo trials and tribulations? Why do these tests have to be so painful?

Let us take a lesson from nature. When digging for oil, gold, or water — or for that matter, anything precious — before that treasure is discovered, dirt and muddy sediment must be unearthed. Simply walking through or contemplating locations for the dig will not yield anything. This same principle holds true for the treasures buried in the crevices of our souls. Unfortunately, no one attains greatness by living a life of ease, going to parties, playing golf, sunning on the beach, and making money. All that does not transform anyone into a better, wiser, kinder, and more sensitive person. Alas, all too often, it does just the opposite.

Even a superficial perusal of history will demonstrate that the great personalities of every generation, to say nothing of our prophets, prophetesses, patriarchs, and matriarchs, suffered and lived lives that were laden with pain. There is a well known saying, "In a desert, there is always sunshine, but for growth you need rain, and for creativity, you need thunderstorms. If we reflect upon this, we will quickly realize that the trials and tribulations that G-d sends our way are tests that are designed to enable us to grow and realize our true potential. If we can do that, we will discover our *flag,* our *banner* — our *identity,* our *unique mission,* the purpose for which our

Creator propelled us onto this planet. If we can accomplish that, we will become "*banners*" for our children, our grandchildren, and all future generations. Thus, everything that the Patriarch Abraham and those who followed in his path experienced were *tests that became banners* — banners that provide hope and direction, banners which, to this very day, serve as beacons of light, banners that lead us to our ultimate destination. Whether we are experiencing personal trauma or we are in the throes of national calamity, it is these banners that keep us going and enable us to cope, overcome, and triumph.

So, when challenging days confront us, when trials and tribulations overwhelm us, instead of sinking into despair or depression, let us ask ourselves, "What is the lesson that I can derive from this? What is the message that G-d is sending me?" Above all, let us remember that that which we are experiencing are tests, tests that we can pass, for even as a good teacher would never test his students on subjects that were beyond their capacity, G-d would never test us with burdens that we could not carry. We need only look to the banners that our ancestors created, and if we do so, we will not only pass the test, but we will emerge stronger and wiser — and more, we will create our own banners as a legacy for our descendants. If we can do this, we will have created the *miracle* that is our lives. Herein is to be found the teaching implicit in the four different meanings of the Hebrew word "test" — "*trials and tribulations,*" so that we may discover our *flag* — our identity, hold up our *banners* for future generations, and create the *miracle* of our lives. But you may protest, how can your life be considered miraculous? Aren't miracles the domain of G-d?

The splitting of the Reed Sea, manna from Heaven, or water gushing from rocks are not miracles — they are acts of G-d, and for the Almighty, they are no more miraculous, no more extraordinary than the bread that He allows us to bring forth from the earth or the water that He allows us to draw from a well. We take those phenomena for granted because we have become accustomed to them, but they are all gifts from G-d.

What is miraculous, however, the miracle that G-d has granted us to realize, is *our discovery of self.* When we discover our own unique banner — our own unique identity — and fulfill our true potential, that is truly a miracle — a miracle of which we can be rightly proud. *That is the miracle of our lives.*

It is to enable us to create that miracle that I have written this book — so that in our journey on this planet, we may pass the many tests that G-d sends our way, *identify our flags, raise our banners, create our miracles,* and fulfill the special calling for which He has created us.

2

Recognize Your Potential

he winter of my husband's passing was harsh and bitter. The snow fell without surcease, and, on occasion, I was obliged to remain at the hospital overnight because the roads to our home on Long Island were hazardous. Despite the weather, however, our children visited their father every day and arranged their visits so that a member of the family was with him at all times.

A few days before my husband's demise, I was in the solarium, waiting, while his nurse cleaned and dressed his wound, when my daughter, Slovie, arrived at his room. Finding the curtains around his bed drawn, Slovie hesitated for a moment, wondering whether she should announce her presence or wait, but before she could decide, she heard the sound of her father weeping.

"Rabbi," the nurse asked, "why are you crying? Am I hurting you?"

"No, it's not you," my husband reassured her, "I'm crying because very soon, I will have to face my Maker, and what will I say to Him?"

With tears streaming down her cheeks, Slovie joined me in the solarium and together, we wept.

My husband was a wise and holy man who lived by G-d's word. His every day was filled with *chesed,* goodness, and kindness. Now, if *he* was worried as to how he would answer the Almighty, how should *we* feel? The question that he posed should challenge all of us, for the confrontation that he feared was one that no mortal can ever escape. And yet we dismiss such thoughts from our minds and we live our lives as if the day will never come when we, too, will have to answer to our Maker for the way in which we lived our lives.

The story is told about the sage, Reb Zeesha, who, like my own husband did, wept and worried over meeting his Maker. "If, on the Day of Judgment," he said, "G-d will ask me why I was not like our father Abraham, I will not fear. I will simply respond, 'Almighty G-d, You never endowed me with the ability with which You blessed Abraham, so I couldn't possibly have become like him.'"

Reb Zeesha went on to enumerate our many spiritual giants throughout the centuries, and, regarding all of them, he said, "I shall not fear for I was never given their gifts. But," Reb Zeesha cried, "if the One above asks me 'Zeesha, why weren't you like Zeesha?' What will I say? How will I answer Him?"

All of us are shaped, molded, lovingly designed by G-d, and imbued with unique gifts. Just as no two people look exactly alike, although they may share the same physical attributes, similarly, no two souls are exactly alike. We are not mass-produced, but custom-made by our Heavenly Father for a higher purpose that only we can fulfill. Before G-d ever created us, He had a clear picture of exactly what He envisioned us to be. Our sages teach that each of us has a letter in the Torah that reflects our souls, and one of the reasons why these letters must be distinctly separated from each other is because we each have a unique mission that only we can fulfill. G-d actually makes a portrait of what He intends us to become and equips us with the necessary tools with which to realize His purpose. All of the tests, trials, and tribulations of our lives are orchestrated by the One Above so that we may fulfill this goal, and if you wonder whether you have what it takes to succeed in this mission, be assured that G-d never makes mistakes — the very fact that it is He Who created you is proof positive that it is within your capability to fulfill this charge.

The Patriarch Abraham had to undergo ten tests before he realized his G-d-given purpose. Each of these tests was designed to tap his inner resources and bring forth the beauty and energy that G-d had planted within his soul. These tests took place at different periods of his life, and proved to be catalysts — "banners" for future generations that to this day inspire and guide us. His final test, the most excruciatingly difficult of all, confronted him when he reached the ripe old age of one hundred thirty seven. It was then that G-d called upon him to offer his son, "Please take your son, your only one, whom you love, Isaac, and go to the land of Moriah; bring him up there as an offering upon one of the mountains which I shall tell you" (*Genesis* 22:2). When Abraham signaled his readiness to fulfill the Almighty's command, his life mission was finally realized; it was then that the angel of G-d called out, "Abraham, Abraham, do not stretch out your hand against the lad, for now I know that you are a G-d-fearing man, since you have not withheld your son, Isaac, from Me" (*Genesis* 22:11,12).

You might wonder why this was regarded as Abraham's ultimate test. In a society in which sacrificing children was common practice, Abraham's willingness to face death at the hands of the barbaric despot Nimrod for the sake of G-d was perhaps an even greater test. But if it is to be truly a test, it must hit you where you feel most challenged, where it really hurts. If you can pass such a test, you will have proven that you are truly in charge of your life, capable of fulfilling the higher purpose for which you were created.

For example — if you feel no desire to smoke, you will easily relinquish that cigarette, but if you are a smoker and despite that, still give it up, you will have passed the test. This principle holds true in every area of life — therefore G-d places us in situations and relationships in which we are provoked and tempted. It's all part of our test.

If you are easily given to losing your temper, you may discover that there is someone in your life who is always pushing your buttons, be it a spouse, a child, a neighbor, or even a stranger. Be aware that this is no coincidence. These situations and people have been placed in your path so that you might master your emotions. Just as you are custom-made, so too are your tests uniquely designed by G-d to challenge you.

The Patriarch Abraham was renowned for his attribute of *chesed* — loving kindness — which was intrinsic to his nature. It distressed him if a day passed and he was not of service to others. At the age of ninety-nine, he was commanded by G-d to circumcise himself. On the third day following his circumcision, when his pain was most intense, G-d sent a blistering hot day so that he would not be disturbed by wayfarers. But more than from his physical pain, Abraham suffered from this spiritual deprivation, so he sat himself at the entrance of his tent, scanning the road for passers-by (*Genesis* 18:1). Three angels disguised as nomads were sent by G-d, and when they appeared, Abraham *ran* to greet them and beseeched them to partake of his hospitality. One of the angels revealed to Abraham that G-d planned to destroy the evil, degenerate twin cities of Sodom and Amorah. The normal reactions of anyone to such news would run the gamut from, "Good! They had it coming to them," to "Who am I to tell G-d how to run the world?" But Abraham arose like a lion to do battle with G-d Himself in an attempt to save those evil inhabitants of Sodom.

It is only by recalling these events that we can fully appreciate the enormity of Abraham's test. It is a devastating ordeal for any parent to be called upon to offer his child as a sacrifice, but for a man like Abraham, who epitomized loving-kindness, to do so, was, indeed, the ultimate test.

Our sages teach that when the angel of G-d called out, "Abraham, Abraham," the repetition of the Patriarch's name was not only an expression of love, but confirmation that Abraham had fulfilled his mission, that the two Abrahams, the one here on earth and the one whose portrait hangs in the Heavenly Gallery, were not only in perfect harmony, but were one and the same. The most terrifying pain, the most hellish experience, is to arrive at the Heavenly Court and behold G-d's portrait of you — to see what you were meant to be, and contrast that with what you actually became.

To bring this message home, consider how you would feel if a friend presented you with the opportunity to invest in a stock, but since you were so absorbed in watching a ball game on TV, you paid no heed to his invitation. The stock skyrocketed! If only you had listened, you could have become a millionaire overnight. You flagellate yourself for your stupidity. How could you have been such an idiot?

The question keeps repeating itself over and over in your mind like a broken record. Now multiply such feelings a thousand times over to understand how you will feel when you see the portrait of what your life could have been, and what it has actually become.

There is an amazing story told about the eminent sage, known as the Netziv. He was the Rosh Yeshivah (Dean) of the most prestigious rabbinic academy in Lithuania and the author of many great scholarly works. It is related that as a young child, he did very poorly in school, and his parents despaired of his ever amounting to anything. One day he overheard them in deep discussion about his dismal prospects.

"It's no use," they agreed, "the boy is just not capable of study, so we might as well teach him a trade and apprentice him to a shoemaker or a tailor." The young Netziv was devastated and immediately applied himself to his studies, It was thus that he developed into the illustrious sage whose very name evokes reverence in all Torah circles.

The Netziv was most fortunate — he heard his wake-up call, but tragically, most of us never get the message. We just glide through life without ever discovering who we really are or who we were meant to be.

When a man neglects or refuses to fulfill his mission, the consequences can be calamitous. In the *Book of Kings*, we find the story of the evil monarch Achav and his wicked wife, Jezebel, who reigned over Israel. Although Achav was immensely wealthy, and possessed much land and property, he craved more, and set his eyes upon the vineyards of one of his subjects, Navos. Navos, however, refused to sell, and this enraged Achav no end. Seeing her husband's troubled mien, Jezebel came up with a "perfect" plan.

"Get rid of Navos — accuse him of a capital crime and seize his possessions!" She put the plan into motion and bribed witnesses to testify against Navos. He was found "guilty" and summarily executed.

The Midrash asks why Navos was so cruelly punished, and the response given is shattering and should prompt us to re-think our lives. Navos, our sages teach, was blessed with a magnificent, melodious voice. When the nation gathered in Jerusalem in celebration of the festivals, Navos inspired everyone with his heart-rending prayers. Then one day, he refused to sing. It wasn't as if he was unwell or some problems precluded his singing — he simply was not in the mood. In vain did the people implore him. He turned a deaf ear to their importuning.

Everything we do here on earth is registered in the Heavens above, so, in a sense, Navos orchestrated his own demise. Since he opted not to fulfill the mission for which he had been created, there was nothing further for him to accomplish, and he was summoned home.

We see this very same teaching reinforced in the story of the prophet Jonah. He too tried to escape his mission, albeit under different circumstances and for different reasons. Nevertheless, the teaching remains constant. We read the story of Jonah during *Minchah* — the afternoon service on Yom Kippur, the holiest day in the calendar year, the day when our destiny is sealed. While the *Book of Jonah* is an electrifying reminder of the power of *teshuvah* — repentance (the evil inhabitants of the city of Ninveh were saved because they repented), it is also there to impress upon us that there is a higher purpose to our lives, a reason why G-d created us, and a destiny from which we cannot escape.

The Vilna Gaon explains that Jonah is not only the story of a prophet, but it is also a profound allegorical lesson. Jonah — Yonah, in Hebrew — means "dove," a bird noted for its loyalty to its mate, and is a reference to our souls which yearn to remain loyal to our Creator and fulfill the mission that He envisioned for us. The story of the Book of Jonah opens with the Hebrew word "*Vayehee*" — which means, "And it was," but that word also connotes distress, meaning that the soul ("Yonah") does not want to depart from its pristine Heavenly abode and must be compelled by G-d to descend into the material world.

Yonah (the soul) fears the struggle between the spiritual and the physical, and rightly so. The world is a confusing place in which it is easy to be seduced and become lost. Yonah succumbs, and attempts to flee to Tarshish, which is not only the name of a city, but a symbol of excess and hedonism. The ship (the body) in which the soul sails is an awesome vessel. If navigated properly, it can lead the soul to its ultimate destination, but if left uncontrolled on the raging sea of life, it can capsize and spell disaster. Yonah is cast into the sea and is swallowed by a whale, which represents death and the grave. There, from the belly of the fish, Yonah (the soul) calls out unto G-d and pleads for another chance, so G-d sends him back to this world to rectify that which he failed to accomplish the first time around. Yonah the prophet did accomplish his mission. He returned to Ninveh and called upon its inhabitants to repent — and they did so.

Like Yonah, we all desire to fulfill our mission — to channel our energies and talents into purposeful lives, but like Yonah, we somehow lose our way — we too sail toward Tarshish, and sell our souls for that which is material and temporary. Too late we discover that we have failed, that our ship is in trouble, that we have allowed the gifts with which G-d has endowed us to lie dormant, misused and abused.

The challenge, then, with which we must all grapple, is to discover *who we really are and what our life mission may be.* This journey of self-discovery is no simple matter. Rabbi Yisroel Salanter, the eminent 19th century founder and spiritual father of the Mussar Movement (a moral movement based on the study of traditional ethical literature) would often say that as unfortunate as it is for a person not to recognize his weaknesses, it is far worse for him to be unaware of his *strengths*, for it is through them that s/he can find fulfillment and realize G-d's master plan. Once we make that determination and identify our own particular strength, we must discover how best to apply it to the needs of our generation, always bearing in mind that nothing is accidental, that there is a reason why G-d propelled us onto this planet at this particular moment in time and placed us in the families and situations in which we find ourselves.

Time and again, looking back upon my own life, I have witnessed the guiding Hand of G-d. One would imagine that, having been born into a rabbinic family, my path would have been mapped out for me. Of *course* I was destined to teach Torah; of *course* it was my mission to reach out to those who were alienated and inspire them to return to their heritage, but, trust me, it wasn't all that simple. Only now, in retrospect, have I come to comprehend how seemingly unrelated events in my life have conjoined to launch me on my life's work in Kiruv (outreach).

In the aftermath of our Bergen-Belsen concentration camp experience, my father was determined that we start a new life in Israel. As committed as we were to the realization of that dream, however, all our hopes came to naught. In those days (1945-47) Israel, then called Palestine, was under the British Mandate and, to appease the Arabs, Jewish immigration was reduced to a trickle. Those Jews who attempted to defy the British quota were shipped off to a British concentration camp in Cyprus, and my father did not wish to subject us children to yet another such ordeal. So we waited and waited for proper documentation. But as weeks turned into months, and the months into two years, our situation became desperate. My parents and younger brother were placed in a D.P. camp in Caux, Switzerland, while my older brother was sent to a makeshift school in Engleberg, near Zurich. I was placed in yet another facility in Bex, near Montreux. Suffering from the scars of the savage treatment at the hands of the Nazis and their cohorts, we yearned to resume a normal family life. We sorely needed the healing presence and loving care of our parents. One would have anticipated that the powers-that-be would have been sensitive to this, but those were turbulent days, and we quickly learned that our return to a semblance of normalcy would take a long time.

My roommate at school was a few years my senior. Her parents had been killed in Auschwitz, and because she was an orphan, she was placed on a priority list for immigration to Palestine. Almost every night, we would have nightmares, and since "lights-out" at night was mandatory, when darkness fell the chairs, the table, all assumed the appearance of Nazis stalking us. As we cried out in terror, we tried to reassure each other, "It's only a chair, it's only a piece of furniture," but when my roommate left, I remained alone and the nights became very long. My parents came to visit and I shared my fears with them. Then and there, they made a decision and declared: "It's enough! We'll go to America and live like a family again."

My aunt and uncle, who lived in New York, had sent us papers that my parents had put aside to be used only if we were unsuccessful in our attempts to reach Palestine, but once their decision was made, they acted with alacrity. The first available ship was an Italian freighter, scheduled to leave from Livorno, Italy to Norfolk, Virginia. Having no clue as to the rigors such a trip would entail in the month of January on the Atlantic, we embarked upon our voyage. For four endless weeks the ship pitched and tossed on the angry swells of the ocean. We were the only passengers on board, and were assigned to a cabin on the lowest deck. To this day I can smell the sickening stench of the diesel engines. We all became desperately seasick and my Mom was so acutely ill that she despaired of surviving, and bade us farewell. This upset my father greatly. *"Chas V'shalom* — G-d forbid! Mommy dear, you are not permitted to say such a thing," he gently chided.

Finally, one morning we spotted land, and the captain announced that we had arrived. We had no idea that Norfolk was some distance from New York — to us, America was America! When we went ashore, we attracted immediate attention — my father with his long beard, and all of us outfitted in ill-fitting hand-me downs that had been distributed by HIAS in Switzerland. We were penniless, famished, and didn't know where to go. Someone called the local police and they, in turn, called the president of the Jewish community, who kindly took us to his home where he assured us that everything was kosher. His wife offered us refreshments, but little did she realize what she had gotten herself into! We were literally starved and in no time at all, polished off three loaves of bread and two dozen eggs. He purchased train tickets for us to New York, and sent us on our way. When we arrived at Penn Station, the same scenario was repeated; once again, someone summoned the police, but this time, the policeman who arrived on the scene spoke a few words of Yiddish, and upon hearing this, we all burst into tears. Imagine, a policeman who was a Jew! This was something that we, who associated a uniform with brutality, had never before encountered. This Jewish member of "New York's Finest" bundled us into a taxi and paid our fare. As our cab wound its way through the streets of New York, we looked out of the windows and marveled at this blessed land where even the policemen were benevolent and compassionate. My parents had not wired, written, or called ahead. My mother, against my father's better judgment, insisted that we surprise her sister. Thus, we arrived at the residence of my aunt and uncle in Brooklyn.

"As long as they don't know we are coming," my mother said, "Let Yanky [my older brother] go first and say that he is bringing regards from the Jungreis family that survived Bergen Belsen." My father looked doubtful, but Mama prevailed. My brother climbed the stairs, we heard his knock, and then we heard a big thump. My aunt had fainted!

We lived with my aunt and uncle for several weeks, but the living-quarters was very cramped, and my parents decided that, no matter what, we had to find our own place. Since we had no means, we moved into a one-room basement flat which my mother divided into cubicles with curtains that she sewed, and then she went to do battle with the cockroaches.

Under the best of circumstances, the new kid on the block has a tough time integrating, but if you are a foreigner, if you don't speak the language, if you are impoverished and live in a dingy basement, the difficulty is intensified. My personal situation was compounded by the fact that, in addition to the aforementioned, I was also a concentration-camp survivor, and in those days, people kept their distance from "*greeners*" (Yiddish term for newly arrived immigrants). But perhaps that which created the greatest gap was the fact that my family was observant, and the neighborhood in which we settled was totally secular, although predominately Jewish. When I walked down the street with my father, I felt the eyes of the children staring at his long beard and rabbinic coat, and as I clutched his hand ever so tightly, I realized that although I was now safe in this blessed land, there were many hurdles yet to be overcome, and my loneliness remained.

My parents enrolled me in Bais Yaakov — a yeshivah for girls quite a distance from our home, so the mere mechanics of getting to school presented a formidable challenge. I had to take two city busses, and invariably, I became sick from the fumes and had to get off until my heaving stopped and then wait for the next bus — so more often than not, I was late for school, which didn't ease the pressure of catching up to my grade level.

None of my classmates lived in my neighborhood or even close by, and I often wished that fate had arranged things so that we could have settled in Williamsburg where many new immigrants and Orthodox Chasidic Jews now lived. Wistfully, I would watch the girls on the block playing stoop ball, hopscotch, or jump rope. I wanted so much to have friends, to be part of the group, but I was the "odd man out." My father urged me to invite the children to our Shabbos table, and as the holidays arrived, to share our *Yomim Tovim* — festivals — with them. I was hesitant, but my father reminded me of our responsibilities to our brethren, and amazingly, they came and loved my father's *Shabbos* and *Yom Tov* table.

I became particularly friendly with a neighborhood girl who was my age and the oldest child in her family. She was a public-school student and I loved talking with her because she was genuinely interested in our way of life. I also enjoyed discussions with her mother, a special warm-hearted lady who took great interest in learning. As a result of our talks, my friend's family became totally observant. Her brothers were all enrolled in yeshivah, and today, they are respected leaders of the Torah community.

I have often been asked when our Hineni outreach organization was established. I can easily pinpoint the year when we were incorporated, but looking back, I now realize that Hineni had its beginnings when, as a newly arrived immigrant, G-d placed me in an environment where I was called upon to explain my Jewishness.

Very often, G-d puts us into situations that are stressful and even hostile. Feelings of frustration and bitterness overwhelm us. We ask ourselves, "Why? Why do we have to contend with all this?"

At such times we must bear in mind that G-d has a master plan, and there is a reason for everything. Certainly, if my parents had settled in an Orthodox Chasidic community, I would have integrated into the environment and never felt challenged. And our Hineni outreach movement, which was a first on the international Jewish scene, might never have been born. So when difficult days fall upon you, do not allow yourself to succumb to despondency or resentment. Rather, ask yourself, "What is G-d trying to tell me? How can I emerge stronger and wiser from this? "What is the message that I should be hearing? How do I pass the test so that I can realize my true potential? How can I create the "flag" that defines my life?" and "How will my flag become a banner to show the way for future generations?

3

Who Are You?

o you know who you *really* are?

I asked that question of Phyllis and Sam Malden (names have been changed to protect their anonymity). They were a popular couple on the New York Jewish social scene. Sam was a well-established businessman and he and Phyllis were active in many charities. Occasionally, I would meet them at dinners or other functions, but their interest lay more in secular causes than in Hineni and I had very little contact with them. I did invite them to participate in our Torah classes, but they politely declined, so I was somewhat surprised when I received a call from Phyllis asking for an appointment for her and Sam.

"We have a serious problem," she said, in a tense, agitated voice, "and we'd like to discuss it with you."

Short of illness, I couldn't imagine what possible problem they could have that would bring them to my office, but then again, they were not people who would come for a blessing, so I concluded that they were probably anxious about their daughter, Kelly, whom I had never met, but had heard was a thirty-five-year-old career-oriented single.

Seeing your children happily married is a goal of all parents — one that transcends religious and social boundaries and is probably one of the major concerns of 21st century Jewry. Over the years, I have been privileged to make countless matches, but unfortunately, they haven't even made a dent in the ever-growing singles population.

A few days later, when I met Phyllis and Sam, they took me completely by surprise. It wasn't Kelly that had brought them to my office, but their own personal crisis. From the moment they walked in, I sensed that something was drastically wrong. They both looked distraught and in place of the air of confidence that very often marks the rich and powerful, they communicated fear, and looked like two trapped birds.

Their discomfort was palpable. "You must be wondering what brings us here," Phyllis said apologetically as they seated themselves. "Actually, it was our mutual friends, Danny and Marjorie Goldring, who insisted that we see you."

I knew Danny and Marjorie well. They had been involved in our organization for several years, but despite their close friendship with the Maldens, they couldn't prevail upon them to participate in Hineni programs. Danny was a successful realtor who, some years ago, went through hard times and was forced to sell most of his holdings. He fell into a spiral of depression, and Marjorie, who from time to time attended my Torah classes, convinced him to see me. Danny began studying with my sons, who are our Hineni rabbis, and discovered the amazing font of wisdom that is the Torah — a wisdom of which he had hitherto been totally unaware. In time, he came to understand that his business problems had been *tests* that prodded him to re-examine his life and chart a new course. Slowly, he rebuilt and proudly told everyone who was willing to listen that those trying days had, in the long run, been a blessing.

It was hard to believe that Sam, renowned as a titan of his industry, was in financial difficulty, but everything about his demeanor suggested that he was.

"So, what can I do for you?" I asked, inviting them to speak.

For a moment, there was silence. Sam squirmed in his chair and signaled Phyllis to begin.

"For the past two years, Sam has been having severe business problems," she explained. "We tried to keep it as quiet as possible, but at this point, our situation has become desperate.

"The rug is literally being pulled out from under us. And what's worse, Sam has become terribly depressed and withdrawn. As much as I try, I can't reach him," and with that, she dissolved in tears.

It was painful to see this once-proud couple so shattered.

"Would you like to tell me about it, Sam?" I asked, trying to draw him into the conversation.

"What's to say?" he muttered under his breath.

"Well, how you see things."

"How *I* see things?" he repeated. "It's a bummer! Every day is the pits and at night I can't sleep. I don't want to wake Phyllis, so I go into the den and turn on the TV until I finally collapse and doze off. But then, I wake up with a start, and reality hits me all over again. I literally can't breathe. So how do *I* see things, you ask? It all stinks!

"You want to hear more?" he added, his voice filled with bitterness. "I borrowed money, I even put my personal assets on the line hoping that things would turn around, but everything's gone down the tubes. My life might as well be over!"

"It's like someone put an evil eye on us." Phyllis interjected. "Look at me," she said, pointing to her dress, "I haven't bought a new outfit in ages. I've stopped going to charity functions and curtailed our social life — it's embarrassing." Her words hung in the air.

"Embarrassing?" Sam repeated. "How do you suppose I feel? I've had to resign from all of my Board positions." Then suddenly, he turned angrily on Phyllis.

"I don't know what we are doing here! You, Marjorie, and Danny talked me into this, but it's ridiculous. What can she do for us?" And turning to me, he said, "Nothing personal, but I really don't see how you can help." And with that, he folded his arms emphatically across his chest.

"Honey, please..." Phyllis protested, and then she turned to me, and said, "We do appreciate your giving us this time..."

"Don't give it a thought," I assured her, "our sages teach us never to judge anyone until we stand in his or her place. I certainly realize how difficult this must be for you and especially for Sam. As a matter of fact, I think it was very big of Sam to have agreed to come. But let's get back to the problem at hand and begin with a question, 'Do you know who you really are?'"

They looked at me incredulously, and Sam repeated, "Do I know who I really am?" And his tone suggested that he thought that I had lost it, but I chose to ignore his innuendo and said, "Perhaps a story will help you to understand what I am getting at."

"Once there was a man who lived in Chelm, the legendary *shtetl* of fools. One day, he decided to visit the *shvitz* — the local bath house. When he arrived, he saw a number of townspeople bathing with great enjoyment, so he decided to disrobe and join them. But suddenly, a thought struck him and he panicked — *Everyone here looks the same! If I undress, I will look just like them, so how will I know who I am? What should I do?*

And then, he came up with a brilliant idea. He would tie a red string around his big toe, and when he looked at it, he would know that *he was the man with the red string on his toe*! Confidently, he entered the pool, but when he emerged from the water, he looked down at his feet and froze. The red string was gone! 'Who am I?' he wailed as he wept over his loss. Terrified, he looked around the room and spotted his string wrapped around the toes of another bather. He rushed over to him, 'I know who *you* are, but can you tell me who *I* am?' he asked."

"It's a cute story, but what does it have to do with us?" Sam snapped impatiently.

"Everything," I responded. "Substitute 'red string' for 'money, business' and you will see yourself. Even as that man from Chelm thought that his identity was that *string*, you too believe that your identity is your business. *But that's your work, Sam, and not who you are.*"

"And Phyllis," I said, turning to her, "forgive me, but to you, it is your clothing, your appearance, that is your 'red string.' We live in a society that recognizes us only through our strings — economic status for men, appearance for women."

"But, Rebbetzin," Phyllis protested, "people do judge you by your appearance, and what you wear makes all the difference."

"You think it does until you discover that it's not all that important. Some years ago, I was invited to speak at Oxford, and when it became known that I would be in England, invitations from London, Cambridge, and Manchester poured in as well. On the heels of that speaking tour, I was also scheduled to speak in Jerusalem,

"You will appreciate that for such an extensive tour I had to pack several changes of clothing. I planned carefully, making certain that for the tail end of the tour I would have a fresh outfit to wear in Israel.

"We arrived in Oxford, my last stop in England, in time for a Wednesday evening program. Following my speech, I remained with the students for a discussion which stretched past midnight. Exhausted, we were shown to our sleeping quarters. Our hosts had very kindly arranged for us to stay in a professor's digs in a centuries-old building on campus. We climbed the narrow, winding stone staircase to our room and to our dismay discovered that the electric grate, which was the only source of heat in the room, had been automatically turned off at midnight. The night was bitter-cold and the temperature in the room was glacial. With chattering teeth, we told each other that the better part of valor would be to sleep in our clothes and cover ourselves with our coats as well as the blankets. On the morrow we would be in Jerusalem and would shower and change there.

"We left Oxford at the crack of dawn after only a few hours of sleep to catch a 10:30 a.m. British Airways flight to Tel Aviv. Having heard of the terrible traffic congestion on the roads, especially during rush hour, we wanted to give ourselves ample time, but despite all our precautions, we quickly discovered that as bad as we had anticipated the roads would be, the reality was by far much worse. We literally sat in bumper-to-bumper traffic, and our poor driver became increasingly agitated as we kept reminding him that we had a flight to catch.

"We finally arrived at Heathrow airport twenty-five minutes before our flight and breathed a sigh of relief. Rushing up to the ticket counter, we presented our passports and tickets only to be told that we were too late for our flight! We thought that we hadn't heard right. How could that be? There was still twenty-five minutes remaining until we were scheduled to take off, but the clerk behind the counter explained that all flights are closed one half-hour before departure for reasons of security.

"'But,' I explained, 'We are Sabbath-observant Jews and we must take this flight or we won't make it for the Sabbath. Additionally, I'm scheduled to speak in Jerusalem on Saturday night.' But the clerk was unbending. 'Those are the rules,' he said officiously.

"My friend, Barbara, insisted that his supervisor be called, and when he appeared, he coldly repeated, 'I'm sorry, but those are the rules. There is nothing that we can do.'

'Is there another flight from a different airline that we can take?' I begged.

"He logged into his computer while we stood there with bated breath, 'The only thing that I can suggest,' he said with his clipped British accent, 'is that I put you on a flight to Copenhagen and connect you to a Tel Aviv flight from there. That should bring you to Israel in plenty of time.'

"Having no other option, we flew to Copenhagen and with only minutes to spare, made the connecting flight to Tel Aviv. When we arrived at Ben Gurion, we rushed to the baggage pick-up, only to watch the carrousel go round and round with no sign of our luggage. Finally, Barbara's suitcase appeared, but mine was nowhere in sight. Patiently, we waited until the last suitcase had rolled by and been unloaded — but still my luggage didn't appear. All my clothing was lost, and the only thing I had was the suit in which I had slept and traveled, which now looked the worse for wear. Weary and dejected, we trudged to the lost-baggage counter, where my worst suspicions were confirmed. My suitcase was lost.

"'Fill out these forms and we'll try to trace it for you. It will most certainly come in on the next flight from Copenhagen,' the woman in the booth assured me.

"'And when will that be?'

"'Next week.'

"'I don't believe this! You don't seem to understand — I need my suitcase *now. Shabbos* is coming — I can't wear this wrinkled traveling suit on *Shabbos,* and I'm also scheduled to speak every day of my stay in Israel.' Then I glanced down at my feet. To ease the trek through airports, I always travel wearing sneakers rather than regular shoes. "What will I do without shoes?" I wondered. I couldn't believe that this was happening, but having no options, we got into a cab to go to Jerusalem. As our taxi made its way to the holy city, I gazed out of the window. As often as I visit Israel, I never cease to marvel at the beauty of the land, and once again, I was overwhelmed at the thought that I, a child of Bergen-Belsen, was making my way to Jerusalem, traveling the same path on which our patriarchs and prophets had walked. When I considered that, I felt silly agonizing over the loss of my suitcase, but still, I was upset.

"In Jerusalem, stores close by midday *erev Shabbos*, so early Friday morning, I went into town to try to buy something to wear. I managed to find shoes, although they weren't what I would normally have chosen, as well as some toiletries and other sundries, but my search for a dress proved to be frustrating and fruitless. I visited several shops, but I couldn't find an appropriate outfit in my size. As it was getting late, we had to get back to the hotel to ready ourselves for *Shabbos.*

"I ironed my suit, thinking to myself that I might try the shops again on Sunday, but when Sunday came, I concluded that it would a pity to fritter away my time in shopping. Whenever I am in Israel, I have a full schedule of programs and I wasn't about to give any of them up because I didn't have a change of clothes. In the past, I had spoken with all manner of handicaps, including a broken ankle and crutches and a broken wrist in a cast; even when I lost my voice and was barely audible, I managed, so I would manage this time as well. Perhaps, I told myself, this was my test. I decided that what I wore was really not all that significant. *I was not my dress*, and the fact that I wore the same outfit day in and day out would not detract from my message. Besides, I reasoned, if my suit was good enough for *Shabbos*, it would certainly do for the remainder of my stay. My suitcase finally did arrive on the morning that we were scheduled to leave for the States, and unopened, it returned to New York with me.

"I tell you this story, Phyllis, because even as I am not *my dress*, you are not *your dress*. *There is more to you than the latest fashion.* When I look at you, I don't see what you are wearing, but I do *see a sensitive woman with a heart, mind, and soul.*"

"Trust me, that's not how the world sees me," Phyllis mumbled.

"That may be," I agreed. "Ours is a society in which most people never get beyond externals, and instead of seeing a woman's inner beauty, we see only her dress. And even sadder is that women never see themselves and learn who they really are. So don't fall into that trap."

"Obsession with appearance is one of the conflicts that pits our Torah values against western culture," I went on to explain. "While it is important to present oneself in as appealing a manner as possible (and I would never minimize that), there's a vast difference between looking good and creating a cult of the body. Our 21st century fashion has objectified women to the point where it eclipses the inner light of her soul, creating a shallow female who believes that she must 'dress' to attract. Women have become so enslaved to their appearance that every new wrinkle, every additional pound, provokes a major crisis that threatens their very identity.

"To appreciate the magnitude of this, let me tell you of a lovely young girl I knew from a fine family, who, at the age of twenty suffered a fatal coronary. Cause of death — anorexia. After several years of self-imposed starvation, her atrophied heart muscles gave out. Tragically, her story is not an isolated one. It is not only in such extreme cases that we are witness to this obsession with appearance — all women suffer from it to one extent or another and the ramifications are far-reaching. It has affected our relationships, our marriages, our families, and the very fabric of our society.

"And Sam," I now said, turning to him, "there is more to you than your money, even if our culture measures a man by the depth of his pockets rather than by the profundity of his mind and heart."

"Tell that to my so-called friends," Sam said bitterly.

"No, it's not your friends. It is *you* who must believe it, and if you are secure in that knowledge, then they too will come to appreciate that there is more to you than money. The way you look at yourself is how people will see you." I went on to relate that when Moses sent scouts to spy out the Biblical land of Israel, they came back with a terrifying report of giants living there. "We were as *grasshoppers* in their sight," they complained (*Numbers* 13:33). Our commentators explain that if they felt that the inhabitants looked upon them as grasshoppers, it was because *they saw themselves* as "grasshoppers."

"Similarly, Sam, if you believe that you and your money are one and the same, then that is how you will be regarded by others. There is no reason for you to have resigned your board positions. Just because you can't make a financial contribution doesn't mean that you have nothing to offer.

"Perhaps," I suggested, "the time has come to acquaint your friends with the real you — but in order to do that, you will first have to come to know *who you really are.*'"

"This all sounds good here in your office, but you know, Rebbetzin, that's not the real world."

"What's the real world, Sam — dysfunctional families, divorce, child abuse, murder, corruption, fraud, infidelity, substance abuse — need I go on?

"Those of our people who survived the centuries have never lived in the real world. As a matter of fact, the very first test with which G-d charged the patriarch, Abraham, was, 'Go for *yourself*' (*Genesis* 12:1), meaning, *depart from the real world* and connect to your inner self — create your own reality based upon the eternal truth of G-d.

"It may be that this is your test — that this is G-d's way of telling you: 'Go for yourself and discover who you really are.' Perhaps G-d wanted you to know that you are more than 'strings?'"

"A very costly test," Sam said acerbically.

"Actually," I said, "financial setbacks are the easiest of all tests."

"You must be joking. What could be worse?"

"May you never experience it, but tests involving illness, tests when you witness the suffering of your children, are much more painful, so despite everything, you have to be grateful, because it's only money, and with G-d's help, you can recoup, and if you don't, your life will still go on, perhaps in even a more meaningful manner."

For a moment, there was silence in the room. "The Rebbetzin is right," Phyllis said. "You can't argue with that."

"But the hardest test," I continued, "and this may come as a shock to you, is when there is no test at all — when G-d gives up on you and considers you beyond redemption. It's like having a parent, a spouse, or a good friend who cares enough to admonish you when you go off the track, who will berate you if you return home at three o'clock in the morning. If, however, there is no one in your life who cares, no one to take you to task; if everyone, including your parents, gave up on you, then your situation is indeed hopeless. We learn this lesson from the Torah.

"When Adam and Eve transgressed, G-d confronted them, chastised them and decreed that henceforth, they would lead a life beset by suffering. Adam would 'eat his bread by the sweat of his brow' (*Genesis* 3:19) and his wife would experience the pangs of childbirth (ibid. 3:16).

"The real culprit of the story however, was the serpent, and amazingly, G-d never entered into any discussion with him. What's more, the serpent is let off easy: 'You shall crawl on your belly all the days of your life, and dust shall you eat... (ibid. 3:14)' guaranteeing that there would always be food at its disposal. As a matter of fact, the serpent is the one creature that never has to hunt for food because it actually wallows in it. G-d makes provisions for the serpent and removes all tests and difficulties from its path because He regards it as hopeless — without potential for growth or change.

"Adam and Eve, on the other hand, are *tested*. They *do* have to struggle; they *do* have to experience pain so that they might probe their souls, grow, and realize their higher purpose in life. Thus, the woman becomes 'Chava,' mother of all life, a source of inspiration and blessing, and Adam does *teshuvah* — returns to his essence and composes songs of praise to G-d.

"Perhaps, Sam, G-d sent you this *test* so that you might re-examine your life, reconsider your priorities, and turn to Him for guidance and wisdom."

"You know, Sam, there is something to what the Rebbetzin is telling us," Phyllis said as Sam mulled over my words.

"I'm not going to argue that," he finally conceded, "but at the end of the day, I've still lost everything."

"Not everything, Sam. I hate to sound didactic, but I must repeat — not everything. And that is what you must bear in mind if you want to recoup. But I must also caution you that if you continue to believe that *you are your money*, then you will have failed the test and indeed, you will have lost everything."

"So, O.K., who am I?" Sam asked.

"Finally!" I exclaimed. "I was wondering when we'd get there. You are '*Chelek Eloka*' — part of G-d. When the Almighty created and breathed life into you, that infinite and indestructible breath of G-d became your *neshamah,* soul (the Hebrew words "*neshamah*"— soul, and "*nesheemah*" — breath, are one and the same). That breath, the *neshamah*, has the capacity to enable you to climb the highest mountain and overcome every obstacle. That soul can never be crushed. Dr. Viktor Frankl, a survivor of Auschwitz, wrote in his memoirs that, while the Nazis tortured his body, they were not able to destroy him, because he was more than the sum total of his physical parts. He was his *neshamah* — his *soul*. I must add that there is nothing new about Victor Frankl's revelation. It has deep roots in our long history, and I myself was witness to it in the concentration camps when I encountered Jews whose spirits were larger than life. You must always remember who you are, and if you do that, you will succeed in withstanding all of life's onslaughts.

"The eminent rabbi, Yaakov Galinsky, who resides in the holy city of Bnai Brak, Israel, relates an amazing story that illustrates this point. During the Communist regime in Russia, he was incarcerated in Siberia. Every morning the rabbi, and the others in his unit, would be marched off to back-breaking slave labor. When they returned at nightfall, they would collapse from sheer exhaustion. Days and nights merged and there was no relief from their dismal existence. Among the prisoners in the rabbi's unit was a distinguished-looking gentleman, who, even in that Gehinnom, somehow managed to retain his dignity.

"One night, while all were asleep, the rabbi was awakened by some movement. He saw this prisoner arise from his pallet and, from under the mattress, remove a uniform with many medals. The man put on the uniform and then took out a mirror, studied himself, whispered a few words, and saluted. Then he quickly exchanged the uniform for his prisoner's garb and went back to sleep.

"Rabbi Galinsky couldn't believe his eyes. He didn't understand what this man was doing and decided that he would wait to see if he repeated this ritual the following night. And sure enough, he did.

"At a loss to comprehend this strange behavior, he decided to ask him what it was all about. The man turned ashen; he was terribly agitated at having been detected.

"'Please don't be frightened,' Rabbi Galinsky assured him, 'I would never betray you — I just want to understand what you are doing.'

"The man confided that, prior to his arrest, he had been a general in the Polish army. 'But,' he went on, "in Siberia, it's easy to lose sight of who I really am, so every night, I put on my uniform and medals and look in the mirror to remind myself that even here in this evil place, I should never forget *who I really am*.'

"Rabbi Galinsky tells this story to teach an awesome lesson: *know who you are*. And that's the challenge with which you must grapple, Sam."

"So what should I do?" Sam asked sarcastically. "Dress up and look in the mirror?"

"Not at all," I answered. "Our uniform is part of us and not something to be put on or taken off. That which the general did in a Siberian prison, we the Jewish people do every day through our prayers, Torah, and our *mitzvos*." And with that, I reached for the prayer book on my desk and turned to the daily morning service.

"Phyllis, why don't you read these words to Sam," I suggested.

"I'm sorry, Rebbetzin, but I don't read Hebrew."

"That's alright," I assured her, "you can read in English."

"'My G-d,' Phyllis began haltingly, 'the soul that You placed within me is pure. You created it, You fashioned it, You breathed it into me, You safeguard it within me and eventually You will take it from me and restore it to me in Time to Come. As long as the soul is within me, I gratefully thank You, my G-d and the G-d of my forefathers, Master of all works, Lord of all souls. Blessed are You, *HaShem*, Who restores souls to all bodies....' That's really beautiful," Phyllis whispered.

"Even more beautiful than the words is the teaching behind them — when you pronounce that timeless prayer, you commence your day by reminding yourself that you are *Chelek Eloka* — a spark of G-d — so even if you messed up, even if you find yourself in an intolerable situation, be it in a prison in Siberia or bankruptcy in New York, your soul remains pure because it is *Chelek Eloka* — a part of G-d. And if you listen to its voice, you will always find your way back to who you really are and the purpose for which you were created."

4

Hearing Your Inner Voice

S am and Phyllis were back in my office. "What are those Hebrew words again? The ones that you said define me?" Sam asked.

"*Che-lek-El-O-Ka mi-ma'al, ne-sha-mah*," I enunciated slowly.

"*Che...lek...*" Sam repeated, stumbling over the words. "That's too difficult for me! I'll stick to *neshamah*. That's a word I remember from my grandmother. It means *soul*, right? I haven't thought about her for a long time, but after our discussion last week, her memory came to mind."

"That's good, Sam, that's your *neshamah* talking."

"I don't know about that. I don't hear any inner voices," he said half-jokingly.

"There are valid reasons for that. As we discussed last week, in our world, everything is based on the material. We identify ourselves through our possessions, and our perceptions are limited to that which is transmitted to us through our five senses. For most of us, our reality is based upon that which we can see, hear, smell, touch, and taste, and since we cannot see the *neshamah,* we deny its existence, but although its voice is not audible, it is nevertheless there. Just visualize a person who is blind, deaf, and dumb — a person whose senses are not there to guide him. Are we to say that he doesn't exist? Obviously, there is a sixth sense, and that is the *neshamah* — the soul."

I went on to relate that on three separate occasions, I had the sad experience of witnessing the *neshamah* depart and the total transformation that takes place in its wake. The first was the passing of my dear, revered father; then, some ten years later, the untimely demise of my beloved husband; and four years after that, I bade farewell to my precious mom. On each of these occasions, I was struck by the sudden change that occurred during their demise.

My father suffered from many ailments: coronaries, strokes, Parkinson's, and a tracheotomy marked the last eight years of his life. Additionally, his Holocaust experiences also took their toll — I can hardly remember when he was free of pain. But throughout, his gentle nature, his warmth, his wisdom, and above all, his faith, never flagged. During the final two years of his life, he was sustained by a feeding tube. He could not ingest anything by mouth lest he aspirate fluid and develop pneumonia. I would often think of how excruciatingly difficult it must have been for him not to be able to moisten his throat with a sip of water, but my father never complained, and whenever visitors arrived, he would insist that they partake of some refreshments.

At the very end, he was unable to speak but just the same, he continued to communicate with his eyes, and those eyes spoke volumes. Two words did remain, however, and I guess that those two words defined his life: *"Baruch HaShem"* — "Blessed is G-d," he would mouth whenever we asked how he felt. I would visit him twice daily — on my way to Manhattan to teach our Hineni classes, and then again on my return home to the South Shore of Long Island. More often than not, by the time I finished my teaching and consultations it was very late, and I would often arrive at my parents' home in Brooklyn well past midnight. The nurse would greet me and, ever so quietly, I would approach my father's bed, careful not to disturb him in case he was sleeping. But invariably, he would sense my presence, and his face would light up with a warm, loving smile. That smile is forever etched on my heart, and how grateful I am today for those visits!

On the Sabbath however, when we cannot travel or use the telephone, there was a communications blackout, and so, on Sabbath eve, as I kindled my Shabbos lights, I would pray, "Please, oh G-d, allow this Sabbath to pass without mishap." When the holy day was over, my first phone call was always to my parents' home.

"How is Tattie?" I would ask with trepidation. And how wonderful it was when my mother assured me that he was still with us. But then came Shabbos Chanukah — the Sabbath that coincides with the joyous celebration of the Festival of Lights. My children and grandchildren had all come to celebrate with us.

On Saturday night, after the stars appeared and we bade farewell to the holy Sabbath and kindled the Chanukah menorah, I ran to the phone for my usual call. When I heard my mother's voice, my heart fell. I knew that something was desperately wrong. "Come quickly," she said, "the *Malach Hamoves* — the Angel of Death — has arrived." We ran — my husband, children and grandchildren, all jumped into our cars and sped to my parents' home. My brothers and their wives and children, who lived nearby, were already there, as was my father's faithful friend and physician. The doctor, an eminent neurologist, a man of great piety and faith, was sitting at my father's bedside, but instead of monitoring his vital signs, he was immersed in the study of our holy books, and I knew that now, it was only the *neshamah* — the soul — that remained.

My father's breathing was heavy and labored. I took his hands in mine, kissed them, and washed them with my tears. I asked him to bless my children, and although he could not speak, I know that he understood, because he attempted to raise his hand in blessing as each child approached his bedside. We all recited the prayers that must be said at such times, and there is no question in my mind that my father heard us. The clock ticked away, and there we were, gathered around his bedside. Midnight became one a.m., two a.m., three a.m., and we continued to recite prayers and psalms.

Suddenly, there was a dramatic change. It's not that we heard a sound, but something happened which I cannot explain — my father stopped breathing as the Angel of Death took his holy soul.

What exactly took place? It's not as though we saw something physical occur, and yet, from one second to another, there was a total transformation. As ill as my father had been, we somehow communicated, and at the very least, were able to hold his hands. But now, in a matter of seconds, his frail, emaciated body suddenly became lifeless. His *neshamah* had departed.

In the Hebrew language, there are many words that translate as "soul," but as I mentioned previously, Hebrew is *lashon hakodesh* — the Holy Tongue — in which G-d Himself spoke and in which no two words are synonymous or interchangeable. Every letter, every word, is definitive and has its own unique interpretation. The very first time the word *neshamah* — soul, is mentioned in the Torah is where G-d blew the soul, *nishmas chaim* — the breath of life — into man's nostrils and he became a *nefesh chayah* — a living being (*Genesis* 2:7). The Zohar teaches that the *neshamah* is part of the essence of G-d, "since one who blows, blows from within himself."

The *nefesh,* on the other hand, is that part of the soul which is closest to the body; it is that which even animals possess on their level. The *nefesh* telegraphs the messages sent by our five senses to us, and dominates our *physical* choices. Our *spiritual* direction, however, is determined by the *neshamah.* The test that confronts every man is to insure that it is his *neshamah* that shapes his life decisions.

It is the *nefesh* that enables us to witness our own funerals and hear the eulogies. The more attached the *nefesh* was to the body during its life, the more it focused on physical and material needs, the more painful the decomposition of the body becomes. As the *nefesh* observes the body disintegrate in the grave, the realization of having made wrong choices, of having wasted a life in futile, meaningless pursuits, becomes a source of anguish, regret, and shame.

Sam and Phyllis appeared somewhat unsettled by my words.

"I'm not telling you this to be morbid or to frighten you," I assured them, "but rather, to underscore the folly of living a life that is centered on the physical and the temporal, at the expense of the *neshamah,* which is eternal.

"So, what do you say," I asked. "Would you like to hear more?"

"Absolutely!" Phyllis said.

"We live in a topsy-turvy world — we agonize over the temporal, the inconsequential, and are oblivious to that which has long-lasting ramifications."

"I'm not sure I'm following you," Sam commented.

"Simple. Just look at yourself. You are crushed at the loss of your money. Mind you, I don't minimize it. It's a terrible blow, a very difficult and painful test, but in all honesty, would you be equally devastated if, for example, you lost your temper and shamed someone in public?"

"Oh, come on, Rebbetzin. There is no comparison. I lost a fortune! How can you possibly equate that with my ranking out some moron who probably had it coming to him?"

"Careful, Sam," I said. "Remember that that 'moron' is endowed with a *neshamah* — the breath of G-d. Loss of money," I went on to explain, "does not follow you into the grave and beyond. Loss of money does not blemish your soul — but shaming someone publically does. As a matter of fact, in the Heavenly Courts, it is regarded as akin to murder. So you're right. There is no comparison, but not in the way you meant."

"I can't relate to that," Sam said, with a wave of dismissal.

"That's exactly my point. As I said, we live in a topsy-turvy world and you will have to re-learn and re-think your priorities."

"I don't know anyone who lives with your priorities," Sam commented.

"To be sure, very few do, but they can be found. Look," I now said, "no one expects you to make a one hundred and eighty degree turn, but the very least that you must do is to try to keep things in perspective.

"Do you remember 9/11?" I asked. "On that day, most of the cell phones in the city were down, but amazingly, those who were trapped in the blazing Twin Towers and those who fought the terrorists on the United Airlines flight heading for the White House, which subsequently crashed in Shanksville, Pennsylvania, got through on their cell phones and left a last message.

"Now, this is something that never happened before. To be sure, throughout the centuries, people have been killed in cataclysmic events — there is nothing new about that, but this was the very first time that we actually had *recorded messages* from those facing death. Incredibly, without exception, they all left behind the exact same message, three little words, 'I love you' — and they each expressed it in their own way. 'I love you, my husband; I love you, my wife; I love you, my children, I love you, mom; I love you, dad.' But it was always, '*I love you.*' There was no talk of business, stocks, real estate, or money. In the end, when we come to the moment of truth and hear the voice of our *neshamah*, we realize that most everything that we agonized and fought over was totally unimportant, for ultimately, only three words count — 'I love you.'

"But isn't it sad that we have to be engulfed in flames in order to come to this realization? Shouldn't we learn to listen to the voice of our *neshamahs* and say, 'I love you' before tragedy strikes?"

"You sure know how to go for the jugular," Sam said ruefully.

"When you touch on *emes* — truth — it's always the jugular," I said, and that's what the *neshamah* is all about — truth. There are many dimensions to the *neshamah* of which we are totally unaware," I went on to explain. "They are discussed in the Talmud and in the books of the Kaballah, but for the purpose of our discussion, let's focus on just one more thought.

"The Jewish peoplehood is comprised of six hundred thousand souls. You may of course protest and ask, 'Aren't there slightly more than twelve million Jews in the world today?'

"Yes, there are, but each and every one of us carries sparks from that original six hundred thousand. Those six hundred thousand all stood at Mount Sinai, which means that all our *neshamahs* heard the voice of G-d, and perhaps that is one of the reasons why, when we study Torah properly, it *feels* so right."

"But wait a minute," Phyllis interrupted, "that sounds like reincarnation to me, and I thought Jews don't believe in that."

"Well then, I have a surprise for you. We do! As a matter of fact, reincarnation is so basic to our faith that every night, before we recite the bedtime *Shema,* we ask forgiveness for any wrongs that we may have committed '*B'gilgul zeh ooh b'gilgul acher,*' in this transmigration or in another transmigration. The literal meaning of *gilgul neshamah* is 'recycling of the souls.'

"You mean to say that people keep coming back?" Sam asked incredulously, repeating Phyllis' question.

"Absolutely. Take, for example, the story of Batya, the daughter of Pharaoh. It is written in the Torah that she *stretched out her hand* to retrieve the basket in which the infant Moses was hidden on the Nile River. There are many levels on which we can understand this, but there is a Kabalistic teaching that Pharaoh's daughter was a *gilgul* of Chava (Eve). Chava brought darkness to the world when she ate the forbidden fruit. Pharaoh's daughter made *tikun.* She rectified the damage Chava caused because she reached out to take the basket that contained Moshe Rabbenu, who gave us the Torah — *the light and hope of the world.*

"Our mother Sarah also carried that spark from Chava in her soul, and she too made *tikun* for that first sin by inaugurating the kindling of the Sabbath lights. Thus, our souls keep recycling until we fulfill our mission,"

"Does *gilgul* apply only to Biblical figures?" Phyllis asked.

"Not at all. If someone was guilty of committing an injustice in his or her lifetime, or did not fulfill his or her mission, the Heavenly Tribunal might decide that that soul must return for *tikun* — rectification.

"Let me tell you a story about the *Ba'al Shem Tov,* the great chassidic master, who lived in the late seventeenth, early eighteenth centuries, that will surely amaze you.

"One *Erev Shabbos* (Friday), the *Ba'al Shem Tov* was approached by a woman who wanted to know if the chicken that she had purchased in the market was kosher. Instead of responding, the *Ba'al Shem Tov* told her to ask the question of a retarded man who was sitting nearby. The woman was taken aback at this strange response, but who was she to question the holy rebbe? So she went over to the poor man and posed her question. He studied the chicken carefully, examining it from every angle, and then proclaimed 'Kosher.' And with that, the man collapsed and died. In shock, the woman turned to the *Ba'al Shem Tov* for insight into this bizarre, traumatic happening. His explanation was even more astounding. The *Ba'al Shem Tov* revealed that in another *gilgul*, this man had been a very distinguished rabbi of great piety. One *Erev Shabbos*, a poor woman brought a chicken to him to pass judgment on its *kashruth*. It was late in the day, and the rabbi had much to do in preparation for the Sabbath, so he didn't take the time to examine the chicken carefully, and without much thought, ruled that the chicken was not kosher."

"When the rabbi arrived at the Heavenly Courts and the days of his life were reviewed, there was only one blemish on his impeccable record, and that was the unnecessary grief that he had caused this poor woman, so he was sent back to make *tikun*. In this reincarnation, G-d placed him in the body of a retarded person, for such an individual is not responsible for the fulfillment of the commandments, and thus his *neshamah* remains unsullied. But now that he had fulfilled his mission, he was free to return home."

"That's heavy duty!" Sam exclaimed. "Who knows who I really am? And who knows who you really are, honey?" he said, turning to Phyllis and trying to make light of the subject. But it was obvious that he was perturbed.

"Don't even attempt to go there. We can't possibly know these things. The only reason that I related this story is to impress upon you that nothing is as simple as it appears to be, so when life tests us, when we feel overwhelmed by the trials and tribulations that come our way, instead of becoming angry, bitter, or depressed, we must ask ourselves, 'What lesson should I learn from this? What is the *tikun* that I have to make? How do I grow and fulfill the purpose for which I was created? How do I learn to listen to that inner voice — my *neshamah*?'"

"Well, that's what I was asking at the very beginning of our discussion," Sam commented.

"I know; however, we first had to get there — so now let's try to find an answer. Actually there are several avenues. For starters, let me ask you a question. When you are troubled by feelings of guilt, what do you do?"

"Phyllis runs to Emily, her therapist," Sam said, laughing.

"And you cold-bloodedly rationalize that they had it coming to them," Phyllis snapped.

"The two of you responded in the way most people react to those gnawing feelings of guilt that tug at the soul — but I'm afraid that both of you are incorrect. Guilt for the *neshamah* is very much like a toothache — it is a blessing because it forces us to seek out a dentist. People who never suffer from toothaches and one day discover that their teeth have rotted away are in serious trouble. Guilt is the voice of our *neshamahs*, reminding us to make amends for the wrongs that we inflicted before it is too late. Guilt is not meant to be talked away, sublimated, or transferred to others, nor is it meant to be rationalized away. In the book of Ecclesiastes, it is written that G-d created mankind upright — but man makes his own calculations and rationalizations in order to justify his aberrations. To be at peace with our *neshamahs,* however, we must address the source of our guilt and rectify it. For example, if you had an altercation with your mother, you can run to your therapist and talk out your feelings, or you can rationalize that you were provoked, and were thereby justified in saying what you did. Neither of these responses will appease your *neshamah*. Your soul will not be satisfied until such time as you make *tikun*."

"How can we know how to make *tikun*?" Phyllis asked.

"Actually, it's quite simple. You have to ask yourself just one question, 'Am I dealing with this problem in accordance with G-d's Will?' So, going back to my example of an altercation with your mom — Torah *requires* that you apologize and rectify the wrong."

"Well, what if the mother was wrong and should be the one to apologize?" Sam challenged.

"It can't happen. The relationship between parent and child is not based on the democratic process, but rather, on the Fifth Commandment, 'Honor thy father and mother.' There can never be justification for being insolent to your parents, so you apologize for no other reason than that she is your mother. As I said earlier, the only way to make *tikun* is to follow our Torah road map. That is the only language to which the *neshamah* responds. Anything short of that, be it medication, therapy, rationalization, or scapegoating, is bound to fail. The pain in our *neshamahs* will continue unabated, depriving us of inner serenity and peace until such time as we fulfill our mission and *tikun* is made."

"But I still don't understand how I can know what my mission is — what I must do to make *tikun*?"

"You cannot know exactly, but there are certain guidelines that you can follow. Let's discuss just one and defer the rest until our next meeting.

"Those things that you find difficult," I explained, "those things that really irritate you and go against your nature are probably situations in which you failed in another lifetime. For example, if you have a short fuse and lose your temper easily, you might discover that there is always someone in your life who pushes your buttons. It might even be your spouse or your child who requires extra patience."

"But how can we be expected to pass tests that go against our nature?" Phyllis interrupted.

"A good teacher would never test his students with that which is beyond their capacity. So too, G-d never challenges us with tests that we cannot pass. When He places something in our path, it means that we are capable of rising to the occasion and passing it."

"But how can that be?" Phyllis protested. "It doesn't make sense. You just can't go against your nature."

"Let's consider that for a minute. Have you ever analyzed exactly what constitutes your nature?" I asked. "Our sages provide us with profound insights into this subject: *'Adom nifal l'fee p'ulosov'* — 'A man is shaped by his deeds,' meaning, if you do something long enough, it becomes second nature, and it is *that* which makes you, *you*. So, for example, if you become accustomed to nasty habits, you become a nasty person. If you become used to venting your feelings, you become an uncontrolled, angry individual. The converse is also true. If you act kindly, eventually, you become kind. If you force yourself to give, in time, you become generous.

"The positive aspect of this teaching is reinforced in our Talmud: *'mitoch she'lo lishmoh, bo lishmoh,'* — meaning that that which you initially do by rote, you will end up doing with sincerity if you persevere. The action will become so deeply imbedded in your psyche that it will actually transform your personality. *It emerges then that it is within your capacity to mold your nature if you truly wish to do so."*

"But doing things by rote, without feeling and believing them, sounds hypocritical to me," Sam protested.

"It is permissible to be a hypocrite in order to break negative habits. And so, if your nature is to be callous or uncaring, pretend to be caring and giving, and if you do so consistently, then one day you will wake up and discover that you have miraculously become a caring, giving person." And to illustrate, I related a story written by the British author Max Beerbohm entitled "The Happy Hypocrite." It is about a gentleman named Lord George Hell, whose name mirrored his personality. His bad temper was reflected in his eyes, his face, his very demeanor, and good people tried to avoid him. Well, one day, Lord George fell madly in love with a sweet, gentle, lovely maiden. But she was so repelled by his appearance that she let him know that she could never entertain the thought of becoming involved with a man whose face was so cruel and angry.

So, Lord George came up with a brilliant idea. He would commission a master artist to create a mask for him that would reflect a kind, benevolent, gentle person. Thus disguised, he called on the damsel, who immediately fell in love with him. They were wed, and lived happily ever after, until one day, an old enemy came to visit. "You think that you are married to a kind, gentle man — I'll show you who your husband really is!" he said with glee. And with that, he ripped the mask off Lord George's face. But lo and behold, the face beneath the mask was identical to that of the mask!

Throughout their marriage, Lord George had pretended to be gentle and generous, so that his conduct would not belie his mask. This left deep marks on his mind and heart and transformed him into the person he had pretended to be.

"A beautiful story," Sam commented, "but it borders on the *miraculous* rather than on reality."

"But miracles can become your reality. That's the beauty of it, Sam. Think about it. What constitutes a miracle? Take, for example, the splitting of the Sea of Reeds. Why was it considered miraculous? Obviously, it is because we are accustomed to seeing the waters of the sea covering the sea bed, but when the sea split, it went *against nature*. The waters rose and formed walls to permit the passage of the

Israelites, a phenomenon that no one had ever before witnessed, and therefore, we regard it as miraculous. But just as the sea went against its nature, every time we *go against our nature*, and pass the tests that G-d sends our way, we too create a miracle. That is why the Hebrew word for "test" — *"nisayon"* is related to *"nes"* — miracle, for passing our tests is the miracle that we are all capable of performing.

"The greatness of man is not measured by the wealth he accumulates, nor by the knowledge that he acquires, but by the way in which he passes G-d's tests. Abraham merited becoming the patriarch of the Jewish people, not because of his brilliant mind or even his generous heart, but by the manner in which he passed the tests that G-d sent his way."

"But I'm not Abraham. I need a mask to pass my test, and masks exist only in fables."

"But that's where you are wrong. We do have masks. The commandments with which G-d endowed us are designed to structure and mold us into better people. *They* are our masks."

Sam looked at me skeptically.

"Try it," I challenged, "and see for yourself. Give me any two things that you find especially difficult and I will show you the Torah mask that is guaranteed to facilitate passing the test and creating the miracle that is your life."

Sam was silent. "I don't know," he said doubtfully, "everything is difficult."

"Well, I *do* know," Phyllis interrupted. "For one thing, he's always moody. I have yet to see a smile on his face. And he also lacks faith. Mind you, I'm not religious either, but I do trust in G-d. The only thing that Sam, trusts however, is money, and now that he's lost it, he's miserable."

"Well, how can I be smiling," Sam protested, "when I am filled with worry."

"Learn from this teaching — force yourself. Pretend!"

"That's easier said than done, Rebbetzin," Sam said. "Believe me, I wish I had reason to smile."

"My husband of blessed memory used to quote a teaching from the Breslover Rebbe: 'When there is no reason to smile, put a smile on your face and G-d will give you every reason to smile.'"

"Sam," Phyllis said, "you must remember that."

"I'm certain that your husband was a wonderful man," Sam said, "but he didn't have to deal with what I do."

"True, everyone's test is different. My husband was a survivor of the Holocaust. His family was wiped out in Auschwitz, and he came to this country a destitute orphan who didn't even speak the language. And believe me, his life was far from easy. To have been the rabbi of an Orthodox synagogue in a young assimilated Long Island community forty-five years ago was a daunting challenge fraught with much aggravation, and yet, I can never recall seeing him without a smile. He understood that his face was public property, that it is wrong to inflict negative moods on others. I'm sure that you will agree, Sam, that it is ill-mannered to sneeze or cough on someone and spread germs. Well, it is even more damaging to crush another's spirit by inflicting an angry or moody expression. Therefore, our sages instruct us, 'Greet every person with a pleasant countenance' (*Mishna*). That's the *mask* you have to wear, Sam, so whenever you come in contact with others, force yourself to smile, and if you prevail, you will discover an added blessing — others will smile back at you and their warmth will be reflected in your heart. 'As water reflects your face, so one heart reflects another' is a teaching of King Solomon.

"Some years ago, I spoke at the University of Pennsylvania, and as is my custom, following my lecture, I stayed to speak to the young people and respond to their questions. A student approached me.

"'May I ask you a personal question?' she asked, hesitantly.

"'Sure,' I responded.

"'You always have a smile on your face, and after reading your book, I know that you went through so much — the concentration camps, the loss of your husband — how can you always be smiling? Tell me, Rebbetzin,' she went on, catching me by surprise, 'where does your smile start? In your heart or on your lips?'

"To be honest," I told her, "I never thought about it, but now that you mention it, I guess it starts on my lips. In my heart I have many worries; in my heart, I know pain, but once I place a smile on my lips, it travels to my heart and makes everything easier. And that's the teaching, Sam. 'A man is shaped by his deeds.'

"As for your lack of faith, Sam, has it ever occurred to you that perhaps you were tested by the loss of your fortune because you placed your trust in your money rather than in the Almighty G-d?"

"Are you telling me that G-d is punishing me?" Sam asked, testily.

"Not at all. G-d is our loving Father. G-d doesn't punish, but He does want us to return to Him. Just imagine a parent who sends a child off to college with a gold credit card and never hears from him. When he tries to call, he gets a machine, and he can't even leave a message because the mailbox is full. So the father decides to close his son's account in the hope that he will call. Sure enough, the phone rings. 'Hey Dad, what's going on? I went for gas and they wouldn't accept my credit card!'

"Let's apply this example to your life, Sam. In vain did G-d call you — He couldn't get through. Your mailbox was full! In all honesty, if not for your loss, would you ever have been motivated to examine your life? Please don't take offense, but in a way, aren't you like that college kid? Aren't you also saying, 'What's going on? Why did I lose my credit card?'"

"You have to admit, honey, that what the Rebbetzin said is true," Phyllis said, in a warm, caring tone.

There was silence in the room. Both Phyllis and I gazed at Sam until finally, with a sheepish half-smile, he said, "So what's my mask for this one?"

"For now, just work on greeting everyone with a pleasant countenance and 'everyone' also includes your wife! As for trust in G-d and faith, we will defer that to our next discussion. Meanwhile, bear in mind that if you really want to know what your mission in life may be, what you must do to make *tikun*, the determining factor should not be that which you *feel* like doing, but that which is *right* to do. So every time you have a moment of difficulty, tell yourself, 'This is a test, and if G-d placed it in my path, then He also made it possible for me to pass it. I need only take hold of my mask, apply it, and the miracle that will enable me to grow into the person that G-d intended me to be, will become my reality.'"

5

To Be a Jew

On a typical Thursday, I see a host of people in my office for private consultations following my Torah classes. There is a common denominator uniting them, and that is the heavy burden that they carry in their hearts. I keep a large box of tissues and loads of comfort food — cookies, cake, and chocolate — on my desk. And on my bookshelf, I have a stock of prayer books and books of Psalms. Over the years, I have been privy to the most tragic and agonizing problems; I doubt that there are many personal dilemmas that I haven't heard

— from the most trivial to the most painful, I have encountered them all.

To be sure, there are situations that seem hopeless and appear to have no human solution. In such cases, I recall the image of my holy father. When people brought their problems to him, and there were no fast or easy answers, he would feel their pain, weep with them, feel with them, and give them a *berachah* — a blessing, from his heart.

I will never forget, when, before the Nazi invasion of Hungary, the Belzer Rebbe, who was at the top of the Gestapo's wanted list, was miraculously smuggled from Poland into Budapest. His wife, children, grandchildren, and in-laws had been brutally set aflame by the Nazis — literally burned to death — and the Rebbe himself was marked for deportation to the death camps. In a harrowing escape, a Hungarian counter-intelligence agent who was friendly to Jews whisked the Rebbe, his younger brother, and his gabbai (aide), into Hungary. Their rabbinic beards and side locks shaven, they were disguised as Russian generals who had been captured at the front and were being taken to Budapest for interrogation. Throughout their 250-mile drive across German-occupied Poland to Hungary, they had one close call after another, but miraculously evaded detection. At one check point they were detained and almost exposed, but then, as if from nowhere, three high-ranking Hungarian officials appeared and ordered that their vehicle be let through.

When the news of the Rebbe's arrival in Budapest reached the Jewish community, there was great excitement. My father, like many others, sought a meeting with him. When it became known in our city, Szeged, that my father was actually going to Budapest to see the Rebbe, countless Jews came to our home, not only from our community, but from the provinces as well. They all brought with them *kvitlech* — petitions — asking the Rebbe for his *berachah*. So it was that my father arrived at the Rebbe's dwelling with a suitcase that was literally filled with these *kvitlech*. But when the Rebbe beheld the suitcase and its contents, he said, "Szegediner Rov [my father's rabbinic title], *gloibt mir, Ich hub nisht kein koyach* — Believe me, I simply have no strength, but I give over to you all the *brachos,* blessings. Whomever you bless, will be blessed."

Looking back upon those years, I have often thought that the Rebbe, with his piercing gaze, must have seen the great love that my father harbored in his heart for every person, and it was that which impelled him to transmit the power of blessing to him. My father accepted this trust with awe and trepidation. He never tired of blessing people, and did so to his dying day. My sons, who spent Rosh Hashanah and Yom Kippur at his side, would tell me that the very short walk from the synagogue to his house would take well over an hour, for my father would stop to greet everyone he met on the way and impart a blessing to them, regardless of who they were or what their level of religious commitment.

Through my outreach work in Hineni, I have had the *zchus* (merit) of bringing multitudes of people from every walk of life back to the fold. I would take them all to my father, who would bless them — and through those blessings, he became not only their *rebbe,* but their *zeide.*

My father never mastered English, and these people did not speak Yiddish, but with his blessings, he transcended all language barriers.

A young man, a student at Columbia Law School who was ensnared in a cult, was literally dragged to my Torah seminar by his desperate mother. My father, who made a point of being present at my classes, spotted him immediately. He embraced him, wept over him, and lovingly said, *"Du bist a tiere Yiddishe kind..."*— "You are a precious Jewish child." As he warmly hugged him and his tears washed the boy's cheeks, he invoked the blessings of our patriarchs — and those blessings worked like magic! In an instant, this lost, assimilated student took a leap that spanned the centuries and returned to his faith. I learned from my father's example that blessings are not just empty words, that when they emanate from the heart, they enter another heart and impart new life. So when people present me with problems, I invoke the *berachos* — blessings — of my father and all my holy ancestors, and I too, bless them.

After more than fifty years of advising people, I still have not developed the thick skin that would render me immune to the suffering of others. I agonize over each and every person, and the plight of Sam and Phyllis was no exception. Financial reversals are never easy to accept, but what was especially difficult for Sam was the unexpected speed with which his world fell apart. Losing the status that came with his affluence and having to make do with less were totally shattering to him.

Mind you, I am fully aware that there are families that are confronted with problems that are by far more traumatic than those of Sam. As I mentioned earlier, when compared to health and life issues, loss of money is probably the easiest of life's tests, but to each person, his own trials are the most painful. Somehow, there is a faulty logic to the adage, "I thought I was poor because I had no shoes, until I met a man who had no feet." My mother, who was renowned for her pithy remarks, best summed it up, "Knowing that someone has more *tsuris* — problems — than I do, doesn't make mine go away. Besides," she would add, "what *nechamah* — comfort — can I possibly have from the *tsuris* of others? If anything, it makes me sadder." True, the awareness that there are those who have far greater problems than ours helps keep things in perspective, but there is no consolation to be derived from such comparisons.

What was especially pathetic about Sam, however, was that he was driving on empty. He had nothing to fall back on, no beliefs to sustain him, no faith to invigorate him and give him hope. I couldn't help but be struck by the sad irony that Sam represented. Here he was, a Jew, the descendent of a nation that had taught all mankind the language of prayer and the power of faith, and in his time of crisis, he had no faith to anchor him....

I realized that for Sam and Phyllis, blessings would not suffice — that if they were to pass the trials that resulted from their bankruptcy and learn and grow from that experience, they would have to examine their own lives and the meaning of their Jewishness, and no amount of blessings could accomplish that. This was something that had to spring from their own hearts, but whether I would be able to ignite such a desire for self-scrutiny in them remained to be seen.

Very often, when school groups visit the museum exhibits at our Hineni Heritage Center in Manhattan, I challenge the students with a question that, due to its simplicity, catches them off guard. "If you had something that was really precious to you, and you were afraid that it would get lost, what precautions would you take to keep it safe?"

They would look at me quizzically, wondering what possible relevance my question could have to their visit, so I tell them that they might begin by placing their names on the object so that if it does get lost, it will be returned. Similarly, I tell them, G-d placed His holy Name upon us, so that we might find our way back to Him.

And with that, I explain that the name "Jew" which is almost the same in every language, "Juif" in French, "Jude" in German, "Zyd" in Polish, "Zsido" in Hungaran, and so on, is a translation of the Hebrew word, "Yehudi," which contains the letters of the Name of G-d.

"It was our matriarch Leah, who actually coined the name, upon giving birth to her fourth son. She proclaimed 'This time I shall praise G-d,' and she called him [her son] "Yehudah" (*Genesis*, 29:35). In the Holy Tongue, Yehuda (Yehudi), literally means 'to praise G-d and offer Him thanks.' So not only is G-d's Name embedded in ours, but so is our mission. For us, *praying to G-d and expressing gratitude is not an option — it's our calling.* It is intrinsic to our lives; it is the very essence of our Jewishness.

"In the Holy Tongue, 'thank you' has another connotation. It also means 'to admit,' 'to confess.' When we say 'thank you' to G-d, we are in essence acknowledging our indebtedness — we are actually admitting that everything that we possess, everything that we are, is a gift from our Creator.

"'*Modeh ani*,' 'I thank You for returning my soul' are the first words that we pronounce upon awakening, and we continue to thank G-d throughout the day. We thank Him for the food that we ingest, for the clothing that we wear, for the knowledge that we possess, for the health that we enjoy — nothing can be taken for granted — *there is a blessing for everything*."

In all my years of teaching, I never had any difficulty imparting this to young people. On one occasion however, a teenager did challenge me. "I can relate to praying, but frankly, I find all these 'thank you's a bit much." Then, trying to be funny, she added, "Do we also have to say thank you for the ground we stand on, for the air that we breathe?"

"Absolutely!" I answered. "As a matter of fact, we have blessings that say just that. And if you think that that's 'a bit much,' ask anyone who experienced a tsunami or a plane crash, or ask the survivors of a mine disaster, and they will tell you that these blessings are not to be taken lightly."

There was silence in the room as many heads nodded in agreement, but she wouldn't let go. "Okay, so I chose a poor example, but if G-d is G-d, if He is infinite and complete, then why does He need all those 'Thank you's?"

"You're right. He doesn't, but *we* do," I answered. "If we are to become better human beings — kinder and happier individuals — then it is essential that we learn the meaning of these two little words and express our thanks with a full heart. It's a simple formula, but its power is immense. If applied regularly, it can actually transform a discontented, depressed person into a contented, happy one, and, mind you, without medication. One of the main reasons why people are unhappy is because they tend to focus on what they do not have rather than on what they do have, However, when they learn to say 'thank you' for all the things they have taken for granted – the expression that you labeled 'a bit much' – it compels them to take inventory of the gifts with which G-d blessed them, and they become better people for that experience.

"Additionally, by acknowledging that everything that we possess is a gift from G-d (and I'm not only referring to our material possessions, but to our talents and energies as well) we will become cognizant of our obligation to give back, and that will lend purpose and direction to our lives.

"Is there anything in your lives about which you feel truly passionate?" I challenged. "What are your life goals? What are the ideals that burn in your hearts? King Solomon, who was renowned for his wisdom taught, '*Ish k'fee m'halolo*' — 'A man can be identified by that which enthuses him, by that which excites him, and yes, by that about which he is passionate.' So ask yourselves, 'What things excite me? What am I passionate about? Sports? Entertainment? Shopping? Music? Cars? Money? What?'

All of these pursuits are a form of self-indulgence — they are all about 'me,' 'me,' 'me' — 'my,' 'my,' 'my,' and by their very nature cannot be fulfilling. We need our daily 'thank you's to keep us focused, to remind us that we have an obligation to give back, since that which we possess is not really ours, but was given to us in trust.

Once you absorb this, you will discover that happiness is not *having* more, but *being* more. And you become more by giving more."

"I wouldn't know where to begin," a girl sadly commented.

"Of course you would," I assured her. "Just tap into your heart and let kindness flow, give love to your parents, your siblings, your friends, your neighbors, your community, your people, and once you master that, you will also learn how to give to G-d. You see, it's all connected," I told her, "In order to express our indebtedness to our Heavenly Father, we have to learn to convey our gratitude to our biological parents and to all those with whom we come in contact.

"I was only four years old when my parents taught me this lesson. In our community, there was a little girl my age who was severely handicapped. My parents instructed me to play with her and teach her what I had learned in kindergarten — a tough demand to make on a four-year-old you might argue, but we are never too young to give. It is with these standards that I raised my own children," I explained, "and today, they in turn are perpetuating this tradition with their children. One of my granddaughters spends her free time after school as a volunteer with autistic children. She takes them on trips, invites them as overnight guests for *Shabbos*, and on Sundays, acts as their bus monitor, helping them in and out of wheel chairs and transporting them — the point being that we all must have goals that are greater than ourselves. And that's what being a *Yehudi* — a Jew — is all about. Ask G-d for guidance; ask Him to show you how you may best give back — the more you pray, the more clarity you will have. So you see," I told the girl, "it's not what you *receive* through your prayers, but what you *become* that is significant.

"There is yet another name that identifies us as a people," I told the students — '*Yisrael*.' That word too, is the same in every language, and there, too, we find the Name of G-d. Translated literally, it means 'to prevail for G-d.' Our father Jacob earned that title when he struggled with the angel of evil and emerged victorious. 'Your name shall no longer be Jacob, but *Yisrael,* for you have striven with the divine and with man and have overcome' (*Genesis* 32:29).

"That battle of Jacob was a cosmic struggle lasting all night until the break of dawn, and left him injured. This lesson once again speaks to us. As *Israelites,* we will always have to fight to preserve our values and our beliefs, and this struggle will continue until the break of dawn — the coming of Messiah. And even if some of Jacob's descendants become 'injured' — lost to assimilation — they too will ultimately prevail and return. As a matter of fact, we have a law, '*Af al pee she'chotoh — Yisroel hu...*' — 'Even if a Jew sins, he is nevertheless still a Jew.' This means that we are never permanently lost, but have an amazing capacity to come back."

"Does that also include someone who converted?" one of the young people asked.

"Oh, yes. Over the years, I have had the privilege of bringing back countless such Jews, be it from cults, Eastern religions, or Christianity."

"How about people who come from religious homes and gave it all up?" another student asked. "I have a cousin like that and it's killing my aunt and uncle."

"The energy of *Shema Yisrael* is engraved upon every heart. So tell your aunt and uncle that one day your cousin will also come back — just let them keep the channels of communication open." And with that, I related the story of Nechama (as always, the names that I use are pseudonyms).

I first met her at our annual Chanukah party. She came with a group of friends, and although there were over five hundred people in attendance, her striking appearance made her stand out.

"I don't think we've ever met," I said, greeting her.

"No, we haven't," she replied, and I felt a certain tension in her voice.

"What's your name?"

"Nikki," she responded.

"Nikki?" I repeated questioningly.

"Actually, my name is Nicole, but everyone calls me Nikki."

"And what's your Jewish name?"

"Nechama," she said, with an edge in her voice.

"I love that name!"

"I'm happy that *you* do, because I don't. That's why I changed it to Nicole."

"I bet that if you knew the significance of your name, you wouldn't feel that way."

"Oh, don't think that I don't. I've heard it a hundred times, and it really doesn't turn me on."

"Perhaps if you heard it for the hundred and first time, you'd like it better!" I joked, "but tell me about yourself. What do you do?"

"I'm an actress."

"Where? Broadway? TV, film?"

"Well, I've had some parts in a few Off-Broadway productions — I'm waiting for my big break."

"So, while you're waiting, maybe you'll try our Torah classes," I suggested.

"Thanks, but no thanks. I've already been there."

"What do you mean?

"Well, I come from a religious family," she confessed. "I went to yeshivah. My family name is _____, you probably recognize it."

Sure enough, I recalled her story immediately. Her parents were well-respected, and when she left home to pursue a career in the theater, it created quite a furor. As a matter of fact, I had often toyed with the idea of calling her parents and offering my help, but since I didn't really know them, I was afraid that my calls would be looked upon as an invasion of privacy. And now, here she was at our Hineni Chanukah party! I couldn't believe it.

"Do me just one favor," I said. "Even if you think that you've heard it all and know it all, give it one more try and come learn Torah with me."

"I'll see if I can find the time," she said vaguely.

"When people say that, it makes me nervous, because I know that they won't. So make a promise that, with G-d's help, you'll come." And with that, I cupped her face between my hands and drew her close to me. "Do it as a favor to me," I urged, looking her straight in the eyes.

To my surprise, the following Thursday, she appeared, and that's how her journey home commenced. From that first class, she came to many more, and in time, she confided that her glamorous life was not so glamorous after all. While she had landed a few parts in off-Broadway shows, they really didn't afford her a livelihood. To support herself, she waited on tables in a restaurant. In moments of depression, she was given to binging, which in turn, led to bouts of bulimia. As for her personal life, she had been through several broken relationships that left her pained and scarred.

"I made a huge mistake when I gave up my family and a Torah life. My former classmates," she said through tears, "are all married with babies, and look at me, I'm nowhere. I thought that I was smart, but I was just plain stupid. I don't know what possessed me, but now it's too late. There's no going back — I cannot undo the past. I guess I'll just have to live with it."

"But you don't! You *can* start all over again. That's the miracle with which *HaShem* endowed us."

"Oh, Rebbetzin, I wish it were as simple as you make it."

"But it is," I said, taking her in my arms. "G-d is our loving Father who wants us to come home. He's not interested in the mistakes you made in the past, but in your resolve to start a new life today.

Your tears are a beautiful offering on G-d's altar, and they are very precious to Him." With that, I reached for a Book of Psalms and read from Psalm 34: 'They cry out and G-d hears, and from all their troubles, He rescues them. G-d is close to the broken-hearted, and the crushed in spirit, He saves.'

"Let go of the past," I urged. "Convert the pain of these past years into wisdom that will enable you to live a more meaningful life. Your name, Nechama, means comfort. Live up to your name. Give comfort to others, but above all, be a comfort to yourself."

"What would you have me do?" she asked in a whisper.

"In a few weeks, it will be *Pesach*. Tell your parents that you will be coming home for the Seder."

"I can't. You don't understand, Rebbetzin. My father will never talk to me. I did so many terrible things. When I left, he warned that he would disown me."

"He just said that to bring you to your senses. Believe me, no father ever disowns his child. Your father may have disowned *what you did*, but never *you*." But no matter what I said, Nechama remained unconvinced, so I took it upon myself to call her father. Having heard of her family's reputation for *hachnosas orchim* — welcoming guests — I felt comfortable enough to ask him if he could accommodate our Hineni organization by taking some of our young people for the Seder.

"I'll have to ask my wife," he answered, "but I'm sure it won't be a problem. How many people are we talking about?"

"Just one girl."

"That will be okay. How old is she and what's her name?"

"She's twenty-five and her name is Nechama."

There was silence at the other end of the line. "Is this some sort of a joke?" he finally said in a tense, trembling voice.

"*Chas V'Shalom* — G-d forbid! I have good news for you. Nechama has been coming to my classes — she is a changed person. I know that she would like to come home for Pesach, but she is afraid that you won't accept her. She's afraid to call you."

There was no response, but I distinctly heard the sound of weeping.

"Why don't you and your wife come to Hineni next week? Go directly to my office and after my class, I'll tell Nechama that I want to speak to her privately, and you will see for yourself that your daughter has come home."

When Nechama walked into my office the following week and saw her parents waiting, she turned ashen. For a moment, daughter and parents just stood there, looking at each other in disbelief. Her mother was sobbing, and her father's eyes were moist with tears. "Mom, Dad," she called out in a trembling voice as she rushed into the open arms of her parents.

"So tell Nechama's story to your aunt and uncle," I now said. "Please G-d, even as she came home, your cousin will come home as well.

"It is written that when our patriarch Jacob was on his death-bed, all of his children gathered around him and he blessed them. G-d had granted Jacob *Ruach HaKodesh* (Divinely inspired insight) — He allowed His holy spirit to rest upon him, enabling Jacob to foresee the future. Suddenly, darkness enveloped him and his *ruach hakodesh* departed. Jacob foresaw that some of his descendants would stray and worship strange gods, and he was terrified. To reassure him, his sons, the twelve tribes of Israel proclaimed in unison, '*Shema Yisrael, HaShem Elokeinu, HaShem Echad!*' — 'Hear, O Israel, the L-rd our G-d, the L-rd is One.'

"Now, this answer is rather puzzling. One would have expected them to say, 'Father, do not fear. We will never abandon the covenant. We will remain loyal to our G-d.' Moreover, what did the brothers mean when they proclaimed, "Hear, O Israel'? Who were they speaking to? And for that matter, *who are we speaking to* when we say *Shema Yisrael?*

"There is a deeper teaching here that is the legacy of all our people. When Jacob struggled the entire night and triumphed over the forces of evil, he created '*Yisrael*' — a '*pintele Yid*' — a Jewish 'pilot light' that flickers in our souls and has become part of our spiritual DNA. So when the sons of Jacob cried out *Shema Yisrael* to their elderly father, they reminded him that, because of his struggle, even if a generation becomes lost, they will nevertheless return because they are *Yisrael,* and the desire to triumph for G-d is forever embedded in their souls. So when we say the *Shema,* we are not only praying, we are making a declaration that we will remain connected to our G-d. We will sublimate ourselves to His will and commit ourselves to the establishment of *Ol Malchus Shamayim* — the Kingdom of Heaven on earth — and the very fact that we are Yisrael is a guarantee that our patriarchs and matriarchs will always be there to help us.

"The '**Y**' in Yisrael stands for Yitzchok and Yaakov; '**S**' stands for Sora; '**R**' for Rivka and Rachel, '**A**' for Avraham, and '**L**' for Leah.

"We are never alone, for they are always walking with us, accompanying us on our every path, helping us find our way back. And more — there are thirteen Hebrew letters in the names of the patriarchs and thirteen in the names of the matriarchs. Thirteen are the attributes of mercy that G-d taught Moses, assuring him that He will forever look upon us with compassion. Thirteen and thirteen equal twenty-six, which is the *gematria* (numerical value) of the Name of G-d in His attribute of mercy.

"It is with *Shema Yisrael* that we commence each and every day. It is with *Shema Yisrael* that the cantor, holding the holy Torah, charges the congregation on *Shabbos* and holidays; it is with *Shema*

Yisrael that we welcome a newborn at the *vachtnacht* — the night before his bris — and that we say farewell to life; it is with *Shema Yisrael* that we enter and exit our homes, for *Shema Yisrael* is written in the *mezuzahs* of our doorposts; it is with *Shema Yisrael* that we conclude the holiest of our days, Yom Kippur, the Day of Atonement; it is with *Shema Yisrael* that we have sanctified the Name of G-d throughout the millennia.

"When, over thirty-five years ago, I founded our Hineni movement, I was treading in virgin territory. There was no precedent for this work. I was keenly aware that to succeed I would need the blessings of our Torah sages. And so it was that, in the company of my dear, revered father, I visited many of the great sages of our generation to receive their *brachos*.

"I recognized that we would have to do something radical to awaken our assimilated, disenfranchised youth, and so it was that we took Madison Square Garden — a formidable undertaking — which miraculously drew a standing-room-only audience.

"But what message could I impart that would enter the hearts and souls of our people? How would I awaken those thousands who were there but no longer remembered who they were? The answer was obvious — "*Shema Yisrael.*" That night, when I called out those eternal words, they reverberated throughout the Garden. Hearts that had lain dormant were suddenly awakened and thousands stood and sang out '*Shema Yisrael*' — and thus, Hineni was born.

"But it was not only in Madison Square Garden that the Shema reawakened dormant souls. I related to the young people the story of the great Rabbi Eliezer Silver, who was one of the first American rabbis to enter the liberated concentrations camps. He encountered the survivors who were living skeletons; he beheld the piles upon piles of bodies, stacked like so much cordwood; he saw the gas chambers and the crematoria in which six million of our people, one-and-a-half million of whom were children, were gassed and incinerated. The enormity of the tragedy was beyond comprehension.

"Rabbi Silver learned that some Jewish children had been hidden in monasteries and baptized, and he made a pledge to seek them out. He traveled to a hermitage in the Alsace-Lorraine region of France where he was told that Jewish orphans were hidden. The monk who was in charge, however, insisted that there were no Jewish children on the premises.

"Rabbi Silver asked for a list of the refugees. Since he was wearing the uniform of a U.S. Army colonel, the monk obeyed him. Among them, he noticed some Jewish sounding names, but he was assured that they were all Germans. Not at all convinced, Rabbi Silver said that he would return to speak to the children in the evening.

"That night, he returned in the company of two aides. They entered a high-ceilinged dormitory room and began to sing '*Shema Yisrael*.' Suddenly, from under the covers of six beds in the room, little voices were heard. They started to sing the *Shema* with him. They remembered it from their mommies and daddies, from their *zeydes* and *bubbies,* and, with tears flowing down their cheeks, they ran to the rabbi.

"'These are my children!' the rabbi exclaimed. 'I'm taking them to their home — to *Eretz Yisrael.*'

"The power of *Shema Yisrael* is such that it resonates in even the most assimilated hearts. Even when all else is forgotten, *Shema Yisrael* remains and guides us home. So when you feel conflicted," I said to the students, "when you are struggling with life's trials and tests and wonder which path you should choose, just remember the names that define you — '*Yehudi'* — ' Jew' — and '*Yisrael,'* and your path will become clear."

Young people never have difficulty understanding this, but I wondered whether Sam and Phyllis would. Would they be willing to accept that, in order to put their lives back together, they would have to learn to pray, study Torah, and thus discover the ideals that enabled our people to proclaim *"Shema Yisrael"* in every generation?

6

But I'm Not Religious!

I must admit that I learned something. I had no idea that the words "Jew" and "Yisrael" had a significance all their own," Sam admitted, but that was as far as he would go.

"Let's not kid ourselves, Rebbetzin — I'm not religious. I went along with this because I was pressured by Phyllis and our friends — I even tried to put on that 'mask' that you spoke of and worked on keeping a smile on my face. But prayer? Frankly, the whole concept seems primitive to me. So I'll pray and by magic, G-d will restore my business? I'm too old for such fairy tales."

"You have it all wrong, Sam. That's not how it works. Try to shed your bias and let's start from scratch. Do you recall that early on, at one of our sessions, I told you that in order to understand any one concept, it is essential that you first define the word in its original Hebrew — in the Holy Tongue? Prayer is not about 'give me'; it's not about bringing a shopping list to G-d, nor is it behaving like a petulant child who throws a temper tantrum until its needs are satisfied. In the Holy Tongue, the term 'to pray' is '*l'hitpallel*,' which literally means 'to judge one's self,' so when we pray, in essence, we are giving an accounting of our lives."

"That sounds kind of contradictory to me," Phyllis interjected. "How can you possibly judge yourself objectively?"

"True," I agreed, "it does sound contradictory. Most of us have difficulty seeing ourselves honestly. Even if we concede that we are guilty of something, we will nevertheless try to paint ourselves in the most favorable light and rationalize that, basically, we are good people, but were either provoked, misled, manipulated, or abused, and therefore, cannot be held responsible. The problem is further exacerbated by our psychology-oriented culture that mitigates against our accepting personal accountability, so genuine self-scrutiny eludes us. But when we stand before G-d in prayer, we cannot 'talk-away' our character flaws. We cannot blame others for our aberrations or whitewash our culpability through therapy. In G-d's presence we have to talk *emes* — truth. We must confront the reality of our actions and our thoughts without excuses or scapegoating, and that is a very humbling experience. It puts us in touch with our *neshamahs*; it gives us a glimpse of who we really are, and, most important, who we must strive to become. So, Sam, if you take upon yourself the discipline of praying regularly, you can truly grow and realize your potential."

"Now, that, to me, is very inspiring," Phyllis said. "I must admit though, that I was always under the impression that the purpose of prayer is to ask G-d to grant us our wishes — sort of like download-ing miracles and blessings."

"That, too, happens," I assured her, "but that is a by-product of prayer and not the reason for it. When G-d grants us our wishes, it's not because we whined and pleaded until, in desperation, He gave in, but because through prayer, *we were transformed and became worthy of a new relationship and status.*

"I can actually relate dozens of stories that I personally wit-nessed that demonstrate the miracles that occur when we allow prayer to recreate us. I have seen people recoup their lost busi-nesses, and in many instances become even more successful; I have seen those who were stricken with terminal illness recover and enjoy a long life; I have seen couples who, for years, were childless and then were blessed with a family; I have seen desper-ate singles who had all but given up hope of finding their soul mates, meet their marriage partners — and it all came about through the miracle of prayer."

"The Rebbetzin should really meet Kelly," Sam now said, turning to Phyllis. "Maybe she could find her a guy."

"By all means. I would love to meet her," I agreed.

"I wish it were that simple," Phyllis said, "but there is no way she would ever consent to come. But, Sam," Phyllis added, "you should really tell the Rebbetzin about your aunt Carol. Maybe she could pray for her."

"What are you talking about!" Sam said with annoyance. "Carol is dying of cancer. She's beyond prayer."

"No one is beyond prayer, Sam," I said. "Prayer works miracles. Let me share with you some stories from my personal experience.

"In the late 1930s there was some sort of epidemic in our city. There was no known cure, and many died. My mother, whose kindness and compassion knew no bounds, was an angel of mercy and reached out to help stricken families. When she returned home from a sick call, she was always careful to wash her hands and change her garments. On one occasion, however, before she could wash and disinfect herself, my older brother ran to her and hugged and kissed her. He soon came down with this devastating illness, which had spread so rapidly that the city health department quarantined the sick in a local hospital. My brother had lapsed into a coma and was a hairsbreadth from death. My parents were told that there was no hope and were sent home to care for their other children.

"My father refused to accept the verdict, and although it was late at night, he went from house to house, awakening the ten most pious men in the city and asked them all to go to the *mikveh* (ritual bath for spiritual purification) and commit themselves to additional Torah study and *mitzvot*. He gathered them under the window of my brother's hospital room where they cried out from the depths of their hearts and recited the entire book of Psalms. Miraculously, as dawn broke, my brother opened his eyes and his first word was 'Tattie'.

"I have seen this life-transforming power of prayer, not only during my early childhood, but throughout my life — even in the concentration camps. Every *Shabbos* eve in Bergen-Belsen, my father would gather us and whisper, 'Close your eyes, my dearest children, close your eyes. We are at home. It is *Shabbos*. Mommy just baked delicious challah.' And as he spoke, he would bring forth some precious crumbs of bread, which at great sacrifice, he had saved from his rations during the entire week. Then, slowly, in his sweet, melodious voice, my father would begin to sing '*Shalom Aleichem*', the hymn welcoming the angels of *Shabbos*.

"On one occasion, my brother cried out, 'Tattie, I don't see any *malachim* — angels — here. Where are the *malachim* of Shabbos?'

"'You, my *lichtige kinderlech* — you, my precious lights — are the *malachim*,' my father answered, with tears flowing down his holy face.'

"Through the power of prayer we transcended our environment and despite the rats, vermin and brutality that surrounded us, we soared and became angels of *Shabbos*."

"So you see, Sam," Phyllis said, "prayers *do* help."

"Honey, we are talking about *terminal illness*. None of the doctors offer any hope — and they're talking about *days*, not *weeks*. Let's get real!"

"Okay, let's get real," I agreed. "Let me tell you about Rochelle, a dear friend of our Hineni organization. She too was given only days to live. I first met her at our High Holy Day services which are held at a hotel in Manhattan. Her two sons, Barry and Bruce, were active in our Hineni Young Leadership program and prevailed upon her and her husband to join us. Rochelle was a sweet, kind, and gracious lady who was courageously battling cancer. She never complained, but I felt her pain. We prayed and looked upon each and every day that passed as a gift, another victory.

"It is our tradition at Hineni to honor outstanding members of our Young Leadership at our annual dinner. Since Bruce and Barry were pillars of the organization, it was natural for us to render them tribute, but I must admit that we had the added incentive of bringing *naches* — joy — to Rochelle.

"At that dinner, we also paid tribute to Elissa, a lovely young woman who had distinguished herself in her commitment. Seeing the young people seated at the dais, a thought hit me. Bruce and Elissa would make a great couple! I got to work immediately, and told Bruce that he must call her. But I wasn't content to leave it at that. Making matches has taught me that, even though most singles desire to marry, they somehow tend to procrastinate, so although it was past midnight when I returned home, I called Barry and put him in charge. 'Make certain that Bruce makes that call tomorrow.'

"Over the years, I have had the privilege of introducing many young couples, but making Bruce and Elissa's *shidduch* and seeing Rochelle's beaming face as she and her devoted husband, Harold, walked Bruce down the aisle, was especially gratifying.

"There were many close calls, but Rochelle continued to fight, and somehow, she always rebounded. But then, one year, just a few weeks before Yom Kippur, Barry called me with sad news.

"'My mother is back in the hospital and the doctors told us that the time has come to make arrangements for a hospice.'

"'No way!' I said. 'We'll intensify our prayers, and please G-d, you'll take her home for *Shabbos*.'

"A few days later, I called her house. Harold answered the phone. 'How is Rochelle?' I asked.

"'Rebbetzin, you won't believe this," he said excitedly, "she's actually in the kitchen making chicken soup for *Shabbos*! Let me put her on the phone to tell you yourself.'

"We laughed and cried as she told me the great news, but above all, we gave thanks to G-d. The cancer however, was unrelenting, and weeks later, as we ushered in the holy day of Yom Kippur, Rochelle was once again back in the hospital.

"On that Yom Kippur, we prayed with renewed fervor, and when services were over, her family went straight to her bedside. I remained at the hotel to wish everyone a good year, and then, I too, rushed to the hospital. It was very late when I arrived, but the family was still there. I took Rochelle's hands in mine and said, 'You are going to be the guest of honor at our Chanukah Women's League Luncheon, and you will tell everyone of the power of prayer and sanctify the Name of G-d.'

"'Oh Rebbetzin,' she answered in a weak voice, tears gathering in her eyes. 'I wish, but Chanukah is a long, long way off. And *me*, speak ? — Oh Rebbetzin!!'

"'With G-d's help,' I assured her, 'it will come true. Let's just pray and connect to *HaShem*.'

"And so it was that Rochelle was our guest of honor. When she was brought to the platform in her wheelchair and took the microphone, a hush descended on the audience. Her words flowed from her heart and entered the hearts of all those present. There wasn't a dry eye in the room, and yes, she sanctified the Name of G-d.

"Our battle for Rochelle's life continued. 'Let's aim for Purim,' I said. 'You'll come to the Purim celebration at my son's home (my son and his wife hold an open house on Purim, and everyone is invited). It seemed like an unattainable goal — from Chanukah to Purim is eons away when you have already been consigned to a hospice, but once again, Rochelle made it. When she was wheeled into my son's home, everyone broke out in spontaneous song in celebration of her courage, her faith, her life.

"It was with this joy of Purim that she once again thanked G-d for His many wonders and miracles.

"'Now we'll go for Pesach,' I told her. 'Please G-d, you'll be at the seder with your family and recount the miracle of your personal redemption.' Such a goal seemed beyond the realm of possibility, but through the power of prayer, the impossible became possible. And so it was that Rochelle sat at her beautiful seder table, basking in the love of her adoring family.

"Seder is a time when we not only recall our past, but we praise G-d for His many bounties. That night, Rochelle expressed her gratitude to the Almighty and thanked Him for the wonderful family that He had given her. She addressed each and every person sitting around her table, and especially thanked her daughter-in-law, Elissa, who had become the daughter that she never had. It was as though Rochelle knew that it was time to go home and was bidding farewell. For over twenty-eight years, she struggled with cancer and defied the odds. Time and again, through the power of prayer, she sent the Angel of Death packing. In the last year of her life, she attained new spiritual heights and left behind a magnificent legacy of faith. Before the year of her passing was up, her daughter-in-law gave birth to a little girl who carries her name. Instead of ending her days in a hospice, Rochelle wove a magnificent tapestry of holidays — from Shabbos to Yom Kippur, to Chanukah, to Purim, to Pesach — it all came about through the power of prayer."

"I must admit it's a touching story," Sam conceded.

"So don't give up on your Aunt Carol," I said.

Sam looked at me pensively. 'If prayer works, Rebbetzin, what happened with your husband? From what I've heard, he was a holy man. Surely he too prayed, and hundreds, if not thousands of people must also have prayed for him."

"Sam!" Phyllis cried out sharply. "How could you?" And turning to me, she said apologetically, "Rebbetzin, please — you must forgive my husband."

"There's nothing to forgive," I assured her. "As a matter of fact, I myself wrestled with this question. You may recall that, at the very outset of our discussion, I shared with you a priceless teaching from our Torah sages: *"Hafoch boh, hafoch boh, d'kula boh"* — "Turn the pages, turn the pages, everything is [to be found] therein" — meaning that when we feel perplexed, when we lack clarity, we need only search the pages of our Torah to gain insight. There is a precedent, a teaching, for every challenge — for every life situation. So I searched in our Torah, and I found illumination in the life of Moses — the greatest prophet to have ever walked on planet Earth. He was the *Ro'eh Ne'eman*, the loving, loyal shepherd of Israel who beseeched

G-d on behalf of his people and was prepared to put himself on the line to protect them. 'Now, if You would but forgive the sins of the people — but, if not, erase my name from Your Book that You have written' (*Exodus* 32:42).

"When his final days approached, for the very first time in his life, he prayed on his own behalf and begged G-d for just one gift — to enter the promised Land so that he might behold its sanctity. And G-d said *no*, but Moses wouldn't let go and continued to pray. He beseeched G-d in five hundred and fifteen different ways, and yet, his request was denied.

"If anyone was worthy of having his prayers answered, it was surely Moses, so how can we understand this? Did Moses' prayers go unanswered? Absolutely not! No prayer is ever lost. G-d instructed Moses to ascend the mountain from where He showed him, not only the Holy Land, but the entire history of our people until this very day — until the coming of Messiah. So G-d did answer Moses' prayers, although not in the way that he may have desired. G-d is not our waiter to whom we can give orders. To be sure, we can put in our requests, but whether we will be served steak, lamb chops, chicken, vegetarian, or dairy, is ultimately His decision, for it is He Who knows what is best for us.

"Moreover, our time is different from G-d's time. Can you critique a film of which you see only five minutes? Similarly, in G-d's time frame, we are here on earth for less than five minutes. While G-d always responds to our prayers, sometimes His response comes only years later — sometimes not even in our lifetime, but in generations to come.

"Every one of our prayers ascends to the heavens above where G-d preserves them so that they may serve as credit cards for our children and grandchildren. Even as our bubbies and zeides created credit cards for us, we have a responsibility to do the same for our descendants.

"Shortly after my husband's death, I found a note written in his hand, 'A long life is not good enough, but a good life is long enough.' My husband had a very good life — not because he was wealthy, went on cruises, played golf every day, or because his life was free of suffering and worry. His life was good because his goodness *made a difference* in the lives of so many, and that goodness lives on.

"Let's face it, Sam. Death never comes at a convenient moment. There is always so much more that we would wish to accomplish, but if we have children and grandchildren to carry on our legacy, if there are people whose lives we inspired and touched, then we did not die — so in a sense, my husband is more alive today than ever before. My children are all following in his footsteps. The prayers that they prayed on behalf of their father sprang from their innermost hearts, and such prayers can never be lost. Those prayers expanded their souls and enabled them to teach G-d's Word with the same love and devotion with which their father taught. At one time or another, we will all have to go, but whether we go on the wings of prayer and a legacy of faith, or in regret and shame, will determine whether we continue to live on.'

"Thank you for sharing that with us," Sam said, subdued. "I hope that I didn't offend you."

"Of course not. I appreciate your candor."

"I do wish I could pray," Sam now confessed, "but I really wouldn't know how to go about it. Like I said, I'm not a religious man — it's just not me."

"But it is you, Sam. It's built into your spiritual DNA. You learn how to pray by praying!"

"You make it sound so simple, Rebbetzin, but it's not. I've seen my friend Danny pray, and I could never do it."

"Of course you can," I assured him. "My sons will teach you, just as they taught Danny. You'll pick it up in no time — and even if your prayers are less than perfect — as are those of most people — nevertheless, the very fact that you are making the effort is, in and of itself, significant. It's like visiting your parents. Not every visit is great, but just the same, spending time with them is meaningful." And to drive home my point, I asked Sam how he would feel if his daughter Kelly were dating a young man who was not on speaking terms with his parents and never visited or called them. "How would you feel about that, Sam?"

"Not good."

"Why not? What does his relationship with his parents have to do with the young man?"

"Everything!" Sam said emphatically. "Someone who has cut off all contact with his mother and father, someone who doesn't recognize their existence, just doesn't have what it takes. That's not a son-in-law I'd be happy with."

"Now, listen to your own words. If you never speak to your Heavenly Father, if you have no relationship or contact with Him, what does that say about you?"

"Sam, the Rebbetzin really got you this time," Phyllis said with a laugh.

"Okay, so I'm hopeless," Sam said, throwing up his arms in resignation.

"G-d forbid! No one is ever hopeless. We don't believe in 'hopeless.' Through prayer we can change everything — and this is not just empty talk."

We once had a righteous king, Chizkiyahu, a descendant of the House of David, who ruled over Israel. One day, he fell gravely ill, whereupon the prophet Isaiah visited him.

"'Put your affairs in order — your days are numbered. You shall die in this world as well as in the World to Come,' the prophet proclaimed.

"Why?" the King asked in dismay. "What sins have I committed? What have I done to warrant such a terrible decree?"

"You failed to uphold the commandment to marry, to be fruitful and multiply."

"But," the king protested, "I did that with the noblest of intentions. Through *Ruach HaKodesh* [prophetic insight] I foresaw that I would have an evil heir who would introduce idol worship and bring calamity upon our people. So at great personal sacrifice, I refrained from marrying and having children."

"It is not for you to delve into G-d's ways," Isaiah answered. "You must do yours — fulfill His commands, and leave the rest to Him."

"'I will repent. Give me your daughter and I will marry her," the king pleaded.

"It's too late. Your death has already been ordained in the heavens above," the prophet answered.

"I learned from my grandfather, King David, that it's never too late — that even if there is a sharp sword at your throat and you are convinced that your situation is hopeless, you are never to give up hope, but must pray and beseech G-d for mercy."

Isaiah rejected Chizkiyahu's plea and left the palace. But no sooner did he depart than the voice of G-d called out to him. "Go back and tell Chizkiyahu that his prayers have been accepted."

"But," Isaiah said, surprised, "Almighty G-d, did You not tell me that a decree has been made?"

"If a man so desires he can alter any decree. Through heartfelt prayers, he can come to see the error of his ways, *change*, and thus annul the decree. It's never too late for a man to return to Me."

Chizkiyahu married Isaiah's daughter and was granted years of good health, but alas, his worst fears were also realized. He sired Menashe, who placed a four-faced idol in the Temple, so that from whichever direction people entered, they would see and worship it.

G-d punished Menashe — he fell into the hands of Assyrian generals who tortured him in a most barbaric and savage manner.

Menashe called out to his idols, begging for mercy, but his pleas went unheeded. And then he remembered his father, King Chizkiyahu, who had taught him to pray and seek G-d's mercy even when all seemed lost. The angels tried to dissuade G-d from accepting the prayers of such an evil man, but G-d allowed Menashe's supplication to reach His Throne and saved him, because through prayer, Menashe became a *different man*. He removed all the idols from the Temple and proclaimed G-d's Law for all to uphold.

"Our Torah and our history are replete with such stories: the people of Nineveh, as recounted in the Book of Jonah; the story of the Jews of Persia as told in the Megillah of Esther, are just two examples."

"I guess I have no excuse," Sam said, "but I can see it now — me, starting to pray, and everyone thinking that I lost it!"

"Sam, I can assure you that no one will think you lost it. On the contrary, they will respect you. To prove it, let me tell you another story."

"Rebbetzin, where do you get all these stories from?"

"Life," I laughed, "just life."

"I don't know — I never experienced such stories in *my* life."

"You will," I assured him, "as soon as you learn to look at the world through Torah lenses." And with that, I related my story.

I am generally invited to speak in South Africa annually. On our trip there two years ago, we had a disquieting experience. We flew from JFK into Johannesburg on South African Airlines. We had been told that a welcoming committee would be meeting us at the airport to escort us to a reception and from there, to our hotel.

The flight from New York to Johannesburg is long and grueling — some fifteen-and-a-half hours — and we were delighted when we finally de-planed. We collected our luggage and proceeded to customs and passport control, eagerly anticipating our meeting with the members of the committee who, over the years, have become very good friends. But we were in for a surprise. While I had no difficulty going through passport control, Barbara, who as you know always travels with me, was stopped. It appeared that every page of her passport was stamped and she lacked a blank page required by South African passport control.

"I'm sorry," the inspector said, "but I can't stamp your passport and you can't go through!"

"What do you mean?" Barbara exclaimed in disbelief.

"Just as I said," was the response. "You don't have a blank page, and I can't let you in."

"Well, how come no one informed us of this at JFK?" Barbara argued, with an edge in her voice.

"I don't know." the inspector shrugged indifferently, "They should have, but just the same, I can't let you go through."

"But I have to go through," Barbara insisted, losing it now. Pointing at me, she said, "This lady has come here to speak. People are waiting for her — there's a whole welcoming committee outside."

"Well, she's free to go, but you cannot!"

"Excuse me," I interjected, "I will not go without my friend. We always travel together."

"Well then, you will have to stay as well," she said flatly.

We argued back and forth, getting nowhere fast. She just wouldn't budge, so we insisted that she call her supervisor.

A middle-aged Afrikaner soon appeared, and when he heard our story, he agreed with the passport control agent, and motioned for us to follow him into a holding room. At this point, Barbara was little short of apoplectic. I glanced at my watch and realized that if I didn't immediately pray Minchah — the afternoon service — it would soon be dark and too late to pray. So I took out my prayer book and went off to a corner of the room to *daven*.

"To be honest, Sam, I wasn't praying to beseech G-d's miraculous intervention. That thought had never even entered my mind. I prayed because we are all obligated to pray in the afternoon. Our services were instituted by our three patriarchs, so when we pray, we not only connect with G-d, but with our forefathers, who preceded us, and in a sense, are praying along with us."

I was engrossed in prayer when I heard the footsteps of the supervisor returning. "This is a serious matter. We really can't allow you to enter the country without stamping a blank page in your passport," he said, repeating his earlier statement. Then suddenly, he spotted me, and I overheard him ask Barbara, "What is your friend doing over there?"

"She's praying."

And with that, I felt the presence of someone behind me, looking over my shoulder. "Now that's a good lady," I heard him say. "When someone prays, everything changes! I'll tell you what. I will hold the airline officials at JFK responsible for this. They will be penalized and fined, and you are free to go."

"Mind you," he added, "I wasn't supposed to be working today but I guess G-d sent me to help you out, because when people pray, help is forthcoming."

"So don't worry, Sam." I assured him. "No one will think that you've lost it if you pray. Besides, I wouldn't have thought that you cared so much about what people say."

"I really don't, but there's still a big world out there."

"If anything," I assured him, "that 'big world' will respect you even more if they see you connect with your faith. It is a promise from G-d that has been substantiated by our history: 'For this is your wisdom and discernment in the sight of the nations...' (*Deuteronomy* 4:6). As a matter of fact, the only reason that I related this story was to show you the *attitude* of that 'big world' that you are talking about — and believe me, the reaction of that supervisor was not an exception, but the norm."

Sam looked at me skeptically.

"I see that you are not convinced," I said, "so I'll tell you one last story."

In preparation for the launching of our Hineni Movement, we were confronted by myriad challenges, not the least of which was filling Madison Square Garden. To generate interest, I spoke non-stop on high school and college campuses. One of the colleges that I visited at that time was New York City's Queens College. I was told to expect a turnout of about fifty students, but when I arrived, over seven hundred had congregated and the program had to be moved from a classroom to the cafeteria — a most unusual occurrence for a city commuter school.

Someone called the *New York Post* and a reporter came to cover the event. The following day, a story appeared which dubbed me, "The Jewish Billy Graham!"

To be honest, when I saw that article, I was somewhat taken aback. I didn't quite know what to make of it. My feelings ran the gamut from puzzlement to annoyance. But then, my husband, in his inimitable wise, sweet way reassured me. "It's *bashert* (meant to be). It can only help. People who would never consider listening to a Rebbetzin will now be curious to hear 'the Jewish Billy Graham,' and you will have an opportunity to kindle the light of Torah in many hearts."

Sure enough, my husband's words proved prophetic. Wherever I went, SRO audiences greeted me, but all that could not compare to the reception the Billy Graham appellation made possible when I visited the Jewish community of _____.

When I arrived, the local paper picked up the story from the *New York Post* and put my picture on the front page under the headline, "Jewish Billy Graham Arrives From the United States!" Not only did that headline create a buzz in the community and on the university campuses, but it opened the door to a most unexpected place.

At our hotel, I noticed a middle-aged couple seated in a secluded corner. There was something terribly sad and forlorn about them. I asked the proprietor of our hotel, who was a Jew and served only glatt kosher, what was wrong. In response, she related a most bizarre story.

It appeared that this couple had a somewhat emotionally unstable son who worked as a security guard at the Israeli consulate — an "in-name-only" position, as in those days, terrorism was virtually unknown. Nevertheless, this young man was convinced that the consulate was vulnerable to terrorist attack and needed to beef up its security. However, no one paid him heed, so he decided that he had to do something desperate to prove his point. He staged a mock attack, called the police and his younger brother, and told them that the consulate was under siege. In his innocence, the brother ran to the aid of his sibling whom he believed to be in mortal danger. A shoot-out ensued, and the brothers were arrested. Their anguished parents sought sanctuary from the media and curiosity seekers in the hotel in which we were staying. I felt for them and decided to approach them to offer some support.

"I hope I'm not intruding, and if I am, please tell me, but I would like to help. If you wish," I added, "I can make an attempt to visit your sons."

The mother looked at me in disbelief and shrugged in pained resignation. "They will never let you in."

"Let me try. You can never tell — I just might succeed."

So, the following day, off I went, armed with a *Siddur* — prayer book — *Chumash* (the Five Books of Moses), and a copy of the local paper. When I came to the prison gate, I introduced myself and pointed to the story with my picture. I was "The Jewish Billy Graham" from the U.S.A. The security guard made a call to his superior, and incredibly, the doors opened and I was allowed to meet with the brother who had come to the aid of his emotionally unstable sibling. He was in a terrible state. His eyes bespoke his despair and pain. I told him that he was never to give up hope, that with the help of G-d, he would again be free. I told him that there was a time when I, too, wondered whether I would ever be able to laugh again and I shared with him my own concentration camp experiences.

"Turn to the Torah for guidance," I urged, "there is a teaching for every situation."

"Not for mine," he said in a low voice.

"You're wrong. When I say 'every situation', I mean, *every* situation. Why do you suppose that we have all these Bible stories about our forefathers if not to show us the way? They underwent every conceivable life experience so that, no matter what predicament we, their descendants, may find ourselves in, we will always be able to draw inspiration from their lives. Our ancestors passed the tests of life so that we might pass *our* tests. They actually created 'banners' — signposts to point us to the path that we should follow. So, yes," I assured him, "there is a precedent for *your* story in the Torah as well."

He sat there, listening, but his eyes told me that he was not convinced.

"You need only study the life of our tribal patriarch, Joseph, who even as you, found himself in prison, although believe me, his situation was far more hopeless. No one in his family knew of his whereabouts; he had no lawyers — there was no one to intercede on his behalf, and worse, he was the only Jew in a country that was notorious for its hatred of Jews. But with all that, Joseph never despaired. He never gave up praying, and placed his trust in G-d. And mind you," I pointed out, "it wasn't as if G-d communicated with him or assured him that there was nothing to worry about. He had no way of knowing that, one day, he would rule over Egypt and save his family, and the entire ancient world. So take your cue from Joseph, and don't lose faith.

"Every morning," I told him, "when you awaken and feel that you can't bear the thought of facing yet another day, say three words: '*Kumu L'avodas Haborei*' — 'Rise up to serve the Creator.' Find something each and every day with which to serve G-d. Pray, study Torah, and relate to everyone with *chesed* — lovingkindness."

"Relate to everyone with lovingkindness?" he muttered under his breath. "Who is there for me to relate to here?"

"Everyone with whom you come in contact," I said. "fellow inmates, guards, visitors, and most important of all, yourself. Don't become an angry person."

"Do you know how Joseph gained his freedom?" I challenged him.

"What does it matter? I am not a Joseph — miracles don't happen for me."

"True. You and I are not Josephs," I agreed, "but miracles can happen to all of us. And remember that that which took place in the lives of our forefathers serves as a message to us. So let's review for a moment the events that led to Joseph's redemption."

There were two ministers from the palace of Pharaoh who were incarcerated with him in the same dungeon. One day, Joseph noticed that their faces were frozen with terror. Obviously, no one who was imprisoned in Egypt's infamous dungeons was a happy camper, but on that particular morning, their eyes were filled with dread. When Joseph beheld their dark, fearful countenances, he felt their pain and asked, "Why are your faces so dejected? Why do you appear downcast today?" (*Genesis* 40:7).

Now Joseph had every reason to be angry and bitter. He had fought and sacrificed to remain loyal to the teachings of his father — the Laws of G-d. And what did he get in return? A devastating prison sentence. If anyone had the right to ask, "Where is G-d?," it was certainly he. Yet, never for a moment did he question the ways of the Almighty. Never for a moment was he bitter. As for his relationship with his fellow prisoners, he certainly had enough on his plate to justify his being indifferent to their plight. Moreover, the Egyptians abhorred Jews, and these two ministers were not exactly his buddies, so why should Joseph have cared? Why should he have given even a second thought to their demeanor?

But Joseph lived with a higher purpose. No matter how fate dealt with him, he never forgot G-d's teaching and the image of his father. It was this awareness that enabled him to feel the torment in the hearts of others, even though his own heart was tormented, and even though those *others* held him in contempt.

The two ministers related to Joseph the frightening dreams that they had had. Joseph interpreted the dreams for them and predicted that the Minister of Bakers would be executed and the Minister of Butlers would be reinstated in his post. And indeed, everything that Joseph foretold came to pass.

Two years after this incident, Pharaoh had a disturbing dream which no one could interpret. It caused havoc in the palace. Pharaoh became moody, irate, and irrational — an alarming state of affairs for the members of his court. It was then that the Minister of Butlers recalled Joseph to Pharaoh. Joseph was rushed from prison and brought to the palace to interpret Pharaoh's dream, which he did, but not before he told Pharaoh, "It's beyond me. It is only G-d who can respond…" (*Genesis* 42:16). It was only after making it totally clear that everything depends on G-d that Joseph interpreted

Pharaoh's dreams and thus became Viceroy of Egypt, a position second only to Pharaoh.

"The lesson that we have to remember," I told the young man sitting before me, "is that this miracle occurred for Joseph because even under the most desperate circumstances, he did not despair. Even in the mire and filth of that Egyptian prison, he never lost sight of the image of his father and his responsibility to serve G-d. It was that service that enabled him to rise above the darkness of his cell, and it is that service that, please G-d, will bring you your freedom very soon. Just remember those three little words, *"Kumu L'avodas Haborei"* — 'Rise up and serve the Creator.'"

This all happened many years ago, and I had all but forgotten the incident, until one evening when I spoke in the city of _____. Following my programs, I usually stay on to talk to each and every person who wishes to consult me, and I do not leave until I have spoken to everyone.

At the end of my presentation, a man approached Barbara and said, "I would like to be the last to consult with the Rebbetzin." Barbara readily agreed, and finally, after the crowd thinned out, and only the rabbi and some members of the committee remained, he approached me. His eyes were glistening with tears.

"Rebbetzin Jungreis," he said, "for more than thirty-three years I've been waiting to ask you a question. What comes first — *Modeh Ani* or *Kumu l'avodas HaBorei*?"

"I stared at him in shock. It couldn't be him, but it was. Memories rushed back — I was speechless and overwhelmed. There were so many questions that I wanted to ask him. How did he make that journey? How did he find his way back from the darkness of prison to the light of freedom? But then I realized that there was really nothing to ask. It's all in the power of prayer. If you connect to G-d, even in a dungeon, there can be light and everything becomes possible. We need only remember never to give up.

"So, how about it, Sam. Can you say those three little words: '*Kumu l'avodas HaBorei*?' — 'Rise up and serve the Creator,' and thereby change your life."

For a few minutes, Sam and Phyllis sat there, silently.

"Honey, please," Phyllis now broke the silence. "Let's say it together." Slowly, Sam and Phyllis repeated the words, and that's how they commenced their journey in prayer and Torah.

Book II

Tests of Relationships

A community, a family, resembles a heap of stones. One stone taken out of it, and the whole totters..."

Midrash Genesis

7

Finding Your Soul Mate

There are certain memories that shall be forever etched on my mind, memories that no amount of time can erase. Such was the night of our deportation. Life in the ghetto was painful and torturous, but just the same, it was life. My father, together with other communal leaders, organized programs to address our needs and maintain a sense of normalcy. There was constant hunger, but nevertheless, we shared our meager rations and there were all sorts of *chesed* and outreach services. We children were prohibited from attending school — but just the same, learning went on daily. Despite the fact that no medicines were available, doctors worked ceaselessly to ease the pain of the sick, and the *bikur cholim* group made herculean efforts to bring them comfort. With every day that passed, more and more people were brought into our ghetto from the provinces, which meant that several families had to be housed in every apartment, no matter how small, and, incredibly, we made room for everyone.

The Nazis spared no effort to degrade and dehumanize us, but they could not succeed in sapping our spiritual strength. We defied their orders, worshiped our G-d, and continued to study His holy Torah. But then, all too quickly, our ghetto existence came to an abrupt end.

We were cruelly awakened one night by shouts of *"Achtung! Achtung! Juden — Raus!"* We were told that we had just a few minutes to get out, and they didn't hesitate to use bayonets, rifle butts, and bullets to show us that they meant business. The sounds of screaming, wailing, and crying were heard throughout the ghetto. The Nazis and the Zsandars (Hungarian Gestapo) barked out orders, *"Schnell! Schnell!"* — "Quickly! Quickly!" They were in a hurry to deliver us to a brick factory, yet another collection station, and from there to the cattle cars that would transport us to the gas chambers. In the midst of all this terror, my father grabbed his siddur, *tallis* and *tefillin,* and the unpublished manuscripts of two of my great-grandfathers, the holy sages, Rabbi Mordechai Benet, *Zt"l,* who wrote on the Talmudic tractates of *Shabbos, Berachos* and *Gittin,* and the *Be'er Yitzchok* — Rabbi Avrohom Yitzchok Glick, *Zt"l,* who wrote on the tractate of *Kiddushin.*

You might well ask what impelled my father to take those manuscripts with him. Did he really anticipate that they would be published in Auschwitz or Bergen-Belsen? Wouldn't it have been wiser to take along something more practical, like a can of sardines? But no, the manuscripts had to survive and become the possession of

Torah scholars for generations to come. People who heard of my father's feat in secreting and preserving those manuscripts marveled at his total faith, but such is the strength of our people.

It wasn't only my father who demonstrated this unswerving faith. The Piacetzna Rebbe wrote his monumental work, *Aish Kodesh*, in the Warsaw Ghetto under the most inhuman circumstances. His wife and children were killed, and as a highly revered rebbe, he was singled out for special torture by the Nazis. Yet, despite all this, he continued writing *Divrei Torah* — Torah teachings. People asked him why he continued to write — no one would ever see his manuscripts — the ghetto would be razed and all its inhabitants killed. Undaunted, the Piacetzna responded, "As long as I am alive, I must study, teach, and write *Divrei Torah*. The rest is up to G-d."

The Rebbe was killed *al kiddush HaShem* — sanctifying G-d's Name — and the manuscript was found in the rubble of the Ghetto by a young Polish boy who sold it to an American soldier for a bar of chocolate. The soldier was not Jewish, but he recognized the Hebrew writing, and he handed it over to the Jewish chaplain of his unit. The rest is history.

As for the *tefillin* that my father took with him, they have special significance for the Jewish people. They are symbolic of the Covenant between G-d and our nation. The Torah refers to *tefillin* as an *"os"* (*Exodus* 13:10 and *Deuteronomy* 6:4-9) — a sign: "And you shall bind them as a 'sign' on your hand and as a symbol between your eyes." Even as a wedding band is a *sign* between husband and wife, *tefillin* reminds every Jewish man of his unique relationship with his Creator. They are comprised of two small black leather boxes that encase four paragraphs from the Torah, handwritten on parchment, that, in essence, embody our faith: the *Shema* — declaring the Oneness of G-d and our acceptance of His holy Kingdom — as well as passages referring to our Exodus from Egypt and our total indebtedness to G-d. *Tefillin* are worn by men during weekday morning prayers and testify that their *hearts, minds,* and *energies* are dedicated to the Almighty.

Throughout the centuries, *tefillin* have been held sacred by our people. No Jewish man would consider traveling without them. My father's *tefillin,* however, had added significance. They were given to him by his own father, the Rabbi of Nadudvar, *Hy"d*, who was killed in Auschwitz. The tefillin had originally belonged to our great-grandfather, the world-renowned sage, *HaRav HaGaon* Osher Anshil Halevi Jungreis, the Csengerer *Tzaddik*, known by the title of his scholarly work, *Menuchos Osher.* When my grandfather presented these *tefillin* to my father, he promised that they would always remain with him, and miraculously, even in the *gehenom* of Bergen-Belsen, the *tefillin* survived.

There is an ancient tradition which calls upon the Jew to demonstrate his love of G-d by rising eagerly each and every morning to worship his Creator: "Do not wait for the morning to awaken you, but let your zeal and fervor for G-d be of such intensity that it awakens the morning and signals daybreak" (*Code of Jewish Law*, Chapter One).

With my very eyes I saw this happen. In Bergen-Belsen, I saw how mere humans can pierce the darkness and through their devotion, bring forth light. At the first sign of dawn, my father would rise and don his *tefillin.* Soon, others would join him and queue up. At great sacrifice and enormous risk, they would wait — not for coffee, nor for bread, but for a moment when they might pray with *tefillin* on their arms and heads and proclaim the ancient words, "*V'erastich lee l-olam*" — "I will betroth you to Me forever; I will betroth you to Me in righteousness, in justice, in kindness and in mercy. I shall betroth you to Me in faithfulness, and you shall know the L-rd" (*Hosea* 2:22).

To have seen and heard this in Bergen Belsen was to have witnessed the eternal spark of faith that glows in Jewish hearts. It was with this faith, symbolized by the *tefillin* and the manuscripts, that my father staked out our new lives in America.

Years later, after we had settled in Brooklyn, my father was visited by the director of a Jerusalem-based organization dedicated to the preservation and publication of precious manuscripts. I was not present at that meeting, but afterward, I learned that when the rabbi arrived at my parents' home, my father told him that before discussing the manuscript, he would like to "talk business." The director was anticipating that my father might request some sort of remuneration, but to his amazement, my father went to the drawer of the sideboard in the dining room and took out a photograph of my daughter who, at that time, had just turned nineteen. "This is my granddaughter," he said with great pride, "the daughter of Rabbi Meshulem and Rebbetzin Esther Jungreis." And he went on to enumerate her many attributes. And then he proceeded to describe the qualities that we were seeking in a prospective husband. "You travel the world," my father told him, "and you come in contact with many fine families. Keep her in mind, and if you encounter such a young man, please let us know.' Not long afterward, my daughter was married to a most wonderful young man, although it was not this rabbi who made the match. My grandfather's manuscripts were published, and today they are studied by Torah scholars throughout the world.

I have related these stories because faith in G-d, love for our Torah, and finding appropriate *shidduchim* for our children are the pillars on which the lives of our people have been built throughout the centuries. Sadly however, such devotion and sacrifice for G-d and Torah is foreign to most in our generation. As for *shidduchim*, young people are left to fend for themselves when seeking suitable marriage partners and miss out on this parental concern and involvement. Left to their own devices, they are obliged to seek their soul mates randomly — on the internet, in the work place, in bars, in schools, or at chance meetings. It is little wonder then, that the singles population has reached unprecedented levels and so many are involved in painful, dead-end relationships.

Kelly, Sam and Phyllis' thirty-five-year-old daughter, was a perfect example of today's career-oriented female. While she was successful professionally, she was unable to attain the same success in her personal life. Nurtured in the belief that marriage was something she had to make happen on her own, she was suspicious of any recommendations coming from her parents.

"Rebbetzin, how can I get Kelly to meet you so that you might introduce her to a nice young man?" Phyllis asked following one of our classes. At this point, Sam and Phyllis were well into their Torah studies, so I suggested that they make a little party to celebrate the first anniversary of their new Torah life. That would be an invitation that Kelly could not refuse.

So it was that I finally met Kelly. She was a tall, attractive brunette who appeared cool and detached, although I sensed a certain vulnerability beneath her air of composure. When I tried to broach the subject of relationships and marriage, she immediately became defensive.

"Did my parents speak to you about me?" she challenged.

I wasn't about to be intimidated and told her how privileged she should feel to have parents who are concerned, who care. Then I related the story of my father and the manuscripts, and I must say that, to her credit, she apologized.

"Don't give it a second thought," I assured her. "Believe me, I understand. It's tough out there. By now you must have had a thousand and one dates that went nowhere."

"You don't know the half of it, Rebbetzin. It's brutal." And as she spoke, I felt her softening.

"With G-d's help, I have made matches for many people, so why not for you? What do you say, Kelly? Let's start all over again. Tell me, what are you looking for?"

"What am I looking for?" she repeated pensively. "Nothing complicated — just a nice, quality guy. Although sometimes I wonder whether he exists."

"Of course he does," I assured her, taking her hands in mine, "but your definition of *quality* may not be realistic."

"What do you mean?"

"Let me share with you an incident that occurred some years ago at one of our Hineni classes, and you'll understand."

A young woman approached me. She was truly beautiful, and many in our group recognized her since she was a television personality. She, too, told me, 'I'm looking for a "quality person," and when I challenged her to explain exactly what she meant by "quality" she enumerated five "musts" on which she was not willing to compromise.

1. Good looking — "Looks are important," she explained. "There has to be a certain chemistry."

2. Bright — "Someone who is well educated, but also has 'street smarts.'"

3. Wealthy — "He has to support me in the lifestyle to which I have become accustomed. At this stage of my life, I can't go backwards!"

4. A great personality and good sense of humor — "I have no patience for moody people. I like a man who is fun and with whom I can have a good laugh." — and finally,

5. Someone who is athletic — "I love tennis."

"Good luck to her," Kelly said, laughing. "That would take five different guys all wrapped into one!"

"That's exactly what I said, but I also told her that her 'big five' was a bunch of zeroes, and did not add up to anything."

"Why?" Kelly asked.

"Simple — zeroes don't add up to anything unless there is a digit in front of them."

Kelly looked at me quizzically, so I repeated, "Five zeros without a digit in front of them, are what we call in Yiddish '*Gurnisht Mit Gurnisht*' — *G. M. G.* — nothing with nothing".

"I don't think that I'm obtuse, but I still don't get it. What digit are you referring to, Rebbetzin?"

"A Torah digit — the first letter of the Torah, which is 'B' — '*beit*', and the last letter of the Torah, which is 'L' — *lamed*. Those two letters spell '*lev*' — heart. If he doesn't have a *good heart,* then his good looks will become repulsive overnight; his sharp mind and wit will be used to abuse and denigrate you; his wealth will control and manipulate you; and his 'great personality' will eclipse and suffocate yours. As for tennis, I told her, 'You can always get him a trainer! But, how will you train him to acquire a good heart?'"

"I never quite thought about it that way," Kelly admitted. "So how *does* one acquire a good heart?"

"That young woman asked that very question and I'll tell you, just as I told her, 'Finding a good-hearted person is no simple matter. As much as we would like to believe that, basically, we are all good people with a few "*shticks*" here and there, the truth is that we are not so good, and *we have to learn goodness.*

"'The heart of man is wicked from his youth' (*Genesis* 8:21).

"We are born seeing only our own needs and must be taught to be sensitive to the concerns of others. This training must start at a tender age. Early on, children must be conditioned to be giving, to be patient, to be considerate, and to be kind. Even simple words like 'thank you' and 'please' *must be taught* and are not to be taken for granted — as evidenced by their absence from the vocabulary of so many adults.

"Unfortunately, in many homes, these values are never imparted. Often, parents regard inappropriate behavior as 'cute' or something that their children will outgrow. There are also those parents who have no clue as to what constitutes a 'good heart'; they raise their children without teaching the disciplines that foster goodness. So it is that there are so many *obnoxious* adults."

"But can't you acquire these disciplines later in life?" Kelly asked.

"Of course you can," I assured her, "but it's very difficult to un-learn ingrained character traits. And for a spouse to undo them is virtually impossible. No one should marry in the hope of changing the other. The best we can do is to change ourselves."

"I wish that I could disagree with you," Kelly sighed. "I guess I had to learn the hard way. I went out with some of those *obnoxious* guys and believe me, they robbed me of many good years. It was only after I suffered much pain and disappointment that I discovered what they were all about. But how can I prevent this from happening in the future? How can I know that the man that I am dating has a 'good heart' before I invest all that time?"

"Do you recall that, when we started to talk, you asked me if your parents put me up to this, and I told you that it's a privilege to have parents who care enough to be involved. In Torah-observant families, children marry early and parents assume direct responsibility for seeking marriage partners for them. Before the young people ever meet, parents carefully research the candidates. Now, I'm not going to tell you that their inquiries are always fool-proof. To be sure, there can be many glitches, but most often, that happens because they do not know what to ask."

"Well, how do you research and what do you ask?"

"It's like 'googling' a person. First you want to know his family background, because like it or not, we are all products of our past. Even if we intellectually reject the disfunctionality to which we were witness in our homes, and swear that we will never repeat the mistakes of our parents — to our chagrin, many of us will discover that, not only did we become carbon copies of our moms and dads, but worse, in addition to *their* aberrations, we have added a few of our own.

"For example, if he comes from a family in which his father was never available, chances are that he will see no necessity to make himself available to his children. And if she comes from a family in which her mother was an absentee, it is very likely that she will neglect her children as well. Or, if he comes from a home in which his parents resolved their conflicts through shouting matches, or by exchanging insults, he may very well do the same. And this holds true in regard to an entire gamut of attitudes. There are families in which everything becomes an *issue,* and there is constant squabbling and acrimony. Admittedly, conflicts exist in every marriage, but in good homes, parents are respectful of one another and require the same of their children, and most important, conflicts are resolved behind closed doors, without the children being aware, or drawn into them. In short," I concluded, "parents try to do a complete investigation with emphasis on character traits."

"And all this before they ever date?" Kelly asked. "In my world, we don't even tell our parents whom we are dating until we are ready to make an announcement! But I still don't get it," she went on. "How can you possibly check character traits? I mean, it's one thing to 'google' someone on the internet — but *character traits?*"

"Admittedly, it's not easy. It takes many in-depth conversations with former and present classmates, dorm partners, co-workers, rabbis, teachers, camp counselors, and friends and neighbors."

"But how can you know that they're telling the truth?"

LIFE IS A TEST

"Here, too, Torah law helps us. While we are not permitted to gossip or speak pejoratively about others, we *are* required to respond *honestly* to *specific* questions regarding marriage partners. For example, instead of asking, 'Is he nice?" — which doesn't mean a thing, we zero in on specific concerns which reflect character and values. How does he get along with his co-workers or classmates? Is he helpful to them? Does he lose his temper easily? Does he hold grudges? Is he moody? Is he dependent on medication in order to function? Does he think that everything is coming to him? Is he possessive and jealous? How does he handle money? Is he the type who is always borrowing? Does he give charity? And it's not the amount that counts, but the *manner* in which he gives — grudgingly, or with an open hand (and this doesn't only pertain to money, but to all forms of giving). Is his word to be trusted? Does he have self-destructive habits? How does he relate to the members of his family? Does he refer to his parents or siblings pejoratively? Does he gossip and malign others? Does he have what we call in Hebrew 'simchas hachayim' — a positive attitude toward life — because in the end, you never know where life will take you, and a positive attitude is one of the greatest attributes that anyone can have.

"And to assess the level of his religious commitment, parents will not simply ask whether he attends daily services, but they will also want to know whether he arrives on time or whether he prays or chats with others during the services. And if he's no longer learning in yeshivah, parents will want to know whether he is *kovea itim* — commits time for Torah study.

"Marriages," I told Kelly, "don't go sour over that which transpires at the UN, in Washington, or in Jerusalem, but they do become battlefields over little things such as these, which in the end, are not so little after all.

"Our sages ask, 'Who is wise?' And they respond, 'He who can foretell the future.' Obviously, they were not discussing prophecy. What they were referring to is the ability to project consequences. Given certain information, we should be pretty well able to estimate what sort of spouse or parent this person will be. Therefore, background checks are vital and this, of course, applies to both genders."

"I must admit that I'm impressed, but isn't all this 'checking' a bit much?"

"Marriage is the most important decision of your life, that will affect not only you, but all your descendants for generations to come. So you cannot be too careful. In the Torah world, we leave nothing to chance, for once *passion* takes over, vision becomes obscured and only too late does the couple discover that they are not suited for one another. Therefore, the Torah has given us disciplines to protect us from such happenings."

"Come to think off it, I did hear that, in the religious community, there is no physical contact until marriage. Is that what you mean?" Kelly asked.

"Yes — and there is a very cogent reason for it. Physical desire is a powerful, magnificent gift given by G-d to men and women to enhance their love and marriage. But, as all powerful gifts, it must be handled with care. When passion is indulged prior to marriage, it can be so blinding that it defuses all logic and reason, and only after much emotional pain does the couple come to realize that they have nothing in common, and are not soul mates.

"So it is, that G-d gave us the discipline that reserves physical contact to marriage. And to illustrate, I related a story to Kelly that occurred many years ago when I was a young rebbetzin.

My husband and I wanted to give our small children a summer vacation in the mountains, but on his meager rabbi's salary, such a luxury was out of our reach. So I came up with the idea of lecturing at a resort hotel in the Catskills, which meant that my family would be permitted to stay at the hotel gratis.

One day, following a lecture on the lawn of the hotel, I received a phone call from a middle-aged Jewish man, the leader of a cult, who was known for misleading many of our young people. In those days, cults abounded among young Jews, but through our program at Madison Square Garden, countless cult members returned to Judaism, and I was viewed as a threat by many cult leaders. On several occasions, I had tried to communicate with this particular man, but he had refused to meet with me. Now, however, he told me that he was ready to take me up on my invitation, and would come with some of his young Jewish cult members. I assured him that they would all be welcome to join us for *Shabbos* at the hotel and prayed that G-d would give me the right words with which to reach their hearts.

They came, however, not to reconnect with their Jewish faith, but to prove to me that I was wrong, and to persuade me to join their ranks. As soon as they arrived on Friday afternoon, they made their agenda quite clear. I told them, however, that I was busy with preparations for *Shabbos*, and that, on the holy day, I was prohibited from "talking business," but as soon as the Sabbath was over I would be happy to sit down with them for a discussion.

Of course, I had my plans — my secret weapons, which were the magic of the Sabbath itself, my lecture on the *Parashah* — Torah portion of the week — and the powerful presence of my parents and my husband, who always came up for the weekend. And those weapons worked! From the moment that we kindled the holy Sabbath lights, the transformation took place and grew with each and every moment. We sang "*Shalom Aleichem,*" the hymn that welcomes the angels of the Sabbath, and before making *Kiddush*, my father, the Rebbe, enveloped them with love and blessed them with the timeless blessings of our people; blessings which were first pronounced by our patriarch, Jacob and by Aaron, the High Priest, and with which to this very day, Jewish parents bless their children. In an instant, their eyes filled with tears, and their armor began to melt away. During the course of the meal, everyone in the dining room joined us in singing and dancing. That *Shabbos* eve became a joyous celebration of the homecoming of these lost Jewish children.

The following morning, after services and *Kiddush*, I taught the *parashah* on the lawn. The portion of that week was *Eikev* (*Deuteronomy* 7:12-11:25), which can be translated as *Footsteps*. I spoke about following in the *footsteps* of our *zeides* and *bubbies*, our ancestors, spanning the centuries, going all the way back to Sinai. And as I quoted the passages of our Torah, the Divine words pierced their hearts.

On Sunday morning we did "talk business" — not about the veracity of our faith but about plans for their future. Robert, one of the young men, told me that he would have to return home for a few days to tell his non-Jewish girlfriend (also a member of their cult), that their relationship was over, and that he was going to New York to study Torah in yeshivah.

Suddenly, we heard my father's voice. In his broken English he called, 'So-nee — Kom here!"

Now Robert was taller than my father, which wasn't too difficult a feat, since my father was no more than five feet tall. Moreover, my father did not speak English, and Robert didn't speak Yiddish, but he was able to communicate better than those with a rich vocabulary at their command. My father took Robert's hand in his and said, 'You go home, *girl give you kiss — you finished man*! Go New York *now* with Rebbetzin and study Torah!' And with those few pithy words, my father hit the heart of the issue — passion can dissolve even the most sincere intentions.

So it was that Robert came to New York with us and began to study in yeshivah. Two years later, with G-d's help, I introduced him to a lovely young girl — his soul mate. He and his wife built a beautiful Torah family, and not long ago, I was privileged to attend the wedding of their eldest son.

My father, a great Rebbe, a spiritual giant, was sensitive to the vagaries of human nature. He understood that while intellectually, Robert accepted that he had been on the wrong path, and that he had to change course and start a new life, nevertheless, when passion would overcome him, in a split second, he could become a "*finished man*." Time and again, history has proven this to be true. Even the most powerful individual can fall under the influence of passion.

"There isn't a week that goes by," I told Kelly, "that I don't receive letters and e-mails from young women who were swept off their feet only to discover that there was no spiritual connection — that the person to whom they had given themselves so totally was unsuitable. And mind you," I added, "these failed relationships are no simple matter. They leave the victims with deep scars, and that is one of the reasons why so many singles carry such heavy baggage."

"I'm one of them," Kelly whispered under her breath.

"I know, sweetheart," I told her, putting my arms around her, "you and thousands of others."

"But if I tell my date that I have been rethinking my values, he'll think I've lost it. And that's one sure way to scare a man away."

"You'd be surprised," I told her. "If you explain to a man that you would like to get to know him emotionally, intellectually, and spiritually — that you are reserving your physical self for your husband and the father of your children — then if he is truly a *quality* person, he will respect that, and if he is not quality, you don't want him anyway. You've been through that already. You don't need another guy to take advantage of you and leave you wounded."

"As crazy as it sounds, it makes sense. I might just give it a try. But suppose I meet someone to whom I'm attracted, and his background check comes up negative? Is it hopeless? Can he be changed?"

"Of course he can, but it's really tough and he will need a lot of reinforcement and help. Actually, that's one of the benefits of Torah study. When you study G-d's Book, you also discover role models to show you the way. Our patriarch Abraham and all our matriarchs came from dysfunctional families. Abraham's father, Terach, was a manufacturer of idols who had no compunctions about throwing his son into a prison when he challenged his paganism and proclaimed the Oneness of G-d. And yet, this same Abraham became the trailblazer for G-d and the architect of *chesed* — lovingkindness.

"Our mother, Rebecca, was the daughter of Besuel, a degenerate, and her family life was further complicated by her wicked brother, Laban. Rachel and Leah, the mothers of the Twelve Tribes of our people, were the daughters of this same treacherous Laban, who is described in the Passover Haggadah as more dangerous than Pharaoh. Yet, despite all this, they became the most noble women to walk on Planet Earth. And more, our patriarchs and matriarchs created *sign posts* — *banners,* from which, to this very day we draw our inspiration and discover how we may overcome our pasts even as they did. So, yes, Kelly, people can most definitely change, but only if they are *determined* to do so. As I pointed out earlier, it never works if that change is made to accommodate a future spouse, for at the first sign of conflict, all their resolve will fly out the window.

"In short, you cannot marry someone in anticipation of re-shaping him. But I will say that, in over forty years of teaching Torah, I have seen the most amazing changes take place. If properly motivated, people have an incredible capacity to grow and become the individuals that G-d intended them to be. The Breslover Rebbe summed it up in three little Hebrew words, '*Eem Rotzeh, Oseh* — if you desire it, you can do it.' There's nothing to hold a person back from growing and changing."

"Well, I must admit that I have seen a tremendous change in my own parents. Since they started to study Torah, the entire dynamic of our relationship has taken on a different face. My Mom has started to make beautiful *Shabbos* dinners, and for the first time, we see each other regularly. I actually feel that we have become a family. In the past, I tried to avoid encounters with my mother — our conversations were always strained and often confrontational. It was like walking on a minefield. I felt that while she *loved* me, she didn't *like* me. But now it's different — we speak almost daily, and I have come to realize that she is probably the only person in the world who cares about every detail of my life — even silly things, like what I had for lunch. But," Kelly added, with a certain resignation, "how does all this help *me* to find my soul mate? I mean, at this point, I can't expect my parents to make a background check on someone for me."

"That's true," I agreed, "but you can investigate for yourself. When you go on a date, instead of making small talk, discussing politics, films, music, diet or sports, ask him some pointed questions such as, 'How often do you call and see your parents and your siblings? How, and with whom do you spend your leisure time?' Find out if his friendships are long-lasting and how often he changes jobs. Though I must caution you that when you pose these questions, be sure to integrate them into your conversation. You don't want to make him feel as if he is being interrogated. No guy wants to marry an attorney who puts him on the witness stand.

"You might also find it helpful to watch out for small but telling signs, such as the manner in which he treats a waiter, doorman or store clerk. When challenged, does he do that which is *right,* or that which is *expedient?* Is he spiritual, or does he care only about himself? Is he sensitive to your concerns? Does he make promises and then proceed to forget them?

"One girl I know broke up with the man she was dating after his car broke down and he lost his temper and kept cursing. Her reasoning was simple — if this is how he reacts when his car breaks down, what will he do when things break down in his life? There are a million and one things to watch out for. But," I added, "bear in mind that, even as you are evaluating him, *he* is also studying *your* character traits, and, mind you, I'm not referring to anything specific, but *not one of us is perfect*. Not too long ago, in a TV interview on this subject, I recommended that, before dating, singles take a good look in a mirror and ask, 'Would I want to go out with *me*?'"

"That's heavy, Rebbetzin. I don't know too many people who would want to go through such self-scrutiny."

"That's true," I agreed, "but dating for marriage requires emotional honesty. It's not only *finding* the right one, but *being* the right one that is important. In the Hebrew language, character traits are called '*midos*', which, literally translated, means "measures." Everyone can make a mistake once in a while, so long as our flaws are *within measure*. But when they become so ingrained that they take over our personalities, then it becomes a serious problem."

"It seems so fatalistic, so hopeless," Kelly said.

"Not at all," I answered. "We have an amazing teaching, which, if applied, can resolve it all. '*Barosi yetzer hara, barosi Torah tavlin.*' 'I created the evil inclination,' G-d says, 'but I also created the Torah as an antidote.'

"Torah acts like a magnifying mirror of our souls. It allows us to be in touch with ourselves so that we may discover who we really are and make the necessary changes for our growth. Torah, like preventive medicine, keeps us in check.

"I guess that means that you want me to come to your Torah classes, right?" Kelly asked, good-naturedly.

"I certainly do! They will change your life. You will learn to look at yourself and others through Torah lenses, and everything will fall into place. I would even suggest that you bring your date along. Instead of going to the theater or for a night out, bring him to Hineni, and test his reactions to the teachings. That will give you insight into his way of thinking, his values, and his priorities. Such discussions can save you much pain, and will enable you to discover early on, if you are suited for one another — if there is something that connects your souls.

"Do you remember the girl I told you about who was looking for the 'Big Five'? That is exactly what I advised her to do. She found her husband at our Torah class, and today, she is happily married with a beautiful family."

"Rebbetzin, you convinced me. You'll see me at class next week. But, if you don't mind, I still have some questions. I was always under the impression that opposites attract, but it seems to me that from what you are saying, you have to be like two peas in a pod if your marriage is to work."

"To be honest, it always helps when 'like marries like.' In Talmudic terms, it is called '*invei hageffen b'invei hageffen.*' There *are* situations however, where two people can be well-suited for one another precisely because they are opposites with disparate temperaments. For example, if one is intense, it is good to have a partner who is more laid back, or if s/he is disorganized, it is helpful to have a spouse who 'has it all together.'

"As a matter of fact, one of the reasons that G-d created the institution of marriage is so that we might complement and balance one another. 'It is not good for man to be alone. I will make a helpmeet *corresponding* to him' (*Genesis* 2:18).

"The Hebrew word for 'corresponding' is '*k'negdo*,' which literally means 'against him,' so, wherever a man falls short, a woman is there to complement him.

"What I have been referring to, however, is not a difference in *temperament*, but in *values*, life goals; and for a harmonious marriage, it is crucial for husband and wife to be on the same page spiritually.

"One of the reasons why Eve, the first woman, succumbed to the seductions of the serpent was that Adam never really accurately communicated to her G-d's command to refrain from eating from the Tree of Knowledge. It was only when Abraham appeared on the world scene that this omission was rectified. Abraham not only discussed G-d's commands with Sarah, but more, he made her his partner in all his undertakings, inviting her to help him disseminate the Word of G-d. Abraham and Sarah were *soul mates*, sharing a common vision and a common bond. Perhaps that is why they succeeded so well in transmitting their legacy to future generations for all time. 'For I [G-d] have loved him because he commands his children and his household after him that they keep the Word of G-d, doing charity and justice' (*Genesis* 18:19).

"In order to transmit a legacy that transcends the centuries, father and mother have to speak in one voice. This sharing of ideas and values was emulated by all our patriarchs. Isaac took Rebecca into his mother's tent and imparted his mother's teachings to her, and when Jacob was told by G-d to return to the Holy Land, he didn't simply order his wives to pack up — rather, he explained G-d's command to them. Our ancestors taught us that the basis of a good marriage is for husbands and wives to become one — not only physically, but emotionally, intellectually, and spiritually. And that, please G-d, can be your gift, Kelly, if you share Torah with your husband."

"Like I said, you convinced me, Rebbetzin. But there is still something that bothers me. I'm a romantic, and all this seems so cut-and-dried. Shouldn't there be an element of 'chemistry' and romance?"

"Of course there should be, and there is. We know that even if everything adds up on paper, it doesn't necessarily mean that those two people are suited to one another. If there is no chemistry, if there is no attraction, there is nothing to talk about.

"Let me tell you about Jonathan and Rachel. I first met Jonathan when I was lecturing in a small Jewish community some distance from New York. Tall, handsome, bright, and charming, he stood out from the crowd. When I spoke to him following the program, I learned that he was from Russia, and like so many Jews from that part of the world, had very little knowledge of our faith. But he was sensitive and intelligent, so it was easy to inspire him to learn.

"You must come to New York and enroll in a serious Torah study program," I told him, "and at the same time, with G-d's help, I will try to introduce you to a nice girl."

"Jonathan took me up on my invitation and one fine evening showed up at our Torah class in Manhattan. Very quickly, he became a much-loved member of our Hineni community. With his keen mind, he became totally absorbed in Torah study, and with his *chein* — charm, he endeared himself to one and all — but try as I might, I couldn't find the right girl for him. Every date that I set up was perfect on paper, but the chemistry was missing. 'She's very nice,' he would concede, 'but somehow, I'm not attracted.'

"Then, two years ago, during Chanukah, I was in Israel. In honor of the holiday, we were giving copies of the Hebrew translation of my book, *The Committed Life*, to the soldiers of the IDF. While there, we also attended a wonderful wedding. The groom was part of our Hineni family, and his bride had taken time off from medical school to study Torah in Jerusalem. It was a magnificent wedding under the open skies of the holy city with the Kotel — the Wall (the only remnant of our holy Temple) — as a backdrop.

"All of the bride's friends were present, and it was there that I spotted Rachel. A lovely young woman with a striking regal bearing, she had come to Israel from Russia via Poland. Her mother died when Rachel was very young, and she had undergone a long, arduous and painful journey to reach Jerusalem. Some people become bitter and angry when fate deals harshly with them, while others grow, become wise, and turn to G-d. The latter held true for Rachel. An artist and designer by profession, she applied her sensitivity to building a new Torah life and quickly became a beloved source of inspiration to everyone. As soon as I saw her, I knew that I had found Jonathan's wife.

"When I returned to the States, I gave Jonathan her e-mail address, but when he questioned me as to how well I knew her, I had to confess that I hadn't spoken to her for more than five minutes, and yet, I just knew that she was the right one. 'Just call or e-mail her,' I urged.

"Jonathan was skeptical, but just the same, he contacted her, and from their very first conversation, they clicked. But the distance from New York to Jerusalem made it seem unrealistic and impractical. Soon afterward, Jonathan called to tell me that he was going to Odessa to commemorate his father's *yahrtzeit* (the anniversary of his father's death). 'There's no way that you can return to New York without stopping off in Jerusalem," I reiterated.

"A few weeks later, I received a phone call from Jerusalem. 'Rebbetzin,' Jonathan exclaimed ecstatically. 'Rebbetzin,' he repeated, and the joy in his voice was palpable, 'Rachel is everything you said and more! How can we ever thank you? We are so happy. You must come to our wedding!'"

"So you see, Kelly, while common aims and goals are the foundation upon which solid marriages are built, there's also a spark, which you refer to as 'chemistry,' but which I prefer to call 'finding your *bashert*' — your soul mate — destined for you by He Who created all of us.

"Over the years, I have had the privilege of making many *shidduchim*, but this one was different — two children without parents embarking upon a long journey home, finding one another, crossing continents and oceans, building a home in Jerusalem, and forging a link in the timeless chain of our people.

"I took this young couple into my heart and had the privilege of walking Rachel down the aisle. As we made our way toward the *chuppah*, her lips moved in prayer and her eyes glistened with tears. Then she turned to me and whispered, 'Thank you — I not only have a husband, but now, I also have an *Eema*.' Since then, every *Erev Shabbos* I receive a call from Jerusalem. Jonathan and Rachel are on the line: 'Good *Shabbos, Eema*. We are so happy. We love you so very much. Thank you!'"

"Do you think I will ever find my Jonathan?" Kelly asked with a twinge of sadness in her voice."

"Of course you will," I assured her. "He is waiting for you, even now."

A few months later, Kelly *did* find him — at one of our classes.

When I think of the story of Sam, Phyllis, and Kelly, I cannot help but be overwhelmed by G-d's many wondrous ways. Sam and Phyllis lost their fortune and underwent what, to them, was a horrific ordeal, but through that ordeal, they discovered their heritage, their faith, their very lives, and recreated their family. And it didn't stop there. Their daughter, Kelly, found her soul mate, and now, please G-d, there will be grandchildren who will carry on the legacy.

If not for those painful, stressful tests, the Jewish life of Sam and Phyllis would probably have come to an end, and with it, a heritage of almost four thousand years.

So when tests come your way, even if they appear to be difficult and bitter, instead of becoming angry or depressed, ask yourself, "What can I learn from this? How can I grow from this? How can I better realize the purpose for which G-d created me?" Indeed, how wondrous are the ways of G-d, Who never gives up on us, but lovingly guides us on the bumpy road of life.

8

When Love Spells Disaster

Morris Berk was agitated, His voice was tense and conveyed urgency.

"Rebbetzin," he said, "we have a major family crisis. You are our last resort."

"If I can, I'll be very happy to help you," I assured him. "Tell me, what's going on?"

"What's going on?" Morris repeated. "The roof is caving in on our heads!"

"Please don't exaggerate," his wife, Alice, interrupted. "From the way you're talking, the Rebbetzin will get the impression that the world is coming to an end."

"Well, my world *is* coming to an end," he snapped, "and so is my father's. And you just don't seem to get it!"

"Oh, I get it all right. Haven't I heard you yelling for the past six months? But I'm trying to be calm and reasonable. My first concern is Jason — that he be happy and well. The rest doesn't really matter."

"Doesn't matter? You see, Rebbetzin, she says this in front of the girls. That's what they learn from their mother!" he said, throwing up his hands in exasperation.

"You will excuse me," I now said, "but I'm not at all certain as to what we are talking about."

"I'm sorry," Alice said. "We should have explained, but, as you can see, my husband is very nervous and loses it quickly."

"How can I not lose it? Our son is planning to marry a *shiksah* (Yiddish term for a non-Jewish girl). My father is a Holocaust survivor, and Jason is his only grandson, the only one to carry on the family name. There is no one else. If he marries that girl, it's the end of our line. It will kill my father!"

"It won't kill your father," Alice interrupted, "but if you're so concerned, don't tell him. Since his last surgery, he hardly knows what's going on anyway, but Jason has his whole life ahead of him and loves this girl like he's never loved anyone before. I don't care what you say," she now added assertively, "I'm not going to allow my son to get sick over this. I've never seen Jason as happy as he is now. Don't get me wrong, Rebbetzin," she said, turning to me, "I'm not in favor of intermarriage — I wish that it wouldn't have happened, but now that it has, I've made up my mind that I'm not going to lose my son over it. Kathy is a very good girl and she has done wonders for him."

As I watched this volatile exchange between Morris and Alice, it became obvious to me that their problem was not only Jason, but their own relationship as well.

"I'm sorry that this has come between you," I now said. "It's one thing to deal with a problem with a child, and something else again when spouses are not united."

"United? That's a joke." Alice sneered. "We haven't been united for years."

"Alice, you're not being fair," Morris protested. "I may not be the best husband in the world, but I haven't been the worst, either."

"I can't believe this! I should be grateful that you haven't been the worst? We've been married for almost thirty years now, Rebbetzin, and I don't think that I can ever remember Morris being there for the family."

"That's an out and out lie! Of course I was there, but I had to work hard — you don't become a senior partner in a law firm by keeping nine-to-five hours. Anyway, who did I kill myself for, if not for you and the kids? Believe me, Rebbetzin," he said, turning to me, "they have all been very happily enjoying the 'good life.'"

Alice muttered something under her breath.

"Are you going to start that again?" Morris said. "I made one little mistake, Rebbetzin, and she continually harps on it, so I might as well admit it. I was stupid. I did things I shouldn't have done. But if Alice had been a little more caring, it would never have happened. Now, I'm not making excuses for myself — I should never have gotten involved. I regret what I did. I've apologized a thousand and one times. I don't know what else I can do."

"*One little mistake*, and you *don't know* what you can do?" she mimicked sarcastically. "Well, I *do* know — I know what it means to suffer in a marriage, and if I see that my son is happy, I'm not going to stand in his way — not for anyone — not for you, and not for your father."

"You see what I mean?" Morris interjected, "and the girls hear this from her all the time."

"How old are your daughters and how do they feel about all this?" I now asked.

"Vickie is twenty and Kate is seventeen," Alice volunteered.

"And they're both on their mother's side," Morris added.

"You're wrong," Alice rejoined. "This is not about being on my side. They love their brother and they want to see him happy."

"Because that's what you drummed into them," Morris said, bitterly.

Their open hostility was embarrassing, and I was pained for them.

"I think that I would like to speak to Alice privately," I now said. "Morris, would you excuse us for a few minutes?"

As Morris left my office, I got up from behind my desk, took a seat next to Alice, and reached for her hand. "May I speak to you as a friend?" I asked. "I understand that you are hurting. It's difficult to overcome a feeling of betrayal in a marriage, but we live in a very troubled world, there are so many enticements pulling at us. It's so easy to get lost and mess up as Morris did. But since your marriage has been challenged, the question that you must ask yourself is 'How do I respond? How do I deal with all this?' You have three options, Alice. 1. You can stay married, seethe with anger, and nurse your wounds; 2. You can sever your relationship and get a divorce; and 3. You can forgive, rebuild your home, and move on.

"The first two choices," I told her, "are not very happy ones. Anger is self destructive, and if you indulge it, not only will it consume you, but it will also consume those who are near and dear to you. As for divorce — in most cases, the only ones who benefit from it are the lawyers. What's more," I added, "after the trauma and expense of the divorce passes and loneliness sets in, you will want to meet someone, but you will discover that there is nothing much out there waiting for you. Almost every week, I see divorcées who are desperately seeking marriage partners — they openly admit that, with each passing day, their exes look better, and if they had it to do all over again, they would think twice. Now, I'm not even discussing the harmful effects that divorce has on children and grandchildren, and the difficulty of finding a new father for them. At the end of the day, children need *one* home, *one* set of parents — not Moms and Dads who have other priorities."

"Rebbetzin," she protested, "my children are already grown. Jason is twenty-six, Vickie is in college, and Kate will soon be graduating from high school."

"Children remain children forever, and never outgrow the need for mothers and fathers who live under one roof. And it's not only children, Alice — grandchildren also need role models. They need to see *bubbies* and *zeides* in a warm, loving environment. In short, the ramifications of divorce can be devastating, with far-reaching consequences. So your best option is to forgive, and get on with your life."

"Are you telling me that people should suffer in a marriage rather than divorce?"

"Suffering, Alice, is a big, big word, and in our self-centered society, it has been totally overused. People see only themselves and have no tolerance for the concerns of others. They want to receive and not to give. They want it *now*, and not later. Self-gratification has become their life-goal, so anything that intrudes on their comfort zone is termed 'suffering.'

"We have a teaching that when husband and wife divorce, in the Heavenly Sanctuary the altar weeps — and the obvious question is why the altar? Why not the ark or the menorah? And the answer given is that the altar is the place on which sacrifices are offered, and it weeps as if to say, 'If only husband and wife had made some more sacrifices, this marriage could have been saved.'

"There are, of course, situations in which there is no option but to divorce, and the Torah makes provisions for such eventualities. But I don't think that this applies to you and Morris. He sincerely regrets what happened and, from what I gather, is committed to your marriage. Morris wants to make amends, so I repeat once again, your best option is to *forgive and move on*."

"It's not so simple, Rebbetzin. I also have a heart. You can't expect me to just forget everything."

"Why not?" I asked. "Is what you're doing now — eating yourself up with bitterness — a better option? Let me ask you, is Morris abusive? Does he mistreat you? Does he withhold financial support?"

"No," she admitted. "I can't say that he does any of those things."

"In that case, there is no legitimate reason at this time for a divorce, and there is certainly no justification for your self-inflicted torture."

"Well, I did *forgive* him," Alice protested, "but that doesn't mean that I have *forgotten*."

"Alice, *if you haven't forgotten, then, in your heart, you haven't forgiven*. Let me share with you our Torah's teaching on forgiveness.

"At the genesis of our peoplehood, we stood as *one* at the foot of Mount Sinai and wholeheartedly accepted the Word of G-d. Moses told us that he would ascend the mountain to receive the Torah, and return after forty days and forty nights. There was a misunderstanding, however, as to exactly when those forty days would commence, and that resulted in a terrible tragedy. When Moses did not return as anticipated, the people panicked and fashioned a *golden calf*.

"I'm sure you've heard the Biblical story about the golden calf, but I would like you to appreciate the grievousness of that sin. It wasn't simply a transgression — rather, *it was an open betrayal of G-d.*

The Almighty had just promulgated His commandments, and on the cusp of that most sacred moment, to dance around the golden calf was an act of perfidy beyond words. The wrath of G-d was kindled, and the very survival of our nation was at risk, so once again, Moses ascended the mountain, but this time, it was to beseech G-d's mercy.

"Not only did G-d forgive, but, in His infinite mercy, *He granted forgiveness for all time by designating that day as the first Yom Kippur.* But Moses, the *Ro'eh Ne'eman B'Yisrael* — the Loyal Shepherd of Israel — was not content. He foresaw that this reprehensible sin of the Golden Calf would resurface in one form or another throughout the generations, so he begged G-d for an additional formula that would guarantee His eternal forgiveness.

"In response, G-d granted us a most magnificent gift — the *Thirteen Attributes of Mercy*, and promised that, whenever we recite them, total forgiveness would be forthcoming.

"Now, was this some sort of hocus pocus — magic words through which all our sins would be expiated? Could it be that simple?"

"I was wondering about that myself," Alice said.

"Well, let me explain the first two attributes, and through them, you will understand how the other eleven work. Actually, it's quite simple, and you can commit it to memory. The first two attributes are the repetition of G-d's Holy Name — '*HaShem, HaShem.*' This is an amazing gift, because it means that, if we truly regret our transgressions, if we turn to Him, He not only grants us a second chance, but He will remove all scars and reminders of our past and look upon us with the same love as He did before we sinned. Hence the repetition of His Name, '*HaShem, HaShem*' — G-d remains the same loving *HaShem* after we sinned as before we sinned.

"So it is that, in these *Thirteen Attributes of Mercy*, the word for 'forgive' is '*nosay.*' which literally means, 'He *lifts up* the sin,' and 'v'nakay' — 'He *cleanses* us of it' — which is a totally different concept from *forgiving*, for, as you yourself said, forgiveness doesn't necessarily mean that you forget. By recalling past injustices, Alice, you create a breeding ground for resentment and you prevent healing from taking place today. Under such circumstances, you can't move ahead, and your relationship with Morris can never be the same."

"Rebbetzin, I'm not G-d — I cannot be so big as to forget."

"None of us are G-d, and He is not asking that we *become* Him, but, if we want this formula to work, if we desire His forgiveness, then we must try to emulate His ways and forgive others even as He forgives us. And who is more worthy of such total forgiveness and cleansing, if not your husband, the father of your children? He has changed, and now it's time for you to change — to wipe the slate clean and start afresh."

Alice was silent for what seemed like a long time. Then she dabbed at her eyes with a tissue and in a subdued voice said, "When you throw all this Torah stuff at me, how can I argue?"

"You can't! None of us can. So, as long as we have that settled, let's get back to our immediate crisis. If you and Morris are not united on this, it will be very difficult to influence Jason."

"But I told you, Rebbetzin," she protested, "I *am* against intermarriage."

"I realize that, but unless you are unequivocal and take a firm stand along with Morris, Jason will interpret your position as an endorsement. When Morris said that this marriage would spell the end of his line, he was not exaggerating. Intermarriage is the new Holocaust that we are confronting in our free world. The numbers are devastating. In the United States, it ranges from 50 to 70 percent, and in Europe it's as high as 90 percent. During the past sixty years, there has been no real Jewish population growth in the U. S., and it's not because there was a Hitler here, or people did not have

Life Is a Test

children, or because there was no Jewish immigration. We have lost it all to intermarriage."

"I had no idea that the numbers were so high," Alice admitted, "and I do appreciate everything that you are saying, but I am a mother — and my first priority must be my son's happiness."

"But you are a *Jewish* mother, Alice, and your first priority must be to transmit Jewish life to future generations. Through intermarriage, the history of your people spanning almost four thousand years comes to an end."

"But what about his happiness?" Alice insisted.

"Let me share with you some simple Torah insights on that as well. During the High Holy Days, we wish one another a *Happy New Year*, but surprisingly, such a greeting does not exist in the Holy Tongue. The expression used is, '*Shanah Tovah*,' — 'Have a *good* year,' or '*K'sivah VaChasimah Tovah*' — 'May you be inscribed and sealed for a *good* year' — the emphasis being on *goodness* rather than happiness — and there is a world of difference between these two words. That which *is good* is based upon responsibility and discipline, giving and sacrifice — taking the harder, more difficult path over the easy, attractive one. Happiness, on the other hand, is a shallow, elusive pursuit that blurs all absolutes. It is rooted in self-gratification and the satisfying of passion, irrespective of the harm it inflicts on others. This pursuit of happiness is at the root of many of the ills that plague us — broken homes, shattered families, indolence, drugs, can all be traced to it.

"Forgive me," I added, "I don't want to pour salt on open wounds, but it was this obsession with happiness that gave Morris license to compromise himself. He felt unloved and that was all the justification he needed. Is this the 'happiness' that you would transmit to Jason? Is this the value system that you want him to live by?

"Happiness, if it is to be genuine, can only be realized through *goodness*, through doing that which is right, moral, and decent in the sight of G-d and man. And this is not my own subjective opinion — it is a teaching of our Torah: '*And you shall do that which is right and **good** in the sight of G-d*' (*Deuteronomy* 6:19).

"And, for your information, the divorce rate among intermarried couples is far higher than it is in same faith marriages — and this holds true even for those spouses who do not regard themselves as religious. So again, I ask you — is this the 'happiness' for which you are fighting?"

The expression on Alice's face told me that she was seriously absorbing my words, so I pushed on. "I hope that you don't mind my saying this, Alice, and forgive me if I'm intruding on your privacy, but I'm speaking to you from my heart. Can it be that you have been so hurt by Morris that you unwittingly derive a certain satisfaction in siding with Jason against him?"

"Absolutely not!" Alice protested. "That's nonsense!"

"I'm certain that you would never do so consciously, but somehow, that's the message that came across to me, and I'm glad to be proven wrong. Just the same," I added, "if you don't mind, I would like to share with you a little story that might prove helpful.

"It's about a chassidic couple, so poor they literally had no bread in their house. They did, however, possess one treasure — an heirloom that had been given to them as a wedding gift by a rebbe.

"When the holiday of Succoth approached, they lacked the money to purchase an *esrog* and *lulav* (the 'four species' mandated by the Torah). The man was so deeply saddened at the thought of being without an *esrog* and *lulav* that he decided to sell the heirloom and buy a beautiful *esrog*. Happily, he took his *esrog* home, and with great care, placed it on the sideboard. When his wife saw it, she asked in amazement, "How did you get that?"

"I bought it," the man answered proudly.

"Where did you get the money?"

"I sold our heirloom," he responded.

"You did *what*?" she shouted in fury. And in a fit of rage, she picked up the *esrog* and smashed it to the ground.

"The man began to tremble, but he took a deep breath and remained silent. In his heart, he thought, 'The heirloom is gone, and now the *esrog* is gone. The only thing I have left is my *shalom bayis* [harmonious husband-wife relationship.] I am *not* going to lose that as well.'

"Similarly, Alice, you may have lost your husband for a very brief period, but does that mean that you should lose the Jewish life of your son as well?"

"I have no intention of doing that."

"I believe that," I said, "but don't you see that if you follow your present course, that will be the result?"

"So what would you have me do?" she asked.

"Stand firm with Morris and prevail upon your daughters to do the same. The entire family must be united on this."

"I cannot speak for them. They are young adults with minds of their own."

"I appreciate that, but if Jason believes that he has support from his family, even if it's only from his siblings, his position will be strengthened and yours will be compromised. And there is yet one more consideration — if you don't voice your condemnation, what is there to prevent your daughters from following Jason's example and marrying out?"

"Okay, I'll try to speak to them. But what if Kathy agrees to convert?"

"We have had many converts in our history who were honored and revered by our people — chief among them was Ruth, the Moabite princess who became the great-grandmother of King David. But she converted because she yearned for G-d, His Torah, and

His mitzvos. She yearned to join the Jewish people and was prepared to renounce her opulent royal life, even to the point of living as a pauper in Israel. But tell me, Alice — what is Kathy yearning for? Why would she convert?"

"Kathy loves Jason," Alice responded and she hastened to add, "Please don't think that she's only interested in his money — she truly loves him."

"I never suggested anything of the sort," I protested. "I never met her, and if you tell me that she is a lovely girl and that she truly loves Jason, I have no reason to doubt that. But you asked me about conversion, and if conversion is to be authentic, it must be inspired by love of G-d, His Torah and the mitzvos, and not by a woman's love for a man. So, once again I ask you, why would Kathy be converting — for love of Judaism or for love of Jason?"

"Well, what about all the converts I hear about?" Alice protested, unwilling to give in.

"There are some who are genuine — who converted even as Ruth did — to become part of our people, to live by G-d's Torah and observe His *mitzvos*. These converts are a blessing, and we welcome them in our midst, but for the most part, modern-day conversions are a sham. We live in a world in which you can find someone to legitimize almost anything you wish. What it amounts to is that you can fool yourself, you can fool others, but you can't fool G-d, and ultimately, conversion is something between the convert and the Almighty.

"And there are still other considerations. Do you really think that it is fair to demand that Kathy sever herself from her family, from the traditions and holidays with which she was raised?"

"She's not that religious."

"Even if she's not, comes the month of December, she will want to have her *tree;* she will want to join her family for holiday celebrations — how do you suppose this will impact on their children?"

"Well, there are families that have both a tree and a menorah."

"Come on, Alice. You know better than that. You know that that would be a total travesty. Faith in G-d is not a game of mix and match. While we respect everyone's religious beliefs and practices, it does not mean that we adopt them as our own. And speaking of respect, how much respect can you have for Kathy if you expect her to give up her faith? You certainly wouldn't want Jason to renounce his."

"Are you telling me that all my ideas are wrong?"

"I'm afraid so — but don't be too hard on yourself. You aren't the only one who has made these mistakes. It's our contemporary Jewish tragedy."

"So what would you have me do?"

"Like I told you — stand firm with Morris, and let's go for damage control."

"Damage control?" Alice repeated.

"Yes. At this point, it's the only way to go, so let's ask Morris to come in and we'll try to brainstorm together."

When Morris rejoined us, I asked him to give me some background and tell me how long Jason had been seeing Kathy.

"Over two years. They met at work. At first, he kept reassuring us that they were 'just good friends.' Then, six months ago, he told us that their friendship had turned into something more serious."

"Did he bring her home during this time?" I asked.

"Oh yes, on many occasions," Alice volunteered, "but like Morris told you, he always assured us that it was just a friendship."

"Frankly, I was suspicious all along," Morris interrupted, "but I was afraid that if I clamped down too hard, I would push him into her arms. I guess I was hoping that the whole thing would just blow over."

"I'm not saying this to throw recriminations at you, but you are coming for help very late. It's best when these things are nipped in the bud. Moreover, these relationships never remain 'just friend-ships,' and once you welcomed the girl into your home, you sent a signal that, even if you weren't happy with the situation, you would eventually accept it. But it is important that we understand what we are up against.

"So, now tell me about Jason's Jewish education," I asked.

"You can't blame *me* for that," Alice protested. "That was strictly in Morris' hands."

"We're not here to cast blame on anyone," I assured them. "I know that you both meant well, but unfortunately, that doesn't eliminate the present problem, so let's try to assess what we have to contend with."

"Wait a minute," Morris protested. "I have nothing to be ashamed of. I saw to it that Jason had a fine Jewish education. He went to He-brew school three times a week, and I even took a tutor to prepare him for his Bar Mitzvah. We always went to synagogue on the High Holy Days and made a seder on Passover. He has been to Israel, and he also knows that his grandfather is a Holocaust survivor — so what else is there?"

"So what else is there?" His question hit me like a ton of bricks. Where do I begin? How could I make him understand the vacuous-ness, the meaninglessness of this so-called "Jewish education"?

"Let me ask you a question," I challenged, "if Jason's *secular* educa-tion had been limited to three hours of instruction a week, from age six to thirteen, and at the age of thirteen, he had to recite a sonnet of Shakespeare, would you feel that he was equipped to face life?"

"What are you trying to tell me, Rebbetzin?" Morris asked.

"I'm trying to tell you that, even as such a secular education would be pitifully inadequate and render him an illiterate, so Jason and his peers are Jewishly illiterate. Unfortunately, however, they have one additional handicap. Because they went through this so-called *bar mitzvah factory*, they assume that they know all that there is to know about Judaism, and have nothing further to learn. The average Jew nowadays has nothing to keep him anchored to his faith, nothing to inspire him to commitment. He has no understanding of the Divinely given treasures that are the heritage of his people — and how could it be otherwise in such a bankrupt educational system? Like you, Morris, many believe that visits to Israel and Holocaust commemorations can substitute for Jewish knowledge. But let's be honest — you don't have to be Jewish to visit Israel, and sadly, even if you live there and speak Hebrew impeccably, it doesn't mean that you know what Judaism is all about. As for remembering the Holocaust — as important as that is, it, too, fails to impart a knowledge of Judaism, even if one's grandfather is a survivor. At best, all that Jason learned from the Holocaust is that there are many evil, satanic people in the world who hate Jews and would like to wipe them off the face of the earth. But that awareness does not enable him to understand what it means to belong to the people of the Covenant. Nor does it impart to him any knowledge of the Torah. So think about it — why should Jason sacrifice for Judaism when he has no clue as to what that Judaism entails? He doesn't even have any sentimental connections — memories of an authentic *Shabbos* or *Yom Tov* that would evoke feelings of nostalgia in his heart and bring tears to his eyes. In short, spiritually, Jason is driving on empty."

"You are painting a pretty bleak picture. Does this mean that our situation is hopeless?"

"Hopeless?" I repeated, "G-d forbid! Our history proves that the word 'hopeless' is not in our lexicon."

"So you think that something can be salvaged?" Morris pressed.

"With G-d's help, *everything* is possible, and we do have our Jewish DNA working in our favor."

"Jewish DNA? That's an expression I've never heard," Alice commented.

"Well, we definitely have it. Let me explain how it works. When G-d sealed His Covenant with us and gave us His Torah at Mount Sinai, all of us — and by that *I mean all of us* — every Jewish soul that was ever destined to be born was present. '*Not with our forefathers alone did G-d seal the Covenant, but with us — we who are here, all of us who are* **alive today**.... *face to face did G-d speak to you from amid the fire*' (*Deuteronomy 5:3-4*). When the Torah says '*today*,' it literally means *today* — in every generation, for all eternity.

"That experience at Sinai ignited a spark in our souls — a spark that neither time nor force can ever extinguish. In Yiddish, we call it the '*pintele Yid.*' It acts like an internal compass, always pointing the way back to Torah. G-d endowed us with many reminders of its presence, and one of them is the commandment to fix a lunar calendar, for even as the moon does not possess its own light, but is a reflection of the sun, similarly, we do not possess our own independent light, since the light that illuminates our souls is that Divine spark from Sinai. And just as the moon periodically disappears from view, only to resurface, that spark from Sinai can never be snuffed out, but resurfaces, and herein is to be found the miracle of our Jewish survival. Consider for a moment, the phenomenon of our own time. Despite the ravages of assimilation and intermarriage, we also see secular Jews rediscovering and reconnecting to their heritage. They are part of a great army of *ba'alei teshuvah* — men, women, and children — who have embraced the ancient faith of their ancestors. Whether we will succeed in inspiring Jason to join their ranks, I do not know, but I do know that we must try."

"So, how do we proceed?" they both asked.

"Let's begin with meeting Jason. Would he be open to seeing me?"

"If I ask him, he will surely say no, but if Alice asks, he might just agree," Morris said, turning to Alice.

"I'm not so sure that I have all that influence, but I can try," she promised.

"Good!" I said. "That's all that we can ask."

But before Morris and Alice left, I once again emphasized that even if Jason agreed to come, it would take a miracle to bring him around, because there was so much going against us.

"So," I told them, "we will need G-d's help to reignite the spark in Jason's soul, and you will both have to do something to stoke the embers.

"Let's start with you, Alice. Do you light *Shabbos* candles?" I asked.

"Sometimes," she answered.

"Make a commitment to light every week, and be certain to *light on time* because you can't kindle the Sabbath lights after the holy day has commenced. Candle lighting is a most auspicious moment when the Heavenly Gates are open and G-d waits to hear from the mothers of our people. So, after you make the blessings on the Sabbath lights, take a few moments and ask G-d to kindle the spark in Jason's *neshamah* and open his heart and mind. And don't just leave it at candle lighting. Make a beautiful *Shabbos* table for your family — bring *Shabbos* into your home."

"And Morris," I now said, turning to him, "do you put on *tefillin* in the morning?"

"When I was Bar Mitzvah, the rabbi in the Hebrew school put them on me."

"My sons are our Hineni rabbis — I'll ask one of them to take you to purchase *tefillin* and teach you how to put them on. Make a commitment, Morris, to go to synagogue every morning and pray."

"*Every morning!*" he repeated. "You want me to go to synagogue *every* morning! That's going to be real tough!"

"It's going to be tough for me as well," Alice hastened to add. "My Fridays are very hectic, and I really don't know how I can get home in time to prepare *Shabbos* dinner and light candles."

Once again, I was overcome by the painful reality of our plight as a nation. How do I make them see the tragic irony of expecting Jason to give up the girl he loves when they themselves are reluctant to give even a little of their time to G-d? How do I make them understand the sad paradox of our 21st century Jewish life? We have homes with state of the art lighting, but we have forgotten how to kindle the sacred Sabbath lights. We have kitchens with conveniences our grandmothers never dreamt of, but we find it too difficult to make *Shabbos* dinner for our families. With the push of a button, we speak to people at the other end of the globe, but we are incapable of pronouncing a simple prayer to G-d. We spend hours on the internet, find time for entertainment, golf, tennis, cards, and the gym, but we cannot find a few moments for our Creator.

Yet even as these thoughts passed through my mind, I also realized that this lack of commitment was not their fault, but was the result of the spiritual deprivation of our generation, so I simply said, "If it's not tough — if it comes too easy — then it has no value. You want to demonstrate to G-d that you are serious, that you are willing to walk that extra mile, but I guarantee that, once you experience *Shabbos*, once you discover the inspiration of prayer, you will realize that our *mitzvos* are not burdens, but a source of great joy and serenity."

"So, is that it?" Morris asked, half-jokingly.

"Not quite," I said, choosing to take him seriously. "There is one more thing to which I would like to ask you both to commit, and that is *Torah study*. Join us at least once a week for a Torah class."

"Come on, Rebbetzin. Enough is enough!" Morris said. "When I asked if that was it, I was kidding, and I certainly didn't mean for you to add more to the package! We came here because we have a problem with Jason, and all of a sudden, *we* have become the problem!"

"Nothing happens in a vacuum. As I said earlier, if Jason is prepared to throw away his Jewish heritage, it is because he was never made to appreciate its value. If our damage control is going to be effective, Morris, you will need to have something more to say to your son than 'My world is coming to an end,' or 'Your grandfather will not survive this.'

"I must confess however that I do have a hidden agenda in asking you to study Torah, and that is to help the two of you recover your *shalom bayis*, because that, too, is part of the healing process. You have to become a family again. G-d did not intend for husbands and wives to live in conflict or in a state of cold war, but that they unite as one in sanctity and love."

"Sanctity?" Alice repeated questioningly. "I don't know of any marriages like that."

"That's because you haven't met any couples who have a real Torah connection and bond spiritually."

"So why can't we pick up a Bible and read it at home?" Morris asked.

"Once you start studying, you will realize how impossible that would be. The Torah is not a book that can be read. Every word, every letter, every dot, every comma, is laden with hidden meaning and must be deciphered. At Mount Sinai, G-d transmitted seventy different ways of understanding His Divine teachings — so this is one study that can never be exhausted. Even if you review the Torah portions a thousand and one times, you never master it — you will always find new insights to inspire and guide you. But you cannot do this alone — you must have a teacher who is not only well-versed in the Torah, but who lives it. Torah study is not an option. Rather, it is the commandment par excellence that supersedes all others. As a matter of fact, G-d says, 'I prefer that you abandon Me, but do not forsake My Torah."

"I don't get it," Morris said.

"Simple — Torah study is our road map — our instruction manual for life — and once we familiarize ourselves with it, everything just naturally falls into place — and of course, we connect with our G-d. However, the converse does not hold true. Many people profess belief in G-d, but make up their own theology, their own sets of rules. Their rationale is simple — 'The only thing that G-d requires of me is that I be happy and fulfilled.' So, instead of worshiping G-d, they worship themselves and rely upon their hearts and minds to be the ultimate arbiters of truth. When you study Torah, however, G-d's Will becomes your imperative, and you live by a higher law. Through Torah study, you will not only connect to G-d, but you will also bond as husband and wife. And more, Torah will enable you to understand that which befell our people throughout the centuries — our exile, the Holocaust, the rebirth of Israel, the in-gathering of the exiles — it is all predicted in the Torah. The histories of other nations are written during or after the events unfold. Our history however, was written up-front, *before it ever occurred* and that, in and of itself, is miraculous and would give every Jew pause if only he would open the Book and study it.

"Every day, as part of our morning service, we recite a blessing and ask G-d to grant us the privilege of understanding His Holy Words, and grace us — not only us, but our children and children's children, and all our people — with His eternal wisdom.

"Would it not be wonderful," I now said, "if all of you — the girls, Jason, and even grandpa, could share Torah study and become united as a family?"

"I don't see that happening," Alice commented dryly.

"You never know — there are people studying with us today whose situations appeared even more hopeless than yours. The main thing is to start, and who, if not you, should show the way?"

"You want to give it a shot?" Morris asked, turning to Alice.

She thought about it for a while and then said, "Do we have a choice? I guess we have to give it a try."

"Good!" I said. "Maybe, just maybe, with G-d's help, we'll see a miracle happen and Jason will come home — and you'll come home to each other."

9

"Who Wins?"

True to their word, Morris and Alice began to attend our Torah sessions, and with every week that passed, they became more involved and committed, but Jason refused to come. From the moment that Alice clamped down on him, he became hostile. As far as he was concerned, Kathy was his soul mate, and he resented anyone who was unreceptive to that. As tensions built, Alice began to second-guess herself, wondering whether she had acted wisely.

"You had no choice, Alice," I assured her. "You cannot bend the truth of our Torah. Jason has to know that you stand for something bigger than yourself, and even if he is resentful now, one day he will be grateful to you for having shown him the way. Hang in there and remain steadfast. Be loving, but strong; invite him for *Shabbos* dinners, keep reminding him of his responsibility to transmit his Jewish faith to future generations, and, please G-d, we will see a breakthrough."

"Oh, Rebbetzin," she said with resignation, "You don't know Jason. He is tough, and can be very stubborn. I'll never get through to him."

But to the surprise of Alice and Morris, Jason called a few weeks later and asked to see me. When he walked into my office, I was somewhat taken aback. From Alice's description, I had expected to see a tall, towering figure, but he was slight of build, with dark intense eyes, best described as an "intellectual type." He had, however, a definite "attitude," and although he didn't say it in so many words, it was apparent that he had come for a showdown. After we exchanged greetings, he got down to business.

"Rebbetzin," he said, "You are responsible for dividing my family, so let me make it quite clear. I'm marrying Kathy. I have no intention of giving her up because *you* say that I can't marry a non-Jew."

"I fully agree with you," I said.

He was so intent on asserting himself that, for a moment, my words flew over his head, but then he paused and asked, "What do you mean, you agree with me? If that's the case, why did you say just the opposite to my parents?"

"Well, I *do* agree with you, and I did *not* give a conflicting message to your mom and dad."

"Am I missing something here?" he asked.

"No, you're not. You heard me right. I would never be so presumptuous as to suggest that you sacrifice and give up the girl you love on my say-so. Even though I wholeheartedly believed what I said, I could still be wrong."

"So, what *are* you saying?" he asked, looking at me quizzically.

"I'm saying that, if this were only my opinion, you could certainly feel free to reject it, but this is not my opinion — this is a command from G-d." And with that, I reached for the *Chumash* — Bible — on my desk, pointed to *Deuteronomy* 7:3, and asked Jason to read the words with me: 'You shall not intermarry with them; you shall not give your daughter to his son, and you shall not take his daughter for your son, for he shall cause your child to turn away from after Me, and they will worship the gods of others....'"

"So you see, Jason, this is not my opinion — this is a commandment of G-d. And G-d even gives a reason for it, which is unusual since most of the time, the Torah does not advance any rationale for the observance of commandments other than that they are the Word of G-d, and, in the final analysis, there can be no more convincing argument than that. Just the same, to make us aware of the deadly consequences of intermarriage, G-d warned us that the children who are the products of these unions will give up Judaism — and tragically, reality has borne this out only too well. Each intermarriage represents a dead branch on our nation's family tree. So you see, Jason, this has nothing to do with *my* opinion. This is a command of G-d to insure our survival as a nation."

"I think that I'm a good Jew, but I have difficulty believing in G-d. If He really exists, how could He have allowed the Holocaust to happen?"

"Forgive me, Jason, but what you just said is an oxymoron. We are Jews by virtue of our belief in G-d. The very word, 'Jew' — 'Yehudi' — means to give thanks to the Almighty. Our mother, Leah, coined the phrase when she gave birth to her son, 'Yehudah.' As for G-d, whether you believe in Him or not, Jason, He *does* exist, and trust me, He doesn't need approbation or recognition from you or me to validate Him. But we do need *His* validation. Without it, you cannot exist, even for an instant. Should He so decide, your life can be snuffed out swifter than the wink of an eye. And regarding where G-d was during the Holocaust, I don't think that you have the right to ask that question."

"Why not?" he protested.

"You just said that you don't believe in Him. Well, if you don't believe in Him, whom are you asking? You can't have it both ways, Jason. You can't say that He doesn't exist and then ask where He was. But as long as we are discussing the subject, let me ask you, what *do* you have faith in? What *do* you believe in?"

"My convictions are simple enough," he said, without hesitation. "I believe in the innate goodness of man, and I believe in the power of culture and education."

"Those beliefs, Jason, are all fallen gods, so if I were you, I would re-examine them. Just study our recent history and you will discover that it was enlightened, civilized Germany that gave birth to the greatest evil ever visited upon mankind. It was scientists, engineers and chemists who built the gas chambers and devised ways to convert our skin into lampshades, our fat into soap, our bones into fertilizer. Many of them were university graduates who listened to Beethoven and Mozart. And it was doctors who conducted barbaric experiments upon us. The Germans were a highly educated, cultured nation — yet it was they who devised a thousand and one torturous deaths for our people. As for the *innate goodness* of man — the entire civilized world participated in this unspeakable crime — some actively, some passively, but, to one extent or another, they all chose to shut their eyes to the evil and thereby condoned it. It was not just six million Jews who perished in the Holocaust, but the foundations of Western culture collapsed, as well. So, as I said, Jason, you had better re-examine your beliefs, and as you do, take a good look at our contemporary world, because nothing has changed. The barbaric cruelty, the acts of terror, genocide, the escalation of anti-Semitism and the demonization of the Jewish people and Israel, are as real today as they were yesterday; so much for the 'innate goodness of man' and the forces of education and culture."

"I guess you got me there," Jason conceded, "*but…*" and his words hung in the air.

"But what?" I challenged.

Instead of responding, Jason shook his head and threw up his hands as if to say, "What's the use!"

"Look," I said. "I am not trying to skirt your question about G-d, but if you are intellectually honest, instead of asking where was G-d, you should ask, 'Where was man?' How was it possible that such evil could have taken place in our enlightened 20th century? And this in no way implies that G-d is absent from history, but He created us as free beings and endowed us with the ability to make choices. The Holocaust was a man-made disaster, even if man refuses to accept accountability for it, and mind you, there is nothing new about this. From the time that Cain, the first murderer, walked on planet Earth, man has tried to shift blame for his evil.

"'Where is your brother?' G-d challenged Cain after he murdered Abel.

"'I do not know — Am I my brother's keeper?' (*Genesis* 4:8-9) was his audacious answer, insinuating that he was not responsible. That G-d, Who *is* the Keeper of the world, should have prevented him from committing this evil deed.

"Thousands of years have passed, but nothing has changed. Man continues to perpetrate the most heinous crimes and then hypocritically asks, 'Where was G-d?'

"Still, if you genuinely wish to understand the Holocaust, and if you are not just being argumentative, then I invite you to come to our Torah sessions, and I guarantee that you will gain clarity. Even if you protest that you don't believe, I will tell you that every human being believes in Him, and how could it be otherwise? It is He Who created us and it is He Who breathed life into us. In the innermost recesses of his soul, no man can be oblivious of Him. So, how, you might ask, is it possible that there are people like you who claim that they don't believe, that He doesn't exist?

"It's all due to *sixteen inches*."

Jason stared at me quizzically and asked, "Sixteen inches?"

"Yes," I repeated, "sixteen little inches that separate our heads from our hearts. A sage once explained that that is the most difficult gap for us to bridge, that the distance from the mind to the heart is as great as the distance of the furthest star from earth, and the reason is simple enough.

"Sometimes, our *hearts* perceive that there is a G-d, but our *heads* refuse to acknowledge Him. We want to set our own agendas and follow our own courses without being bound by His higher Law. And the converse can also be true. Sometimes, we intellectually recognize the *truth*, but lack the emotional stamina to follow through. It's like knowing that smoking is detrimental to our health but being incapable of stopping, because we simply lack the discipline to control ourselves. So, whichever way you look at it, Jason, denial of G-d's existence is most often rooted in an inability to close *that sixteen-inch gap*. At Sinai, Moses, our teacher, warned us about this conflict, 'You shall *know* this day and take it to your *heart*, that *HaShem*, He is G-d' (*Deuteronomy* 4:39). In other words, our hearts and our minds have to act in consonance in acknowledging Him. This principle is so basic to our faith that we proclaim it three times a day in *Aleinu* — the prayer that closes the three daily services."

For what seemed like a long time, there was silence as Jason mulled over my words, so I decided to share with him an experience that I had on a flight to Dallas, Texas.

Whenever I travel, I take my office with me — I like to use my time on planes as expeditiously as possible. The absence of ringing phones gives me the opportunity to recite Psalms and to write uninterruptedly. I was engrossed in prayer when I heard the flight attendant ask Barbara, who was seated next to me, "Are you going to Dallas on business or pleasure?"

"Neither," Barbara answered, "My friend never goes on vacation. She is going to Dallas to speak."

"Speak about what?" he asked curiously.

At this point, I had just completed a psalm, so I joined the conversation and told him that I would be speaking about G-d.

"Ahh —" he exclaimed, "that's a topic that I can relate to. What is your religion?"

"Jewish," I responded.

"I'm not Jewish, but just in case there is someone in your audience who doesn't believe in G-d, let me tell you a story. Some years ago, prior to my becoming a flight attendant, I was in law enforcement. One of my closest buddies on the force was an atheist. Whenever we got into a discussion, he would loudly protest that he didn't believe. Well, one day, in a big rainstorm, I was on duty when a call came in reporting a major collision involving five cars and a motorcycle. I raced to the scene, and the sight that greeted me was one that I never again want to see. Bodies were strewn all over the road, and lying in a ditch near the embankment was my buddy. It was his day off, and he had taken out his Harley. In the blinding rain, he skidded and was thrown into a ditch. He was lying in a pool of blood, but was conscious. When he saw me, he gathered all his strength and gasped, 'I'm so happy that it's you. I have to tell you something. You know how I always used to say that I don't believe in G-d? Well, it wasn't true. In my *heart*, I believed in Him all the time, but my mind was afraid to embrace Him. I just couldn't handle it. Now, I'm going to have to face Him. Pray for me, and ask that He forgive me and accept me.' By the time the ambulance arrived, he was gone."

"Whenever I hear someone say that they don't believe in G-d," he concluded, "that story comes back to me, because *in our hearts*, we all believe in Him. We just look for excuses to escape our responsibilities."

"I have often repeated that story," I told Jason, "and it resonates with all audiences. Belief in G-d is intrinsic to every man, and if this holds true for all people, how much more so is it valid for you, Jason, a Jew who stood at Mount Sinai and heard the voice of G-d."

"Now, that's one of the things that I object to," Jason pounced at my reference to Sinai. "This Jewish exclusivity smacks of racism!"

"Racism? Not at all. If there is any faith that is *not* racist, it is ours. We believe that all people are assured of their place in Heaven as long as they adhere to the seven Noahide laws of morality, such as not committing murder, not stealing, etc. We do not require anyone to convert to Judaism to be saved, and this is not just something theoretical — some pollyana-ish teaching. Our Torah commands us to relate to all people with kindness, respect, honesty and integrity.

"'… and you shall *love the stranger* as yourself, for you shall remember that you were strangers in the land of Egypt' (*Leviticus* 19:34). So, when I said that we, the Jewish people, stood as one at Mount Sinai and entered into an eternal Covenant with G-d, it had nothing to do with racism. Rather, I was referring to a charge, a responsibility, given to each and every one of us to live by G-d's Covenant and transmit it to future generations. That revelation at Sinai is historical fact — Christianity, Islam, and their offshoots all built their faiths on it. None of these religions has ever disputed the authenticity of that moment, nor has any other nation ever claimed to have had a similar national experience. What's more, it is all documented. You can check it out:

"'Inquire now regarding the early days which preceded you from the day when G-d created man on the earth, and search from one end of the heavens to the other end of the heavens and ask, "Has there ever been anything like this great thing, or has anything like it been heard? Has a people ever heard the voice of G-d speaking from the midst of a fire as you have heard and survived?"' (*Deuteronomy* 4:32-34).

"That world-shaking moment, when G-d revealed Himself and established His Covenant, is unique to our people, but anyone who wishes to be a part of it, may do so, provided it is *love of the Covenant* that impels him or her to commit, and *not love for a man or a woman.*"

"Kathy is more spiritual and kinder than any Jewish girl I ever dated," Jason protested.

"I won't dispute that. I'm sure that she is everything you say, but that has nothing to do with taking on the responsibilities of our Covenant — a Torah life."

"Well, what if she converts?"

"Jason, we just went through all that, and I explained it to your Mom as well. All those who love our Torah and are prepared to observe its *mitzvos* — commandments — are welcome to join us, but they must be truly committed and prepared to live a Torah life. Kathy's commitment is to *you* and not to Judaism. What's more, she has no intention of living a Torah life, so what would she be converting to? And let's face it, Jason — you, yourself, have no clue as to what Judaism and Torah are all about. You don't even know whether you believe in G-d, so what can you expect from Kathy? Why should she give up her religion in favor of yours?"

"I may not know too much about Torah, I may be ambivalent about G-d, and I may not be religious, but I would never give up being Jewish," Jason protested adamantly.

"But Jason, if you follow your present course, you *are* giving it up. I know you would never do so consciously — when push comes to shove, there are very few who would deliberately and openly renounce their faith, but Jason, that's simply not good enough! I once heard someone compare our contemporary Jewish life to a sports team that has a host of enthusiastic fans but no good players. If a team does not have good players, it is doomed to die, and soon, even its fans disappear. So, it's very nice that you are a *fan*, Jason, but that just won't cut it. We need *players,* and *good players* at that! If our people are to live and thrive, we need players who will take the field and play with passion, strength, and commitment, players who will not only relate to Torah, but who will *live it* and be willing to sacrifice for it. Just the same," I hastened to add, "I can't fault *you* for not feeling that commitment."

"I can't believe you're being so charitable," Jason said, somewhat sarcastically.

Choosing to ignore his sarcasm, I told him that I wasn't being at all charitable — I was just being realistic. "I can't very well expect you to sacrifice for something that you have no knowledge of and do not love."

"Well, I'm glad that you understand, Rebbetzin."

"Of course I do, but that doesn't give you license to turn your back on your people and cast away your G-d-given heritage. Whether you choose to believe in G-d or not, one day you will have to face Him, and when you do, He will not ask you about the doubts that plagued you, but He *will* want to know why you did not search for answers, why you lost your heritage by default. Why you did not bring Jewish children into the world. So I'm asking you to set aside just a few hours for Torah study and find out who you really are."

Jason did not respond.

For a while, we sat there in silence, and then I asked, 'Why are you so afraid? What are a few hours in the scheme of things?"

"I'm not afraid," Jason shot back, "but I'm very busy and Torah sessions are not exactly at the top of my agenda."

"Come on — that's just a cop-out. If you want to, you can find the time, but I will take your words at face value, and I will ask one of my sons to give you a Torah class at your office. You won't have to travel anywhere — you can study in place."

But Jason wasn't ready to commit even to that.

"Didn't you just tell me that you would never renounce being Jewish?" I asked him. "Don't you see that if you follow your present course, you will be doing just that? If your children don't have a Jewish mother, it will all be over. We are minuscule in number — less than thirteen million in the world, and of that thirteen million, there are few *players*, and many are not even *fans*. Consider that intermarriage is constantly escalating — add to that, assimilation, alienation, and Torah illiteracy, and you have the makings of a spiritual Holocaust.

"Throughout our history, from the days of our Egyptian bondage, we have triumphed over persecution, oppression, and yes, even a Holocaust, but a spiritual Holocaust is different. Those who become its victims simply disappear without a trace. There is no one to memorialize them, no one to say Kaddish for them; no one to carry on their names." I went on to tell Jason that my own grandparents, uncles, aunts, and cousins were all murdered in the gas chambers of Auschwitz, but they are all alive today because my children and grandchildren carry their names and live by their legacy. "But a spiritual Holocaust leaves no legacy — not even a name, not even a Kaddish." To illustrate, I related a story that I once heard from the former Chief Rabbi of Israel, Rabbi Yisrael Meir Lau.

As a young child, he and his older brother, Naphtali, were shipped to Buchenwald concentration camp. In the death camps, children were systematically taken to the gas chambers, but Naphtali had made a promise to his parents, who had been murdered by the Nazis, that he would take care of little Yisrael Meir. There are many amazing stories about the herculean efforts of Naphtali to preserve the life of his younger brother. Miraculously, both boys survived and made their way to Israel, where eventually, Naphtali became an ambassador, and Yisrael Meir the Chief Rabbi.

The story that Rabbi Lau related concerned a fellow survivor, a colleague, also a rabbi, to whom I shall refer by the pseudonym, 'Reb Chaim.' At the end of the war, like all survivors, Reb Chaim searched for remnants of his family, and soon discovered that his entire *mishpachah* had been slaughtered. He also learned that his beloved rabbi had been killed, and that none of his family had survived, except for one daughter who was living with her young child in Belgium. When he made inquiries about her, he was told that she had placed her son in a Catholic monastery. This news devastated Reb Chaim. "How could this be?" he asked himself. "How could the rebbe's daughter do such a thing?" He wrote to her, but all his letters were returned unopened. He verified the name and address, and they checked out, so he wrote once again and even sent telegrams, but all his correspondence was sent back. Having no other options, he decided to travel to Belgium to seek her out. He felt that that was the very least he could do to honor the holy memory of his rebbe.

Arriving in Antwerp, he took a cab from the airport and headed straight to the town where she lived. Without much difficulty, he found her house. As he knocked on her front door, he thought he saw someone peering through the curtains, but there was no answer. Again and again he knocked, and still, there was no answer, but Reb Chaim refused to give up.

The cab driver, who had accompanied him, suggested that perhaps there was no one home.

"I know that someone is here," Reb Chaim insisted. "I'm not budging, even if it means camping out on the doorstep," he shouted as loudly as he could, hoping that the woman inside would relent and open the door.

Finally, the door slowly opened, and in a sharp voice, a woman said, "I know who you are. I know why you came. Please go away! I don't want any part of that life anymore, so please go away."

"I've come a long way," Reb Chaim pleaded. "Could I just come in for a glass of water?"

Her natural compassion overcame her. "Please come in," she said to Reb Chaim and the driver. "I will make you both a cup of tea."

"No, no," Rabbi Chaim protested. "A glass of water would be fine."

As he lifted the glass to his lips, he loudly pronounced our timeless blessing, "Blessed art Thou L-rd our G-d — *shehakol ne'heyeh bidvaro* — through Whose Word everything comes to be."

When she heard those familiar holy words, something must have resonated in her heart, for she said, "Do you know what they did to my father, your rebbe? Do you know how they killed him?"

"No, I don't, but please tell me."

"They came into the ghetto at dawn, shouting, shooting and screaming. They stormed our small apartment and broke down the door. My father was immersed in prayer, wrapped in his *tallis*, with his *tefillin* on his head. His face radiated sanctity and kindness, but those beasts never saw that — to them, my father was just a sub-human Jew, to be crushed, exterminated. With their rifle butts, they smashed my father's skull, and as they did so, they roared with laughter. My father fell to the ground — his *tefillin* rolled into the pool of blood. And that was the last time I saw my father, your rebbe. I don't want that life for my son. I've turned a new page, so please, just go away!'"

Reb Chaim was overcome by tears and could not speak — Finally, in a low voice he said, "Yes, I will leave. But before I go, please answer just one question: WHO WINS?"

"What do you mean, 'Who wins'?" she repeated.

"I mean, 'WHO WINS'?" Reb Chaim said again. "If you place tefillin on your son's head, then your father and the Jewish people will have triumphed, but if you raise your son as a non-Jew, then Hitler will have won. So I ask you, 'WHO WINS'?"

And with that, Reb Chaim left. He got into the cab and told the driver to pull away ever so slowly. "I have a feeling that she will come outside," he said, and sure enough, the door opened and she ran to the car.

"You're right," she said, weeping, "but you must make me a promise. There is no one left from my family...no one to teach my son. Will you put *tefillin* on my son's head?"

The woman and her son returned to Jerusalem with Reb Chaim, and today, that child is an eminent Rosh Yeshivah — the dean of a highly respected rabbinical academy in Israel.

"To paraphrase Reb Chaim," I now said to Jason — "I too would like to ask. WHO WINS? Will you be yet another statistic in that spiritual Holocaust? Will you disappear without leaving a trace or will you become a living branch on your family tree and give new life to your people? Life is a test, Jason, and this is *your* test. It is for you to decide — *who will win*?"

Jason's eyes were moist.

"It's a tough call, Rebbetzin," he said in a voice filled with emotion. "Like you said, it's not easy to bridge those *sixteen inches* that separate my heart from my mind."

"I know," I said, "and I don't expect you to give me your answer now, but I am asking you to make a commitment to study Torah."

"When is the next session?" he asked.

"Tomorrow evening."

"I will be there," he promised.

I walked him to the door, and when we came to the lobby of our building, I asked him to read the inscription on the wall. "This is My Covenant with them.... And these words that I have placed upon your lips, shall not depart from your lips, nor from the lips of your children or your children's children, forevermore.... Thus saith the L-rd." (*Isaiah* 59:20-21).

For thousands of years, we have repeated those words of Isaiah. They are part of our daily morning service. But more significantly, they are engraved upon our hearts. Just consider the miraculous survival of our people — cast to the four corners of the world, absorbed by every civilization and culture — yet the promise has been kept. When a Jew is reminded of his Covenant, a spark ignites in his heart and he passes the test.

10

Not the Horse I Wanted

There is a Hungarian folk tale about a little boy, born into an impoverished family, who dreamt of having a rocking horse. But such a toy was far beyond the reach of his parents, so his wish remained just a dream.

One day, his mother fell ill. Her condition deteriorated rapidly, and she died. In Hungary, in the non-Jewish community, it was a tradition for the funeral procession to be led by a carriage drawn by black horses. The little boy was standing by the window, weeping silently, when the hearse pulled up to the house. When he saw the black horses, he cried out bitterly, "That's not the horse I wanted!... That's *not* the horse I wanted!"

Very often in life, it happens that our hopes, our aspirations, do not materialize as we anticipated, and just like that little boy, we too cry out, "*That's not the horse I wanted!*" When we are young, and envision the family we will one day have, we dream of loving mates and perfect children — children who are healthy, handsome, bright, gifted, considerate, and successful in all their endeavors; children who are always respectful and never give us grief. But life is full of disappointments. Seldom do things turn out as we planned. There is always the unforseen: "Many are the thoughts in the heart of man, but it is the Will of G-d that prevails" (*Proverbs* 19:21). If we look back upon our lives, we must concede that the unexpected often happens — that *the horses that pull up to our homes are seldom the horses we wished for* — and nowhere is this more apparent than when it comes to raising our children.

There is yet another Hungarian tale that is relevant to parenting. It is about a young man who falls for a girl who tells him that she will marry him only on condition that he deliver his mother's heart to her. The young man is so infatuated with the girl that he complies with her wishes. As he runs to the girl with his mother's still warm, palpating heart, he hears her voice, "My dearest most precious son — please be careful. Don't run so fast — I don't want you to fall!"

The moral of the story is obvious — sometimes the disappointment that parents feel is so wrenching, so agonizing, that they feel as though their hearts have been cut out. Yet, despite it all, a parent remains a parent forever. Even when rejected and hurt, even when overwhelmed by pain, parents continue to worry about their children and place their welfare above their own.

But it is not only parents who struggle with this pain — in a sense, G-d Himself experiences it. Just consider how you would feel if your children never greeted you, never gave you a hug or a kiss, never said thank you, never so much as acknowledged your presence, and yet, expected you to do everything for them. Sadly, that is the reality of the relationship that most of us have with G-d. We fail to recognize that it is G-d, our Heavenly Father, Who gives us life, Who sustains and nurtures us, and every day grants us a new lease on life.

Like all fathers, G-d hoped that Adam and Eve, His firstborn children, would be perfect. He created them to be beautiful, brilliant, loving and kind — free of jealousy, greed and hatred. He even provided an ideal setting for them — a utopian paradise, so that they might live and thrive eternally. G-d made only one little request of Adam and Eve, and that was that they refrain from eating of the Tree of Knowledge. But they rebelled and thus G-d became the first parent to feel the pain of disappointment in His children.

But, you might argue, surely, G-d, Who is all-knowing, Who foresees that which will occur in the future, was well aware that Adam and Eve would violate His instructions, and that He would banish them from the Garden of Eden. So, if He knew beforehand that His plan was doomed to failure, why did He go through with it? Why didn't He just bypass the Garden of Eden and immediately place Adam and Eve into a world of struggle, toil, and sacrifice?

Perhaps one of the reasons was to offer us a lesson in parenting so that we might be fortified and better prepared when our children do not turn out as we had hoped. When reality does not mesh with our dreams, when the pain is so intense that we actually feel as if our hearts had been cut out, at such times, we must remember that, if G-d can be disappointed, who are we to complain? And if *He* does not give up on us, who are *we* to give up on our children?

To be sure, G-d's original plan had been derailed — He had to shut down the Garden of Eden, but He never ceased loving us. Even as He banished us from Paradise, He fashioned protective garments for us and lovingly clothed us (*Genesis* 3:21), promising that, if we willed it, the Garden of Eden could become our possession once again. So just as G-d locked the Garden of Eden and made alternate plans, so too, must we often abandon the Garden of Eden that we hoped to attain for our children, deal with the new reality and continue to love them.

Eli and Marilyn Gordon came to see me with David, their teenage son. When Marilyn called for an appointment, she explained that there was a crisis in their family. David had been cutting classes, inappropriately using the Internet, and staying out late into the night. And worse, they had received a letter from his principal, warning that, unless David got his act together, they would have to look for a different school for him.

When they walked into my office, my heart went out to them. Eli and Marilyn looked so distraught — their suffering was etched on their faces and reflected in their eyes. David trailed behind them — angry and defiant — and without saying a word, he slouched into a chair.

"So, tell me," I said, trying to break the tension. "What's happening, and how can I help you?"

"Our son is having some issues," Marilyn said, nervously. "Would you like to tell the Rebbetzin about it, David?" she asked, turning to him.

But David remained obstinately silent, so I repeated Marilyn's question and asked him if he would like to tell me what happened.

"I have nothing to say," he snapped. "*She* can tell you!"

"Forgive me, David, but who is *she*?" I asked

"*She*," he repeated, tilting his head toward his mother.

But I wouldn't let go, and persisted — "Who is *she*?"

It took quite some time to get him to finally say, "My *mother*," but even as he pronounced those words, he grumbled under his breath,

"Anyway, what's the difference!!! *She, mother* — what do I care? It's all the same."

"David," Eli interrupted, "speak respectfully to the Rebbetzin."

"Get off my back, already!"

"Please, David," Marilyn said, her voice quavering with tears.

"He's always on my case!" David retorted angrily.

"I wouldn't have to be on your case if you would be a *mentsch* and didn't come home at 3 a.m.," Eli said.

"If you hadn't taken away my computer, I wouldn't have been out at night."

"You know very well why I took away your computer," Eli shot back sternly.

"Yeah, I'm a bum, a thick-headed moron who will never amount to anything!" David exclaimed with disdain.

Eli's face reddened. It was obvious that it was all he could do to control himself.

"David, please," Marilyn begged. "You know that Daddy didn't mean that — but you provoked him."

"Yeah, I know. I've provoked him from the day I was born."

"Let's all calm down," I said. "If anyone provoked anyone, it was probably me, since it was I who insisted that you say 'my mother,' instead of 'she'. So, why do you think I made such a fuss about that, David?"

"I haven't the faintest idea," he mumbled under his breath.

"When you refer to your parents as 'he' or 'she,' you depersonalize them, but when you say, '*my* mother,' '*my* father,'' you are referring to the two people in this world who care most for you, who will stay up all night worrying about you, praying for you, shedding tears for you. Only your mother and father carry your burden in their hearts, only they will go to sleep with your pain and wake up with your pain. Whether they are at work or at a party, whether they are in the privacy of their home or in company, they never forget — even for a minute. If you have a problem or a crisis in your life, friends may offer sympathy and commiserate with you; they may even shed tears for you, but, in the end, they will go on with their own lives. For your mother and father, however, there can be no peace if you are not at peace, no joy if you are unhappy — but when you regard your parents as 'he' or 'she' you lose sight of all that."

Marilyn broke down and wept openly, and Eli fought hard to hold back his tears.

"Your father loves you, David. If he didn't care for you, believe me, he wouldn't be here tonight. This is more painful for him than it is for you. And if he called you those names, it is not because he believes that in his heart, but because he doesn't know how to get through to you, and in his desperation, he lost himself. Trust me, if you were a stranger, he would be very calm and never say a word, but *you are his son*. You mean everything to him and if you fall apart, he falls apart. Just look at your mother and father, David — they are both crying. If they didn't love you, why would they be crying?"

David could not bear to look at his parents, and he tried to avoid my eyes. "I just want to be left alone," he said in a barely audible voice.

"David, I promise you," I said, "that's the one thing you don't want — you *don't* want to be left alone. Do you know how many people there are who live alone and would give anything in the world to have a mother and father who care, and yes, who are '*on their case*' — who ask, "Where were you? Why did you come home so late? What are you doing to yourself?" But there is no one to say those words to them. They can come home dead drunk at 4 a.m., freaked out on drugs, and no one will say a word, because *no one loves them enough to care*, and that, David, is the most devastating pain of all."

But David just sat there, stone-faced.

"Tell me, David, why are you so self-destructive?"

"I'm not self destructive — I just want to have fun," he answered defiantly.

"Come on, David, let's talk honestly. When you cut school and stay out at night, when you surf the internet, you're not having *fun* — you're just trying to escape from reality, because there is something that is making you very unhappy. As much as you try to put up a *cool* front, I know that in your heart you are suffering, and when you do finally get to sleep, there are tears in your eyes, even if you don't allow anyone to see them."

"I'm okay. Don't worry about me, and don't try to analyze me."

"I'm not trying to analyze you. I am worried about you because I want you to be more than just 'okay,' but perhaps it would be better if we spoke privately. I'm sure that your mother and father would excuse us for a few minutes."

"We'll wait in the hall," Marilyn and Eli volunteered, obviously relieved to escape the tension in the room.

As they left, I turned to David and asked, "Tell me, what hurts you?"

"Nothing hurts me," he protested indignantly.

"So tell me what bothers you."

"What bothers me? Lots of stuff!"

"David, 'lots of stuff' doesn't mean anything. Break it down and identify it. Is it your school? Is it your home? Is it your friends? Why are you so angry?"

"It's nothing that you would understand."

"Try me — I've been through a lot. There's almost nothing I haven't heard. So, let's start with school. What *Gemara* (tractate of the Talmud) are you studying now?"

"Don't ask me — I sleep through class, or the Rebbe kicks me out."

"Why?"

"I guess it's because the Rebbe agrees with my father. I'm a bum."

"Don't do that to yourself, David," I interrupted. "Neither your father nor the Rebbe thinks that. Their choice of words may have been unfortunate, but parents and teachers are human, and humans are not perfect — under stress, they will say things they don't mean."

"Oh, they meant it all right!"

"You're wrong, David, The only reason they said what they did is because they couldn't get through to you, and in their frustration, they lost it. Your father believes in you and wants to see the *real you* emerge. That is what he is hoping and praying for."

"That's a good one," David sneered, "the 'real me'. Tell me, Rebbetzin, who is the real me?"

"I'll be happy to tell you," I responded. "You are *chelek Eloka me-ma'al* — a part of *HaShem* — custom made by Him for a special purpose that only *you* can fulfill. There is no one in this world, David, who is quite like you, so *HaShem* needs you to do *your thing*, to realize His greater plan for mankind, and those who love you, can't bear to see you throw your life away."

"There is no one in the world who is quite like me, and *HaShem needs me*," David repeated mockingly. "Come on, tell me another one!"

"I stand by what I said, David. There are billions of people out there, and yet no two look exactly alike. Similarly, no two *neshamahs* are exactly alike. So yes, *HaShem needs each and every one of us,* and to remind us of our special calling, the Torah tells us that He commanded Moshe Rabbeinu to take a *census*."

"What does a census have to do with it?" David asked testily.

"Everything — but why don't you ask me the reason for a census to start with? After all, if G-d is infinite and all knowing, why would

He need a census? Surely, He knew the exact number — so why did He command that we be counted again and again?

"And there is yet another puzzle — the words the Torah uses for counting is '*S'eu es rosh*' (*Numbers* 1:2), which literally means, 'Lift up the head.' How would you explain that one, David?"

"I wouldn't know," he responded unenthusiastically.

"Well then, let me tell you. G-d wished to convey His love for each and every one of us, so He commanded, 'Lift up the head [of each] of My people' by *counting them* — by letting them know that *they count*, that they are *precious to Me — vital and irreplaceable*. What's more, G-d commanded that this counting be done through our *families*, through our *fathers' houses*, and through our *names*, teaching us that the family, the community, is incomplete unless *every individual member contributes to the whole the unique gifts that are embedded in his or her name*. Every name represents a mission; every name has a corresponding passage in the Torah; so you see, David, your family, your community, the school at which you study, and G-d Himself need you."

"Come on, Rebbetzin. No one needs me, and I doubt very much that G-d even knows that I exist."

"But of course He knows, and of course your family needs you. Why do you suppose that your parents are so upset. Didn't you see their tears? You can fake a laugh, David, but you can't fake tears. As for G-d being aware of you — tell me, do you *daven* (pray), every morning?"

"Not really," David shook his head.

"Well, if you prayed, you would realize that G-d is very much aware of you, because you would be familiar with *Tehillim*, Psalm 147, '…G-d counts the stars and calls each by name….' If *HaShem* can count the stars — and there are zillions of them — if He can call each by name and assign each a unique mission, then surely, He can lovingly count you, call you by your name, and invest you with your mission. But if you have no understanding of this, if you don't see a higher purpose to your existence, then there is only emptiness in your soul, and that is very painful.

"The psalm itself testifies to this, for it says that 'G-d heals broken hearts,' teaching that the most powerful balm for a broken heart is the awareness that we count, that we are needed and loved. Everyone hurts, David, when they think they are not needed. So even though you refuse to admit it, I know that you are hurting, and that is why you keep running, trying to find excitement and fun. But if you had studied Torah, you would have found your fulfillment within yourself because you would have realized how vital you are, how much you count."

"Rebbetzin, I've studied. Don't forget, I go to yeshivah — I study Torah."

"You may be in yeshivah, but that doesn't mean that the yeshivah is in *you*. If you slept through your classes, you never studied Torah, you never 'got' it. Torah is different from all other studies. It is the only wisdom that is actually embedded in our souls, that we mastered before we were ever born."

"How do you know that?" he challenged.

"Simple. All our souls were at Sinai and we all heard the voice of G-d — and to reinforce that teaching, during the nine months that our mothers carry us, G-d assigns a special *malach* — an angel — to teach us Torah."

"So how come I don't know it?" he said mockingly.

"Well, there's a good reason for that. At the time of our birth, the angel taps us on our lip and we forget everything we learned."

"That's the most ridiculous thing I ever heard. What's the point of learning if we forget it anyway."

"I knew you would say that, but once we master something, David, we can never really forget it. On a conscious level, perhaps, but not in our souls — that wisdom is always there, so if you open your heart and mind to Torah, you will discover profound truths that will *speak* to you. Come to one of our Torah sessions, and see for yourself."

"I don't think so," he said flatly.

"Just one class," I pressed. "It will not only open your heart, but it will change your reality — your very life."

"Rebbetzin, I've been there. I'm not one of your *ba'al teshuvahs*."

"Do you know what it means to be a *ba'al teshuvah*?

"I think I have a pretty good idea."

"But you don't, because, if you did, you wouldn't have made that remark. We all have a mandate to be *ba'alei teshuvah*. That is the angel's final instruction as we are about to be born. '*Be righteous and not wicked. Even if the entire world tells you that you are righteous, in your own eyes you should always consider yourself as wicked!*' — meaning that, despite all our attainments and accomplishments, we should never rest on our laurels and never delude ourselves into believing that we are complete and no longer in need of self-improvement, but must grow and endeavor to perfect ourselves throughout our lives. That, David, is what it means to be a *ba'al teshuvah*.

"So how about it, David? Become a *ba'al teshuvah* and begin by improving your relationship with your parents. And this doesn't only mean to refrain from referring to your mother or father as 'he' or 'she.' That's just one small part of it. We have a whole gamut of *mitzvos* in regard to honoring parents.'

"Yeah, I know — but all that stuff is for the *nerds,* not for me."

"You're wrong, David, all that 'stuff' is for you, for me, for all of us. Honoring parents is so basic to human nature that even if we never studied Torah, even if we were unaware of the Fifth Commandment, our hearts, our very beings, should prompt us to honor them. Just think about it — following birth, every creature becomes independent in no time at all, and goes off on its own. But we humans are totally helpless and dependent — the tiny infant is fragile and in need of constant nurturing and care. It takes many years before s/he becomes self-sufficient. Just think, David, about the continuous sacrifices that parents are called upon to make for their children — why do you suppose that G-d created the world this way? Surely He could have made babies as self-sufficient as puppies. But the Almighty wanted us to feel gratitude and indebtedness toward our parents so that we should *want to honor them* and *express love for them*. One of the most famous stories in the Talmud regarding the lengths to which we must go to show reverence for our parents, is about Dama ben Nesina, a non-Jew. Although he never studied Torah, he sensed that he had to revere his parents. Dama possessed a precious stone on which he could have made a huge profit, but he passed up the opportunity because the key to the vault in which the stone was kept was under the pillow on which his father was sleeping. Dama refused to disturb his father's sleep for all the money in the world."

"Anyone doing that today would be considered nuts!"

"I wouldn't say that at all, David. I'll tell you a story from today."

I have a niece in London, a chasidic rebbetzin, who, on a return flight from the U.S., had her seat upgraded to business class. She found herself seated next to a woman to whom the stewardess was super-attentive. Every few minutes, she came over to offer her special delicacies and asked whether she needed anything When the pilot also came to greet her and invited her to visit the cockpit, my niece concluded that she must be seated next to a celebrity. After a while the lady dozed off, and my niece very discreetly asked the flight attendant who the woman might be.

The attendant's face lit up with a bright smile. "Oh," she said proudly, "*that's my mother!*"

David thought about the story and then said wistfully, "That's not my family."

"Why not? If you will it, David, it *could* be your family. You need only allow your parents' love to enter your heart."

"My father gave up on me a long time ago. It's too late for all that now." But even as he spoke, his voice told me that I was finally getting through.

"It's never too late, David," I assured him, "that's what being a *ba'al teshuvah* is all about — elevating your life, improving your relationship — and I assure you — no parent ever gives up on his child. No matter what, no matter how painful the betrayal may be, a father, a mother, will never renounce their own flesh and blood, but will love their children unconditionally — and to prove it, let me tell you another story that was reported by three Israeli soldiers during the 1982 Operation Peace for Galilee War.

The soldiers were searching for a dangerous terrorist and went to his house, but found only his wife. When she saw them, she protested that she was Jewish, but they didn't believe her. "It's easy to say, 'I am Jewish' when confronted by Jewish soldiers," they told her.

"Please, you must believe me," she pleaded, and showed them a necklace with a star of David.

But the soldiers remained unimpressed. "Anyone can purchase a Jewish star."

"I promise you, I'm Jewish, she insisted. "I'll prove it." And with that, she began to chant the Yom Kippur "Kol Nidrei" prayer.

For a brief moment, the soldiers were taken aback, but when, after a search of the house, they found a recording of Jan Pierce's *Kol Nidrei* under her mattress, they said, "So that's how you learned the prayer!"

"Yes, that's how I learned it," she admitted, "but I promise you, I'm really Jewish. Please listen to my story. I'm an American, and in college, I met my husband, who was an Arab student. We fell in love, and when I told my parents that I was planning to marry a Moslem, which meant that I would have to convert to his faith, they became furious. We had terrible fights, and they gave me an ultimatum — either I break up with him or they would disown me. But I was in love, and didn't care. We married, and he told me that the time had come for us to return to his country. I didn't even say goodbye to my parents, but somehow, my father found out that we were leaving. Just as we were about to pass through airport security, I heard my father's voice calling me. I turned around, and sure enough, there he was, waving to me and holding up this recording of 'Kol Nidrei.' I ran back to him, and in the midst of tears he hugged me and said, 'On Yom Kippur, we are all forgiven for our sins, and we all come home. Never forget Yom Kippur, my daughter — come home!'

"There was no time for further conversation. My husband was calling me.

"At that time, I didn't know that he was a terrorist, and once I found out, it was too late — he wouldn't permit me to leave. My new life was full of pain and disappointment, but the recording kept me going, I listened to it over and over again, and that is how I know it by heart. Please help me return to my family and my people," she pleaded.

The soldiers investigated her story, and it all checked out. They took the young woman back to Israel and she was reunited with her family and her people.

"So you see, David, even when parents experience the most devastating pain, they never give up, but await their child's homecoming. As much as you believe that your father gave up on you,

I can assure you that he, too, is waiting, hoping and praying that you will allow him to love you as only a father can. Only you can help your parents create a strong, warm, loving family. *You count*, David. Think about our conversation while I speak to your mother and father."

David did not answer, but his eyes told me that he heard me loud and clear.

11

As Smart as A Rooster

li and Marilyn awaited me with bated breath, even as parents await a surgeon in the waiting room of an O. R. Their anxiety was palpable. "I'm almost afraid to ask, Rebbetzin, but were you able to reach him?" Marilyn asked.

"I don't know," I told them honestly. "It's much harder with turned-off yeshivah kids than with those who have no background at all. It's like writing on a crumpled piece of paper rather than on a crisp, new one. But," I hastened to add, "don't lose heart. We won't give up. Please

G-d, we will reach him — we need only persevere."

"I wish I could believe that," Eli commented. "He's my son, and it hurts me to say this, but there is something twisted in his brain. I've tried in every way — with kindness and with toughness. I promised him gifts, trips and tickets to ball games, and when that didn't work, I yelled, I punished, but nothing helped. Please don't take this personally, Rebbetzin, but I told Marilyn that it was ridiculous to come here. There is nothing you can do that we haven't already tried."

"Eli is bitter. He and David don't get along," Marilyn explained apologetically.

"I'm not bitter, I'm a realist, and if we don't get along, it's because I don't take his nonsense like you do," Eli said pointedly.

"I don't take his nonsense," Marilyn protested. "I see what's going on, but I've discovered that sometimes it's better to remain silent."

"Sometimes? How about 24/7?" Eli retorted sarcastically.

"Well what do you accomplish with your yelling and screaming 24/7? He just runs out of the house, or into his room to surf the internet."

"I already took the computer away from him," Eli said.

"I know, honey, but what did we gain with that — now he's out all night."

"That's what I'm trying to tell you — it's no use. He's a bum!"

"Hold on," I interjected. "We are all on the same page, so let's brainstorm and see what we can come up with. And if you don't mind, Eli, I must tell you that anger is counterproductive. It's not only damaging to David, but harmful to you as well. There is nothing to be gained from it. As for calling him a bum — if you do it often enough, it could become self-fulfilling prophecy, and he might just come to believe that that's what he is."

"Rebbetzin, I know all that. I've tried complimenting him. We went for counseling. We've been through it all, but no matter what I say or do, nothing makes an impression on him."

"I beg to differ with you. Your calling him a '*bum*' *did* make an impression, but I'm afraid, the wrong one. Why do you suppose he brought it up so often? Forgive me, Eli, I don't mean to preach, but our Torah warns us against '*ona'as devarim*' — using hurtful words. Children have feelings, just like adults, and sometimes more so. Don't get me wrong. I realize that David pushes your buttons, that he makes it difficult for you to control yourself, that you say what you say out of desperation. But as far as David is concerned, he believes that your words truly reflect your feelings, and this most certainly has exacerbated the hostility between you."

"So maybe I should pat him on the back and tell him how wonderful he is," Eli said sarcastically. "Or maybe I should tell him it's okay to come home at 3 a.m.; that it's okay to cut school and fail every subject; that it's okay to browse the 'net? Rebbetzin, I said it before and I'll say it again — he's just plain no good!"

"You're wrong, Eli. Every child is good. In every *neshamah*, there is a *pintele Yid*, a Divine spark. It's all a matter of tapping into it."

"It sounds great, Rebbetzin, but it's not reality."

"But it is, Eli. Our reality is not what we see with our physical eyes — our reality is not rooted in the here and now; our reality spans the centuries and is rooted in our Torah, in our history."

"Well, I haven't seen *this* in our history or in our Torah."

"In every generation, the challenges are different, but the problems remain the same. Rebellious children are nothing new. Our history is replete with them, but when push comes to shove, that *pintele Yid — that holy Jewish spark* — always emerges from their hearts and it triumphs. Take, for example, Yosef Meshissa, the Hellenist Jew who lived in the days of the Second Temple. He was so evil that he actually advised the Greeks to plunder and desecrate the

Beis HaMikdash — the Holy Temple. The Greeks however, were terrified of the consequences of invading G-d's Sanctuary, so they made a deal with him — anything that he brought out from the Temple would belong to him.

"Brazenly, Yosef Meshissa entered the Holy Sanctuary and exited carrying the magnificent, majestic Menorah. When the Greeks beheld it, they were awed. 'That's a gift fit for a king!' they exclaimed. 'We can't possibly allow you to keep it. But you can go back and take something else for yourself.'

"Amazingly, Yosef Meshissa refused to comply. 'I can't go back,' he cried. 'That place is sacred. We dare not desecrate it. I did it once. I won't do it again!'

"The Greeks became infuriated and threatened to kill him if he didn't go back, but Yosef Meshissa refused. They tortured him in a thousand and one ways, but still he would not submit to their demands and he died an excruciatingly painful death.

"The question that must bother everyone who hears this story is 'What happened to Yosef Meshissa? How could it be that the man who had plotted to defile and loot the holy Temple should suddenly undergo such a transformation and be willing to die *Al Kiddush HaShem* — sanctifying G-d's Name?'

"The esteemed Ponevezher Rov gave the answer to this enigma: *Yosef Meshissa entered the Beis HaMikdash.* Once he experienced its sanctity, once he breathed its holy air, he was totally transformed. From an evil, traitorous, Hellenist Jew, he became a totally committed Jew, willing to give up his life for his faith.

"We have to apply this teaching to David. We have to create an environment for him in which he can connect to something holy — an environment that is devoid of anger, an environment that will keep him anchored, an environment that will leave an indelible impression on his mind, heart, and soul."

"And how would you propose that we do that?" Eli asked skeptically. "We don't exactly have a *Beis HaMikdash* at our disposal."

"That's true," I agreed. But as you well know, despite the *Churban* — the destruction of the *Beis HaMikdash* — every home is designated as a *mikdash m'at* — a sanctuary in miniature."

"But we *do* have a Torah home," Marilyn protested, "even if David has done everything to destroy our *shalom bayis*."

"I understand that, but under such circumstances, the dynamics of family life become very complex and we have to turn to our Torah for guidance if we are to recapture that which was lost."

"Rebbetzin, we are not *ba'alei teshuvah*," Eli now said. "We *know* what a Torah home is."

"Just a few minutes ago, your David said those very same words to me, and I pointed out to him that as knowledgeable as we may be, we all need reminders on how to resolve our problems the Torah way. There is no *nisayon* — trial — that our *Avos* and *Eemahos* — patriarchs and matriarchs — did not experience. They underwent every ordeal so that we might learn how to cope with our *own* life challenges. So let's focus on a few of their teachings and see if they can guide you in your relationship with David.

"When our father Yaakov had problems with his son, Reuven, he refrained from chastising him because he feared that Reuven, in an impetuous fit of anger, might leave home to join up with wicked Uncle Esau and become totally corrupted. Therefore, Yaakov did not admonish his son until he was on his deathbed (*Genesis* 49:3-4).

"To apply this to David, Eli, you want to be careful not to criticize him to the point where he feels compelled to flee to the wicked Esaus of today and join up with the worst elements of society. Moreover, when Yaakov did admonish, he was careful to condemn only the *actions* of his sons, but never their *persons*. And even then, his criticisms were always couched in positive terms. For example, he showed Simon and Levi how to convert their passion and temper to benefit the nation (*Genesis* 49:5-6). He made them the teachers and Levites so that they would teach their brethren to care for one another.

"And I must tell you, Eli, that this is not just theory. I saw it in practice during my childhood, for this is the way in which my own beloved father raised us. When my brothers and I misbehaved, my father would look at us lovingly and say in Yiddish, '*Es pas nisht* — this conduct is unworthy of you — my precious children.' And mind you, my father never addressed us simply by our given names, but always added a Yiddish adjective of endearment, such as '*ty'ere lichtikeit*' — precious light; '*shefele*' — little lamb; '*zees kind*' — sweet child, or '*heilege neshamah*' — holy soul. So no matter what we did, we never had any doubt about who we were. We were '*heilige neshamahs*' — holy souls — and that's a whole different ball game from being called a *bum*."

"That just won't work with David," Eli said, shaking his head.

"You'd be surprised," I answered. "I know countless families who took me up on these suggestions, even secular ones to whom Yiddish was alien, and it changed the dynamics of their lives."

"Look, Rebbetzin, I could call him '*zees kind*' from today till tomorrow — it won't make a difference."

"Try it," I insisted.

"Please honey, the Rebbetzin is right. You must give it a chance," Marilyn prodded.

"Alright, alright — I'll give it a try," Eli assented, albeit unwillingly. "And what else would you like me to do?" he added testily.

"It's not what *I* want you do — it's what our Torah *teaches us* to do. When Yaakov blessed his grandsons, Ephraim and Menashe, he had a painful vision in which he foresaw future generations of rebellious sons. '*Mee e'leh?* — Who are these?' he cried out in anguish. To which Yosef replied, 'They are my sons, whom G-d gave me with *this,*' pointing to the *ketubah* — marriage contract — meaning that they were his legitimate descendants."

"'*Bring them* to me,' Yaakov said, 'so that I may *bless* them, *kiss* them, and *hug* them' (Genesis, 48:8-11)

"Thus we learn from the patriarch Yaakov, that the way to react to obstreperous children is to nurture them with love. But to fully understand Yaakov's example, it is important that we review the sequence of his actions.

"Step 1: 'Bring them to me.' — No matter what, we must reach out and bond with them. Step 2: 'Bless them' — We must articulate our love, our blessing, so that they may hear it and absorb it.

"Steps 3 and 4: 'Let me *kiss* them and *hug* them' — With that kiss, Jacob sealed the blessings, but he did not stop there. He hugged them and enveloped them in love. A hug, Eli, is all-embracing, symbolic of total acceptance and commitment.

"Tell me," I now asked." When was the last time you blessed David?"

Eli just shrugged.

"We have a most beautiful tradition of blessing our children every *Shabbos* eve. So why not try it, Eli? No matter how our relationship deteriorated during the week, on *Shabbos* eve, just before we make *Kiddush* over the wine, we place our hands upon our children's heads and invoke the ancient blessings of the Patriarch Jacob and Aaron, the High Priest — and there is a codicil to this — the priestly blessing can only be conferred *b'ahavah* — with love, and for a father, that should be easy enough."

"Rebbetzin — I don't think you get it," Eli said, with a tinge of bitterness in his voice. "Do you for a moment imagine that David comes to the *Shabbos* table?"

"Well, if he doesn't, go to his room and find him," I said. "And if he's not home, bless him when he *does* return, *but* — and this is the *big 'but'* — you must do so without arguments, recriminations, or fights. It's *Shabbos*. Your home is now a *Beis HaMikdash* in micro-cosm. So no matter what, tell David that you cannot allow *Shabbos* to pass without giving him your *berachah*.

"I can assure you, Eli, that if you follow this formula, if, after you give your *berachah*, you kiss and hug David, the effect will be more powerful than all the shouting, screaming and fighting that he has come to associate with your relationship."

"It all sounds good here in your office, Rebbetzin," Marilyn interjected, "but, in all fairness, I don't see how Eli can apply it. The relationship between him and David doesn't lend itself to such de-monstrativeness. And David is not a little boy whom Eli can put on his lap and hug and kiss."

"We never outgrow the need for a hug, a kiss, and a parental blessing," I told her. "Even when I became a grandmother, I continued to seek my father's *berachahs*, and to this day, I can still feel his gentle hands on my head. Although he has been gone for many years, I can still hear his voice lovingly whispering blessings — and this held true, not only for my father and my generation, but my husband interacted with our children in this very same way, and today, they raise their own children with blessings, kisses, and hugs."

"I have to agree with Marilyn. I just cannot see it happening between David and me," Eli responded.

"That's because you've never tried it. What have you to lose?" I asked. "Your way hasn't worked, so why not try the Torah way? And as long as we are exploring different options, I would also recommend that you come as a family to our Torah classes."

Marilyn and Eli looked at me in disbelief. "Rebbetzin, you must be joking! Bring David to a Torah class!"

"I know, but that is precisely why we must get him to come — I would like to see him *fall in love with Torah*, and if we can do that, we will be on our way."

Had I suggested that they visit the planet Mars, I don't think they would have been more shocked.

"You want David to *fall in love* with Torah by coming to classes?" Eli repeated incredulously.

"Absolutely," I confirmed. "That's the key to this entire problem. If he comes to love Torah, he will also come to love you and understand his purpose in life. If Torah is to impact on him, however, he must be inspired to open his heart and embrace it with love. Just as we make *Kiddush* over the wine on *Shabbos,* and hold the goblet in an *open, cupped hand* rather than with a *closed fist*, so that we may *receive* the blessings of *Shabbos*, so too, must we learn Torah and receive it with an *open heart*. Unfortunately however, all of David's experiences have been *close-fisted*. In school as well as at home, he felt that everything was crammed down his throat, so he has never opened his heart to receive *HaShem's* gift. That is why I would like you to come as a family and share a new way of learning that could be life-transforming."

"Rebbetzin, I don't know. I can't imagine that he would agree," Marilyn objected.

"I don't know either, but let me suggest it to him. As I said, what have we to lose? It's an easy, painless, and cost-free formula, and I have never seen it fail. But before we call David in, I would like to share with you an encounter that I had with a troubled young man that I believe could prove helpful to you."

At the inception of our Hineni movement, a distraught mother approached me. Her son, a whiz kid, whom I shall call Kenny, had talked his way into a summer job on Wall Street. In a few short weeks, he managed to embezzle a huge sum of money. Since the boy was a minor, with no previous record, the court agreed to release him on his own recognizance, provided a reputable agency or organization would agree to supervise him. So it was that this unfortunate woman came to ask if Hineni would assume this responsibility.

It was a daunting challenge, but I couldn't very well refuse. My conscience wouldn't allow me to live with the thought of Kenny going completely astray in the company of other delinquents in some correctional institution.

At our first meeting, I laid down the rules. I told him that I expected only one thing from him — *that he be as smart as a rooster!*

He looked at me in shock, obviously wondering whether I had lost it. So, I opened the prayer book and showed him that one of the first blessings in our morning prayers is to thank G-d for having granted wisdom to the rooster.

Kenny began to smirk, as if to say "What nonsense."

Picking up on it, I said, "I grant you that of all G-d's creatures, the rooster is probably one of the most brainless, but if you acquire its wisdom, I will be very satisfied, and you can be content in the knowledge that you made it."

The smirk remained fixed on Kenny's face, so I proceeded to explain that there are three reasons for this curious blessing. First of all, the rooster knows how to distinguish between night and day. Similarly, we must learn how to differentiate between right and wrong — between that which is honest and that which is corrupt, between that which is compassionate and that which is cruel. "A high IQ," I told him, "a brilliant mind, success in amassing a fortune, are all meaningless if you do not absorb this simple basic wisdom of the rooster. *It's not the knowledge that we have that defines our lives, but our ability to make good decisions.* We all know people who are so smart that they outsmart themselves. They lack the simple discernment of the rooster. They cannot distinguish between night and day."

The second lesson to be learned from the rooster is consistency. Rain or shine, day after day, the rooster crows. He never tires, he never gives up, he's never in a "mood."

To be a Jew, I told him, is to live with that value system. Just as a rooster greets each and every day and tackles the work at hand, similarly, we must go to our posts and assume our responsibilities whether or not we are in the mood.

And finally, the last lesson that we must learn from the rooster is to have faith. No matter how dense the darkness of the night may be, the rooster knows that morning will come and never gives up.

So even if we feel discouraged, and believe that our situation is hopeless, we must have faith that everything can turn out right, and this is yet another lesson that we learn from our Torah.

When we went forth from Egyptian bondage and triumphantly crossed the Reed Sea, Miriam the prophetess, with tambourine in hand, led the women in song and dance. But where did she get a tambourine in the dessert?

Miriam prepared the tambourine while her people were in the slave labor camps of the Auschwitz of Egypt. She actually first used the tambourine at the wedding of her parents, Amram and Yocheved. When Pharaoh promulgated his barbaric decree declaring that all new-born males be killed, husbands and wives separated so that no child might fall victim to such a tragic fate. But little Miriam challenged her father: "Perhaps G-d will grant us the child who will be our redeemer, who will lead us forth from this cursed place."

Overwhelmed by his daughter's pure faith, Amram remarried Yocheved; Miriam celebrated with the tambourine at their wedding. Moses was born, but the darkness of Egyptian bondage became more dense and the torture more intense. Nevertheless, Miriam held on to her tambourine and said, "One day, we will be redeemed, and on that day, I will again dance with my tambourine."

So when darkness envelops us, when we wonder whether the sun will ever shine again, instead of becoming discouraged and depressed, remember Miriam's tambourine. Take hold of it and know in your heart that the day will come when you will again dance and celebrate.

"These were the three lessons of the rooster that I taught Kenny. If he wished to succeed, I told him, he needed only to master them.

"Kenny did succeed, and today, he is teaching his own children how to be as smart as a rooster. That's the lesson that we must try to impart to David," I told Marilyn and Eli.

"And how would you propose to do that?" they asked.

"The best teacher is personal example. You must prove to him that you yourselves have absorbed the wisdom of the rooster."

"I don't see how this 'rooster wisdom' applies to our situation," Eli remarked.

"But it does," I assured him. "Our American value system adulates success. Everyone has to be 'Number One,' We all have to be winners and the ripple effect has been felt in our yeshivah world as well — our children must all excel. So we have to rethink our priorities. First, instead of focusing on David's grades, focus on his ability to make 'right decisions,' to distinguish between night and day.

"Second, be consistent. Just as the rooster crows in rain or shine, you must show him that you are his parents, and no matter what, your love is *unconditional*. But to make it credible, you will have to change the dynamics of your family."

"What do you mean by that?" Eli asked.

"Forgive me," I said, "but I felt such tension emanating from you when you were with David. Mind you, I don't blame you, and I am certain that you don't realize it, but you look at David with such resentment and bitterness that, in his mind, he surely thinks that you hate him.

"So, once again, let's borrow a page from our father Jacob. When the Patriarch blessed his children, he imparted a very special *bera-chah* to Judah that has great significance to us today, because to one extent or another, we are descendants of Judah — that is why we are called *Yehudim* — Jews.

"The blessing was, 'Red-eyed from wine and white of teeth from milk' (*Genesis* 49:12) meaning that while milk is the most nourishing food and can sustain a baby, even more nourishing is the white of teeth — a smile. We never quite outgrow the need for someone to smile at us. Wine, in turn, is a wonderful drink. It warms us; it lifts our spirits; it makes us happy — but more than wine, kind warm eyes that communicate love can make our spirits soar. So force yourself to look at David with a smile and warm kind eyes, so that he may believe that you really do love him.

"Finally, even if the night is long and the darkness is thick and heavy, you cannot give up, but must learn from the rooster that morning will surely come and the sun will yet shine. *HaShem* never gave up on us, so how can we give up on our children? How can you give up on David?"

"Rebbetzin, you're an idealist, and I admire and respect you for it, but I live in the real world. How can I smile and look at him with loving eyes when he is giving me such grief?"

"I'm not telling you that you should go around with a smile plastered onto your face, but if you want to have a relationship with David, he has to see you looking at him with love, and when you feel that you have no choice but to reprimand him, do as the Chofetz Chaim did."

There's a well known story about a young man who studied in the sage's yeshivah in Radin, Poland. He, too, was rebellious, and was found smoking on *Shabbos* — an unheard-of transgression for a yeshivah boy. The Chofetz Chaim called him in to speak to him. A few minutes later, the young man emerged from the meeting and vowed that he would never again smoke on *Shabbos*.

A contemporary rabbi, serving as a guest lecturer at a Miami synagogue, related this story in the course of his sermon and remarked,

"I would love to have been privy to what the Chofetz Chaim said to bring about such a magical transformation."

Following the davening, an elderly gentleman approached the rabbi and said, "I can tell you exactly what the Chofetz Chaim said."

Amazed, the rabbi urged, "Please tell me."

"The Chofetz Chaim," the elderly gentleman related, "took the young *bocher's* hand in his and lovingly said just one word, '*Shabbos*'. But as he did so, the young man felt the warm tears of the sage on his hand, and those tears penetrated his innermost being and left an indelible mark of love on his soul. It was *that*, that did it," the old man concluded.

"How do you know all this?" the rabbi asked curiously.

"I know, because I was that young man!"

"Eli," I concluded, "try the Chofetz Chaim's way — *sad, but not mad!* When it comes to disciplining, loving tears are by far more powerful than shouts and threats."

"What can I say, Rebbetzin? I'll try."

"We will all try," I told him. "And now, if you are ready, let's call David in."

Eight long years later, I received an invitation to David's wedding and emblazoned on it was a *rooster.*

12

Why?

Seldom does a week go by that I am not confronted by the question, "Why?" There are many underlying causes for this question: illness, financial crisis, crippling accidents, abusive relationships and marriages, frustration in finding soul mates, rebellious children — the list goes on and on, and to each person, his own affliction is the most painful. As if this were not enough, our generation is also challenged by global "*whys.*" Catastrophic natural phenomena, such as tsunamis and earthquakes, cataclysmic events like 9/11, and barbaric acts of terror have all left their marks, and can be summed up in one word — *suffering*. The relentless specter of suffering makes no distinctions. Its long tentacles reach every segment of society — young and old, wealthy and poor — all are equally afflicted. At one time or another, suffering strikes us all, and when it does, we call out in bewilderment, "*Why?*"

As prevalent as the question is, it cannot be answered with certitude, for in this world, there are no definitive answers. Moses himself asked *why*, and G-d told him, "You will see My back, but My face may not be seen" (*Exodus* 33:23), meaning that we humans cannot possibly comprehend the events that unfold before our eyes. Our lives here on earth are like a split second in eternity, and just as we can't judge a film after arriving in the middle and viewing it for just one minute, similarly, we cannot comprehend G-d's master plan for us. We can understand only that which is before us, and even then, our perception is limited to that which our intellect, our hearts and our eyes allow us to see. It is only with the passage of time that we can hope to gain a measure of illumination. For example, our forefathers in Egypt, who cried out in agony under the lash of their cruel masters, could not comprehend the *whys* of their suffering, but today we can appreciate that that brutal Egyptian bondage prepared them for Sinai. Only a nation that experienced pain and suffering could champion the cause of justice, compassion, and love; only of such a nation could G-d demand, "You shall not wrong or oppress the stranger, for you were strangers in the land of Egypt" (*Exodus* 22:20). And further, "You shall *love* the stranger, for you were strangers in the land of Egypt" (*Deuteronomy* 10:18).

This same pattern is repeated throughout our history. When Ruth, the Moabite princess, was reduced to abject poverty and instructed by her mother-in-law, Naomi, to gather forgotten sheaves of grain in the field of Boaz, she had no way of knowing that her great-grandson would be King David — that she was laying the foundation for the Kingdom of David, from whence Messiah would descend.

The saddest period in our Jewish calendar year is the "Three Weeks," which commences with the seventeenth day of Tammuz, when the walls of Jerusalem were breached, and culminates with Tishah B'Av, the ninth day of Av, when the Temple was destroyed. Our sages teach that seventeen in gematria* — numerology — is *tov* — good, and the letter "**T**es," is symbolic of good, for when the letter "**T**es" appears for the very first time in the Torah, it is written that "G-d saw that the light was **T**ov — good" (*Genesis* 1:3). This suggests to us that from those horrific catastrophe on the seventeenth day of Tammuz and Tishah B'av, **T**ov — good — will yet emerge. The name of the month is also symbolic — "Av" (Father) reminds us that we are not alone in our sorrow — our merciful Father is with us.

Ours is a generation, however, that is short on faith, and when dark clouds envelop us, when our "whys" continue to plague us, we have difficulty coping and envisioning a better tomorrow.

And here, too, we turn to our Torah for guidance. G-d told Moses, "Behold, there is a place near Me. You may stand on the rock.... I shall shield you with My hand until I have passed..." (*Exodus* 33:21, 22) — meaning that until such time as we have clarity, we must fortify ourselves by standing on the rock of faith and clinging to G-d.

But you may ask, "Is that realistic? Can someone who is really hurting be sustained by faith?" As a survivor of Bergen-Belsen, as one who has personally experienced pain and trauma and knows the meaning of struggle and suffering, I can testify that faith is the *only* formula that *can* work. When uncertainty besets us, when we

---

In the Hebrew language, every letter has a numeric value — hence the word '*Tov*' consists of 9 + 6 + 2 = 17. The very first time that a letter appears in the Torah alludes to its definitive meaning. The *Tes* first appears in *Genesis* 1:3 in the word *Tov*, good.

fail to understand our individual "whys," the knowledge that G-d is guiding our lives enables us to go on. If, however, we see ourselves as victims of fate and view our suffering as *happenstance*, we would have to conclude, as the existentialists do, that all of life is *absurd*, and we would succumb to depression. A well-known Holocaust author and psychologist reduced this concept to a formula: S minus M = D — suffering minus meaning equals depression.

Early in this book, I wrote that when we wish to have clarification on any given subject, in addition to turning to the pages of our Torah, it is also important that we understand the literal meaning of that concept in Hebrew, for Hebrew is the *Holy Tongue*, and therefore every word is definitive. The Hebrew word for *suffering* is "*sevel.*" There are two other words that share the very same root, and yet have totally divergent meanings — *sabal* — porter, and *savlanut* — patience. The connection between these three words became very clear to me when I was on a speaking tour in Russia. My book, "The Committed Life", had been translated into Russian, and was very warmly received by the Jewish community. At the end of the tour, we decided to take several cartons of the book back to the U.S. for distribution among our Russian-speaking brethren, but Barbara and I could barely lift the cartons, so we called for a *sabal* — a porter. Do you think that he was dismayed when he saw those heavy cartons? On the contrary — he was delighted. He informed us that his price for carrying each carton was fifteen *dollars* — not *rubles*! So, instead of viewing those cartons as a burden, he saw them as an opportunity to earn a sizeable sum of money.

It occurred to me that our suffering is very much like that, for even as the *sabal* — porter — cheerfully carried his heavy load, knowing that he would be compensated, similarly, we are buoyed by the knowledge that our *sevel* — suffering — is not in vain, but has a higher purpose and represents an opportunity for growth — for realizing our unique potential. We need only have *savlanut* — patience — to see it.

This concept not only holds true for the word *"sevel"* but is to be found in all Hebrew words that connote suffering. For example, the word for *crisis* in modern Hebrew is *"mashbir,"* which, in Biblical Hebrew, means "birthing stone," teaching us that, if we respond to a crisis positively, new life can come forth. *Just as a rose has thorns, but produces a beautiful flower, so too, from the thorns in our lives, magnificent flowers can bloom.*

To be sure, very often our pain is so overwhelming, the storm that envelops us is so intense, that we fail to see the hand of G-d, and it is then that we need *savlanut* — patience — to find strength in the knowledge that all that has befallen us is ultimately for our good, even if that good is not readily apparent.

Two great Torah giants embodied this belief — Rabbi Akiva and Nochum Ish Gamzu. Rabbi Akiva taught that *"all that our merciful Father does is for the good,"* while Nochum Ish Gamzu asserted, *"This, too, is for good."*

At first glance, they both appear to be teaching the same concept. But there is a fine difference, Rabbi Akiva propounds that everything our merciful Father does is for the best, even if we presently fail to understand it. We trust in G-d and know that all our travails are for our benefit. Nochum Ish Gamzu, on the other hand, taught that we do not have to await the future to see the good, because that which befalls us is *already* good.

It is important to note that both these sages suffered immensely. Their teachings were not abstract concepts — they actually lived them. Rabbi Akiva was an impoverished, illiterate shepherd, who commenced his schooling at the age of forty. His declaration stemmed from an experience he had while on a journey. When night fell, he sought lodging in a village, but none of the inhabitants were willing to offer him hospitality. Having no recourse, he went to a nearby field and lit a candle so that he might study. But the wind blew it out, so he went to sleep. During the night, wild animals killed his only possessions, his rooster and his donkey, leaving him totally destitute. In the morning he discovered that, during the night, bandits had raided the village and plundered and killed all its inhabitants, but he had been saved by the fact that neither a lit candle nor his animals had attracted the attention of the thieves, causing him to proclaim, "All that our merciful Father does is for the good."

Nochum Ish Gamzu, on the other hand, was blind. His legs and hands had been amputated, his entire body was covered with boils, and he lived in abject poverty, yet he taught, "*This, too, is for good.*" His disciples asked him why he, a holy man, was so afflicted. Nochum related that, one day, when he was on a journey with three mules laden with all kinds of delicacies, a starving man approached him begging for some food. He told the man to wait until he finished unloading his mules, but while he was unloading, the man collapsed and died. Devastated, Nochum pronounced his own sentence, and asked G-d to inflict these punishments on him for having failed to respond with alacrity to this poor soul. When his disciples heard the story, they cried out, "Woe is us, that we see you like this, our master!" To which Nochum replied, "Woe would have been to me if you had not seen me like this" — meaning that it is much easier to pay in this world than in the next! Hence his teaching, "*Gam Zu L'Tova* — This, too, is for good."

This, then, is the fabric from which our Jewish spirit is woven, the spirit that enables us to meet the many excruciatingly difficult tests of life that have challenged us throughout history. These teachings of Rabbi Akiva and Nachum Ish Gamzu resulted in two popular Yiddish sayings "*es vet zein gut*"— "it will be good," and "*es iz shoen gut*" — "it is already good." I heard these words from my own revered father in the ghettos and in the concentration camps; I heard these words as he struggled to create a new life for us here in America; I heard them when he was in the throes of debilitating illness — a prisoner of his hospital bed, and I can hear them even now — "*es vet zein gut*" — "it will be good," "*es iz shoen gut*"— it is *already* good."

On the Sabbaths that we bless the new month, I teach Torah to the women of my community. On one of these Sabbaths, I awoke to the sound of thunder, lightning, and torrential rain. The storm continued unabated throughout the day. The walk to the synagogue from my home is a good twenty minutes, but there was no way for me to cancel the class since we are not permitted to make phone calls on *Shabbos*. So, wrapped in my raincoat and accompanied by my granddaughter, who insisted on coming with me, off I went to teach. I was positive that no one would attend, but amazingly, the synagogue was packed. When the class ended, we were all on a spiritual high, invigorated by the knowledge that more powerful than the storm was our desire to study the word of G-d.

I was about to leave, when a kindly looking woman in her forties, whom I will refer to as Lillie, shyly approached me. "Rebbetzin," she said, "you see that rain? That is how my tears are falling." And with that, Lillie proceeded to relate a sad story. She was the mother of six, two of whom were disabled and needed special schooling. Her oldest son was bright and capable, but in all sorts of trouble and a source of terrible tension in her home. Additionally, her husband had lost his job, and to top it all off, she had found a growth that her doctor said looked suspicious and needed to be removed and biopsied without delay.

"Rebbetzin," she said, "I'm falling apart. I don't know where to turn. Someone suggested that I examine my life and see why all these terrible things are happening to me. I know that I'm not perfect," she cried, "but I don't know what I did to merit such terrible punishment."

I took Lillie in my arms and blessed her. People who are hurting need others who will share their pain rather than make sanctimonious pronouncements as to why they are deserving of their fate. I assured her that, very often, G-d's most difficult tests are reserved for his most trusted and beloved servants.

"Just consider our matriarchs," I said. "Have you ever thought about how much they suffered? How they all underwent the most painful tests. Take, for example, our mother, Sarah. She was forced to wander from place to place; famine in the land of Canaan forced her and her husband, Abraham, to descend to Egypt where she was abducted by Pharaoh's soldiers. And her ordeal did not end there, for her most agonizing test was her inability to have children. She desperately yearned for a child, and when she saw that the years were quickly passing by, she made the ultimate sacrifice and asked her husband to marry her handmaiden, Hagar, in the hope that, through her, Sarah might have a child to raise. But her plan backfired, for no sooner did Hagar conceive, than she proceeded to mock her mistress. She arrogantly told everyone, 'Sarah is not the righteous woman that you believe her to be, for why else would G-d have deprived her of a child?' Hagar gave birth to a son, Ishmael, but here too, Sarah suffered disappointment, for he was a wicked, destructive presence, who had to be sent away.

"It was only at the ripe old age of ninety that Sarah was miraculously blessed and gave birth to Isaac — but her life tests were still not over. She awoke one morning to discover that Abraham had ascended Mount Moriah to offer their son, Isaac, on the altar. Upon hearing this news, she cried out in anguish — her heart gave out and her soul departed.

"Would you regard this as a sorrow-free life?" I asked Lillie. "And yet, for Mother Sarah, her sojourn on this planet was one of complete joy, and the Torah assessed the years of her life as *'Kulon shovin l'tova'* — 'all her years were equally good.'"

"But how could they all have been equally good?" Lillie protested.

"That's exactly the point," I answered. "From a human perspective, Sarah underwent the most horrific ordeals, but when you consider G-d's greater design, you will realize that Sarah's trials and tribulations became *banners* that illuminated our paths throughout the centuries; banners that showed us the way and forged us into a nation that lives by G-d's covenant. So, yes, *'Kulon shovin l'tova'* — all her years were equally good."

"It is not only from our matriarchs and patriarchs that we can learn this powerful lesson," I told Lillie, "but from all the giants of our past."

Just consider Iyov — Job. His life reflected the ultimate in suffering. There was no affliction with which he was not tested. He lost his vast fortune; he lost his wife and all his beautiful children. Destitute, he was tormented night and day, for not only was his heart broken, but he was wracked by unremitting pain from horrendous sores that covered his body. Just like you, Lillie, Job had insensitive friends, who advised him to examine his life and discover *why* he was deserving of Divine punishment. G-d was displeased with those friends — this was not the way to comfort someone who was hurting, and Job, himself, derived no solace from their words. Nevertheless, he searched his soul — but could not find any satisfying answers. "*Why?*" Job kept asking, "*Why?*"

In response to his cry, G-d spoke to Job out of a whirlwind and asked him a simple question, *'Efoh hoyisa b'yosdi aretz?'* — 'Where were you, Job, when I laid the foundations of the earth?' (*Job* 38:4-6).

G-d continued posing question after question, and Job could not respond to any of them. Humbly he recognized his inability to fathom the Divine, and was comforted. No longer did he ask *why*, but rather, *how*. Yes, how do I serve my G-d in faithfulness and love? How do I become wiser from my suffering? How do I rebuild my family?

And Job did rebuild — and his second life was even more splendid than before, because he built it on the pillars of his new found wisdom and faith.

"I realize, Lillie, that all this must seem somewhat far-fetched to you — that you must be thinking — 'Job is a legendary figure, and ordinary people are not capable of rising to such heights. But just think of that which we witnessed following the Holocaust.

"If any human experience could be termed Job-like, it was surely the Holocaust. Take, for example, the Klausenberger Rebbe, *zt"l*. He lost his wife and all eleven of his children, and not only did he rebuild his personal life, but he also built a dynasty for the Jewish people — splendid communities in the United States and in Israel with outstanding schools and institutions. He had a vision to build a hospital in Israel, and so, the Laniado Hospital in Netanya came into being. At the ground-breaking ceremony, the Rebbe said, 'I can already hear the cries of the countless babies who will be born here and give new life to our people!'

The story of the Klausenberger Rebbe is not an isolated case. You need only visit Jewish neighborhoods throughout the world, and see for yourself — synagogues and yeshivas with odd-sounding names. Once they were the names of *shtetlach* where Jews studied Torah. If just one Jew survived, he built a yeshiva, where today, the voice of Torah resounds once again.

The great Kabbalist and sage, Rabbi Moshe Chaim Luzzatto, in his monumental work, *Mesilas Yesharim — The Path of the Just* — wrote, "All that befalls us in this world — the good as well as the bad, are *tests*."

"So, Lillie," I said, "instead of torturing yourself with the 'whys', ask yourself, 'How can I pass the test that G-d placed in my path? How can I become stronger from it?"

"Rebbetzin, I really wouldn't know where to start."

"Well, you might begin with those problems that are the greatest cause of your grief, like bringing your oldest son back into the fold and cementing your family."

"I wish I could, but it's impossible to talk to Benny."

"Did you tell him about your upcoming surgery?" I asked.

"No, I'm trying to keep this from my children as long as I can."

"I agree that you should shield your little ones, but as far as Benny is concerned, he should definitely be told, and don't be ashamed to tell him that you *need* him now. You should also let him know about the tough times that his father is having. Perhaps this will be a *wake-up call* for him and your family will emerge stronger and better from it all.

"Rebbetzin, I don't think you begin to understand how bad things are between us. Benny hardly talks to us."

"That's all the more reason why you must speak to him now."

Lillie looked doubtful.

"If you wish, I could call him, but I still think that it would be more effective for you to have a heart to heart with him. Just sit him down and reach out to him. Tell him the plain truth, and don't be afraid to cry. You may just be surprised at how well he will respond. As for your other problems, we will intensify our prayers and, please G-d, you will have a complete recovery, and we'll put out feelers for a job for your husband. With G-d's help, something will come up."

"Oh, Rebbetzin, it's so humiliating — I'm so embarrassed!"

"There's nothing to be embarrassed about," I assured her. "It would be embarrassing if he didn't *want* to work, or if he did something wrong. But people lose jobs — things happen, and who knows, but that this might just prove to be a stepping stone to a better position."

"I don't know, Rebbetzin — I'm so frightened! " I just feel as though my world is falling apart."

"Don't be frightened," I said, putting my arms around her, " just repeat four little words from *Adon Olam* — '*HaShem lee v'lo eeroh'* — 'G-d is with me, I shall not fear.'

"But let me share with you one more teaching from our Torah to help keep you going."

If there is anyone whose world fell apart, it was Noah. Everyone and everything in his world vanished. He was confronted by a total Holocaust. How does a man survive in an ark while the entire world is disappearing in front of him? G-d commanded Noah to place a *tzohar* in the ark for illumination. What is the exact translation of this word? Some of our sages suggest that it was a special jewel of such brilliance that it illuminated the entire ark; others say that it was a window that brought in light. We have a tradition regarding varying biblical interpretations of our sages. They all represent the living word of G-d. Therefore, even if there appears to be a disparity, all are equally valid.

The word *tzohar* contains the same Hebrew letters found in the word *tzorah* — terrible problems, and *rotzo* — desire. When someone says, "I have *tsores*," it's never a matter of simple difficulties. It's more like, "I've run out of gas and I feel I have nothing left" — that's *tsores!* To witness your entire world disappear before your very eyes is to experience *tsores* beyond description, but Noah was given a prescription for survival. If he so *desired (rotzoh)*, he could *convert his tsores — pain, into a window of opportunity* through which he could perceive his mission with greater clarity. Noah however, never quite got that message. When he emerged from the ark and found total devastation, he planted a vineyard and became drunk. So Noah never made it into the ranks of our patriarchs and matriarchs who viewed life as a *test* that must be passed with honor.

"This then, is your choice, Lillie — to pass the test with which you have been challenged or collapse and succumb to depression. Once you learn to view your *tsores* as windows through which you can create a jewel, you will find illumination and purpose."

"Thank you," she said, her voice barely above a whisper. "I will try to keep what you said in mind. But Rebbetzin, I'm still not at peace. Isn't it true that when difficulties befall us, we have to probe our lives because they are *punishments from G-d?* Maybe this is not a test, and G-d *is* punishing me.*"

"Lillie," I said, taking her hand in mine. 'Listen to me well — G-d is our merciful Father whose love is infinite and whose compassion always encompasses us. And this is very clearly stated in the Torah; 'You shall know in your heart that, just as a father chastises his son, so too, G-d chastises you' (*Deuteromy* 7:5). This very same concept was taught by King David, whose suffering was without measure. There was no affliction with which he was not tested, but instead of becoming angry, bitter or depressed, he created psalms, 'G-d is my shepherd, I shall not want.... Even though I walk through the shadow of death, I shall fear no evil, for You are with me. Your rod and Your staff shall comfort me...' (Psalm 23).

"David understood that even as the shepherd uses his staff to keep his flock on the right path and prevent them from straying, so too, G-d's rod and staff are not *punishments*, but *corrections* to keep us on the right path. Even as no father wants to see his child suffer, G-d would never want to cause us pain. He is our shepherd, who uses his rod to protect us and show us the way. So you cannot think of G-d's punishment in *human* terms. As for examining your life — that is something that *we are all called upon to do daily*. We must constantly strive to grow, to improve ourselves, and if we do so, we will discover that much of the grief that we experience does not come from G-d, .but is self inflicted — the result of our own bad choices, our own neglect and abuse. Now mind you, Lillie, I'm not suggesting that you did something to bring this upon yourself, but to one extent or another, we are all self-destructive, even if we refuse to admit it. So, as I said at the beginning of our conversation, instead of tormenting yourself with 'why,' ask yourself 'how?' And always remember that G-d is with you. He hears your prayers; He sees your tears — they were not shed in vain, for 'the gates of tears are never closed.'"

Lillie had her procedure, with Benny and her entire family at her side. Thank G-d, her tumor was benign. In time, her husband found a job, and she was able to echo the words of Rabbi Akiva and Nochum Ish Gam Zu. 'Everything that our merciful Father does is for the best, and it's *already* good.' — "*Es iz shoen gut*!"

Book III

When Tests Are Wake-Up Calls

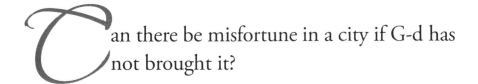

Can there be misfortune in a city if G-d has not brought it?

Amos 3:6

13

Wake-Up Calls

While we may not have definitive answers to our "whys," we can say with certitude that nothing that happens in life is coincidental. That which befalls us as individuals, as well as that which we experience as a people, are not random happenings, but wake-up calls from G-d. Many of us have difficulty with this concept. We pride ourselves on being reasonable, rational individuals and look askance at those who would suggest that there is a Divine power calling us. We delude ourselves into believing that we are in charge of our lives, and even if things happen that are beyond our comprehension, we convince ourselves that *they happen simply because they happen.*

The Torah warns us against attributing events in our lives — be they negative or positive — to "*keri*", the Hebrew word for *happenstance.* If we term that which befalls us "mere coincidence," then G-d will relate to us in like manner, and we will encounter "*chamas keri*" — a "fury of casualness" (*Leviticus* 26:27-28) — meaning that with each successive calamity, it will become more and more difficult for us to identify G-d's signature in our lives.

As our forefathers were about to enter the Promised Land, the closing portion of the Book of *Bamidbar* — Numbers — enumerates all their journeys and encampments throughout their forty-year trek in the wilderness. The Torah would never record a travel itinerary unless it meant to convey a profound message to all of us for all time: All our personal experiences — our frustrations and our sufferings, our joys and our celebrations, are *journeys* designed by G-d, to lead us to our own promised land. Our highs as well as our lows — the hills and valleys of our lives — are all part of the journey that G-d has mapped out for us. Moreover, each person's journey is custom-made, designed specifically for his or her individual needs. If we bear this in mind, then our lives will take on a totally different dimension, for we will view *all* our experiences as opportunities for spiritual growth and fulfillment. And I'm not referring only to traumatic and dramatic moments, but to every aspect of our lives. Our struggles in finding our soul mates, earning a livelihood, raising our children, our battles in overcoming discord and illness, are all part of the journey, custom-choreographed by our Maker for our own specific needs. Therefore, when this portion of *Bamidbar* is read in the synagogue, it is chanted to a sweet tune, for even the most arduous journey can become a song if we bear in mind that G-d is directing it all.

I was asked to lead a group of secular Israeli college students on a tour of Auschwitz and Treblinka, and I invited my daughter and granddaughter to join us. I wanted them to see and remember the places where their grandparents, uncles, aunts, cousins — six million of their people — were slaughtered. My daughter, Chaya Sora, was keenly aware that she was on a journey — she didn't only absorb the horror that was, but she searched for something that could be salvaged. *Shabbos* morning, we prayed in the only functioning synagogue in Warsaw. It was a pathetic sight — a building that had once been a bastion of Torah, where Jewish life had flourished and thrived, was now a bare relic of the past, with just a handful of middle-aged and elderly people. But in that emptiness Chaya Sora spotted a sweet young girl to whom I shall refer as Tova, praying with great fervor. Curious as to who she might be, Chaya Sora approached her and discovered that Tova, age fifteen, and her mother were *righteous converts* who embraced Judaism wholeheartedly. "My dream," the girl said wistfully, "is to study in a Bais Yaakov school" (a school for Orthodox girls).

"Why do you want to study in a Bais Yaakov school?" Chaya Sora asked, surprised that she even knew of it. And her answer was even more amazing: "So that one day, I might be able to marry a true *ben Torah*" (a young man committed to Torah). Chaya Sora was overwhelmed by the girl's sincerity and was determined to bring her to the States, not only to study in a Bais Yaakov school, but also to enable her to spend the summer in a camp where she would meet like-minded girls her age. It took Chaya Sora almost a year, but she got Tova out of Poland, and the rest is history. Today, Tova is an outstanding student in Bais Yaakov, and, please G-d, is on her way to establishing the Jewish home for which she yearns.

I have shared this story, because, if we are aware that *life is a journey* mapped out for us by G-d, then we will realize that there is a purpose to our being in any one place at any one time. Even if we are visiting or just passing through, there is a reason why we are there. We need only be alert, and we will discover that, wherever we are, G-d places many opportunities in our paths through which we can make a difference.

King Solomon was the wisest of all men. When he was a mere lad of twelve, his father, King David, died. To be King of Israel, to sit on the throne of David, would be a daunting challenge for anyone — how much more so for a twelve-year-old? So G-d appeared to Solomon in a dream and said, "Make a wish and I will grant it."

Now, if you were a child of twelve, summoned to reign over Israel, what would you request? A great empire, a powerful army, enormous wealth, success, fame, wisdom, peace? Young Solomon asked for none of these. Instead, he beseeched G-d for the gift of a "*lev shomea*" — "a listening heart."

"A listening heart?" you might protest. "Isn't that somewhat incongruous? Do we not listen with our ears?"

But even as a child, Solomon, who was destined to become the wisest of all men, understood that what we merely *hear* goes in one ear and out the other, but when we listen with our hearts, we can hear G-d's wake-up calls and realize our purpose in life. If we know how to listen with our hearts, messages will come to us from the most unlikely places, even from inanimate objects.

At the age of forty, Rabbi Akiva was an illiterate shepherd in the employ of Kalba Savua, one of the wealthiest men in Jerusalem. Akiva's wife, Rachel, the magnificent daughter of Kalba, challenged Akiva to study Torah.

He smiled sadly — how could he overcome years of ignorance and neglect? How could he ever catch up? How could he, in his mid-years, go to school with small children? He took a walk in the forest to contemplate his plight and came upon a brook in which he noticed a large stone with many indentations. *From whence did those dents come?* he wondered. Then he realized that they were made by water dripping on the stone.

If a stone, which is hard, can be penetrated by soft drops of water, then surely, my mind can be impacted by words of Torah, which are as powerful as iron, he reasoned. And with that, he returned home to act upon Rachel's offer, and went on to become one of the greatest Torah sages of all time. If one has a listening heart, everything becomes possible, and one will receive messages even from a rock.

The greatest event in the annals of mankind, which forever changed the course of history, occurred when G-d revealed Himself at Sinai and gave us His Torah. That awesome moment is recorded in the Book of *Exodus* in the portion of *Yisro*. At first glance, it is difficult to understand how it was that Yisro merited such a distinction, for although he was the father-in-law of Moshe, he had also been a heathen priest who converted to Judaism. Would it not have been more appropriate for the portion to have been named in honor of Moshe?

This great privilege was granted to Yisro because of the one little word with which the *parashah* opens, "*Vayishma*" — *and [Yisro] heard.* But surely, the entire world heard the same messages — the Exodus of the Jewish people from Egypt, the miracle of the splitting of the Sea of Reeds, Israel's amazing battle with the Amalekites. These were not hidden events — everyone was aware of them. But just the same, only *Yisro heard,* only *he* was moved to *act* and come to Sinai.

If we know how to listen with our hearts, we will know how to make the right choices, choices that will impact not only on us, but on all our descendants. If we know how to listen, not only world-shaking events, but even inanimate objects and casual conversations can become life-transforming experiences.

A rebbe once traveled from *shtetl* to *shtetl* teaching Torah. When night fell, he stopped at an inn to rest his weary bones. The innkeeper showed him to his room, and as he prepared to retire, he heard the wife of the innkeeper call out to her husband, "Yankele, finish your work while the candle is still burning."

The rebbe was shaken to the core — the words kept echoing in his mind — "Finish your work while the candle is still burning " — accomplish what you can while you are still alive; while you still have your faculties and your energy.

At the inception of Hineni, I sought the blessing of our Torah sages. Accompanied by my father, I visited many saintly men, and that was how I met Rabbi Yosef Eliyahu Henkin, *z"tl*, just a few weeks before his demise. He was very elderly, blind in both eyes, and quite ill, with an IV in his arm. His *gabbai* – attendant — led him ever so carefully to his chair in his humble, lower East Side apartment. My father and I stood in awe as he painfully made his way.

Rabbi Henkin and my father embraced — they had been close friends for many years. Then, my father informed the sage that I was also present and had come to seek his blessing for our newly established outreach organization.

"You will surely succeed, my child," he assured me, "but I would like you to remember what you see here today," and pointing to his sightless eyes, he said in Yiddish, "*Tzvei shtick fleish* — Two pieces of flesh. Tell everyone to study Torah while the 'flesh' can still see." And with that, he reached for the volume of the Talmud on his table and quoted passages which his eyes did not see, but were nevertheless clearly engraved on his mind and heart. I have often related this story, but sadly, very few have the receptivity in their hearts to absorb the message and apply it to their lives.

At one time or another, we all receive such wake-up calls, but we have become so immersed in our materialistic pursuits that we can

Life Is a Test

no longer hear them. Not only do we not know how to listen, but we do just the opposite — we are masters of *selective listening*, and hear only that which we want to hear.

How often does it happen that, while reading a book or attending a lecture, we say to ourselves, "This is just for my wife/husband, sister/brother, friend/neighbor." But somehow, we never realize that those words were meant *for us*. This holds true for our personal messages as well as for cataclysmic world events. It is only when tragedy strikes us personally, that we wake up — but even then, we are more likely to feel sorry for ourselves and bemoan our fate than to recognize the hand of G-d.

A classic example of this human frailty is the generation that built the Tower of Babel. They had first-hand knowledge of the flood that had engulfed the world in Noah's time. In fact, Noah was still alive to tell them that the deluge had not been a case of nature gone haywire, and yet, that is exactly what they preferred to believe. They rationalized that the heavens collapse every 1656 years, so they decided to build towers to hold up the skies and prevent future catastrophes. G-d's message to Noah was totally lost on them — this, despite the fact that Noah and his sons were living testimony to the devastating consequences that result from rebelling against G-d.

There have been great moments in our history however, that have been exceptions, when we *did* get the message and rose to the challenge. Such was the time in ancient Persia when our people heard Haman's decree to exterminate young and old alike. United in prayer, our people re-accepted G-d's covenant and converted darkness into light, curse into blessing, and proclaimed the joyous festival of Purim for all time.

This, then, is the choice that confronts us all — to follow the example of the ancients of the Tower of Babel or the path of our forefathers who reaffirmed G-d's covenant and transformed tragedy into triumph.

Ours is a generation that has been challenged again and again. We have had so many wake-up calls — some subtle, some more obvious, but perhaps none has impacted like 9/11. For a very brief moment, it appeared as though we were actually listening, and realized that our lives were not only about business and the pursuit of pleasure, but about timeless values, mature love, and sacrifice. On that day of infamy, we rose above the flames of the Twin Towers and united in fellowship and kindness. In Torah language, we call this *chesed*. G-d built the world on pillars of *chesed* (Psalm 89), for that is the energy that justifies the continued existence of mankind.

Chesed is more than making a charitable contribution. *Chesed* means giving of ourselves and placing the needs of others before our own. *Chesed* means smiling at someone even if our own hearts are breaking. *Chesed* means imparting words of encouragement even when we are consumed by our own fears. *Chesed* means a desire to *give*, not necessarily because someone is in distress or deserving, but because our hearts overflow with love and we feel a *need to give*.

On September 11, we felt that need. We examined our lives; we evaluated our priorities; we became kinder and gentler — we did *chesed*. Our newfound kindness was evidenced even in the way we said hello. Instead of the usual cursory nod, we actually greeted one another from the heart. Everywhere there was a willingness to help, from the heroic firemen, to the police, the mayor, the president, and the man on the street. People were actually listening with their hearts to the voices of family members, friends, neighbors, and even strangers, but all too soon, as the intensity of our pain subsided, we reverted to our old ways, and it was business as usual.

In his monumental work, the *Pri Tzaddik*, Reb Tzadok HaKohen, teaches that G-d sends wake-up calls through many channels. We need only learn to be sensitive to them, and we will discover that messages resonate all around us.

Soon after 9/11, a letter was circulated on the Internet asking people to give thought to the number *eleven*, starting with the date, 9/11 — nine plus one plus one equals *eleven*.

The Twin Towers, standing side by side, resembled the number *eleven*.

The towers had one hundred and ten floors — drop the zero, and once again, we have *eleven*.

September eleventh was the two hundred and fifty-fourth day of the year — two plus five plus four equals *eleven*.

The flight number of the first plane to hit the towers was *eleven*; ninety-two passengers were aboard — nine plus two equals *eleven*. The flight had *eleven* crew members — two pilots and nine flight attendants.

Sixty-five passengers were aboard the second flight — once again, six plus five equals *eleven*.

The American Airlines flight which crashed into the Pentagon was airborne for ninety-two minutes before it crashed — once again, nine plus two equals *eleven*.

The United Airlines flight which crashed in Shanksville, Pa. had thirty-eight passengers — three plus eight equals *eleven*.

Shanksville, the site of the crash, has *eleven* letters.

New York City has *eleven* letters.

Afghanistan has *eleven* letters.

Saudi Arabia, birthplace of Bin Laden, has *eleven* letters.

"The Pentagon" has *eleven* letters.

The term "*eleventh* hour" connotes crisis.

911 is an often-used call for help.

And the e-mail listed many more elevens, too numerous to mention, but I'm certain that by now you get the drift.

Our young people at Hineni asked if this had any application in Judaism.

My natural inclination was to say, "It's hokey! You can't take anything like that seriously." Besides, 9/11 was not the date on the Jewish calendar, so what was the point of searching for Jewish answers? But then I began to think about it and I realized that the corresponding Hebrew date to 9/11 was the twenty-third of Elul, and that also added up to *eleven*, since Elul is the sixth month of the Jewish calendar year and six plus two plus three equals *eleven*!

What does it all mean? What should we make of it, and how should we respond?

I turned to the portion of the week that we read during 9/11 and combed the pages to determine whether the number eleven came up in that *parashah*. Sure enough, there it was! "The hidden things are for Hashem, our G-d, but the revealed things are for us and our children" (*Deuteronomy* 29:28). And over the words "to us and our children" are *eleven* cantillation dots!

What does it all mean? I was determined to dig deeper.

As I explained earlier, in the Hebrew language, each letter of the alphabet has a numerical value. *Aleph* is not just "a," but is also the number one. *Beit* is not just "b," but it is also the number two, and so on. Thus, we can gain greater understanding of the meaning of words through their numerology. The Hebrew word for repentance, return to G-d, is *teshuvah*, the numeric value of which is seven hundred thirteen (seven plus one plus three), once again adding up to *eleven*.

I started to examine other elevens in the Torah, in our prayers, and in our literature, and discovered that they were *all somehow connected to teshuvah — repentance*. Can these elevens be wake-up calls imploring us to re-examine our lives, our priorities? Is it not written in the Talmud that in every catastrophe that is visited upon the earth, there is a message for us?

Life Is a Test

In the Holy Temple in Jerusalem, the priests offered a special incense service on the Golden Altar. The incense had *eleven* spices, and were offered every morning and evening. The service was so sacred that we still recall it in our daily prayers and enumerate all eleven spices. The great Kabbalist, the Arizal, taught that sincere recitation of that service brings one to repentance.

The *Book of Psalms* was written by King David, but what is less well known is that Moses also composed psalms, and David included them in his book. How many psalms did Moses write? You guessed it — *eleven*!

Moses imparted his last will and testament to the people in the *eleventh* month and reminded the nation that the journey from Mount Sinai to the Promised Land normally takes *eleven* days (*Deuteronomy* 1:2-3), and a journey to the Promised Land is not just a *physical* journey, but a journey upon which we must *all* embark.

Joseph is the Biblical figure who paved the way for the descent of his brethren to Egypt. He was the *eleventh* son of Jacob, and in his dream, he saw *eleven* stars that foretold the future. According to our tradition, that which befell our forefathers is bound to recur in the lives of their children. At the end of days, someone from the House of Joseph will once again pave the way for the messianic period.

The numerical value of the Hebrew for *Rachel Imenu* — "Mother Rachel" is three hundred thirty-five. 3 plus 3 plus 5 equals eleven! Regarding Mother Rachel it is written, "A voice is raised on high — wailing and bitter weeping, Rachel is crying for her children. She refuses to be consoled, for her children are gone. Thus said the L-rd, 'Restrain your voice from weeping and your eyes from tears — there is reward for your labor.... Your children shall return to their borders.'" (*Jeremiah* 31:14-17). Mother Rachel, to whom G-d gave this unconditional promise, died on the *eleventh* day of the Hebrew month of *Cheshvan*.

In the *Book of Daniel*, in which Kabbalistic concepts and prophecies are related, eleven horns are mentioned. These horns are symbolic of the different regimes with which we will have to struggle in our exile. Our Sages explain that the "last horn" before the coming of Mashiach will be the eleventh horn. This *eleventh* horn will represent the new religion of Islam, which will be small at its inception, but will grow very quickly and be haughty. This eleventh horn will claim that he is a prophet and will try to overturn the world and the law.

There is a Kabbalistic teaching that the force of evil in the world is symbolized by Amalek, and we are commanded to obliterate all traces of this evil. Only thus can Messiah come. When Moses imparted this teaching (*Exodus* 17:14-15), he referred to the Throne of G-d as "*Kes*" rather than "*Keesey*" and to G-d's Holy Name as Y-H, rather than Y-H-V-H. Thus, he omitted a letter from G-d's Throne and two letters from His Name. This teaches that as long as evil prevails, G-d's Name and Throne are incomplete. The two letters that Moses omitted from G-d's Name are the *Vov* and *Hey* (6 + 5 = 11). Can all these elevens be attributed to mere coincidence? Even if we are skeptics, shouldn't it all give us pause?

But it is not only through the number eleven that messages have come to us. There have been many other couriers.

During the summer of 2002, a terrible tragedy occurred in a bungalow colony in New York's Catskill Mountains. A mother had just bathed her infant and put her into her carriage for a nap. Suddenly, from out of nowhere, a wild bear appeared, snatched the baby from her carriage, and made off with her. The shocking story appeared in newspapers and the media, but somehow, it failed to make an impression, yet our Talmud clearly states that the generation that witnesses a wild beast snatching a baby from its cradle should sound the alarm with a *shofar* to awaken the people. But the shofar was *not* sounded and we were *not* awakened.

During the last few years, the number of catastrophes has multiplied to such an extent, that we have all but become immune to them. Natural disasters like the tsunami, Hurricane Katerina, volcanic eruptions, earthquakes, global warming, hitherto unknown diseases, barbaric acts of terror, and nuclear tests that threaten the very survival of our civilization have all come to be accepted as the norm. "It is what it is," we tell ourselves with resignation, and we go on with our lives as usual. But can all this be attributed to mere coincidence? Shouldn't these afflictions give us pause?

There is a story about a Hasidic rebbe who was walking with his disciples when he noticed a little boy behind a tree, crying bitterly.

"Why are you crying?" he asked.

"I'm hiding, and no one is looking for me."

The words of the child were like a sharp knife in the heart of the rebbe. "Woe is us," he said to his students, "G-d is waiting for us to find Him, but we have failed to search for Him. Woe is us!"

Maimonides taught that, when suffering is visited upon us, we are commanded to cry out and awaken our people with the sound of the *shofar*. Everyone must be alerted to examine his or her life and commit to greater adherence to Torah and *mitzvos*. Maimonides warned that, if we regard the tragedies that befall us simply as "the way of the world" — "natural happenings," we will be guilty of *achzarius* — cruelty.

At first glance, it is difficult to understand why Maimonides would choose the term "cruelty" to describe those who view trials and tribulations as "natural happenings." Such people may be unthinking, apathetic, foolish, blind, or obtuse, but why accuse them of cruelty?

The answer is simple. If we regard our pain and suffering as "mere coincidence," we will feel no motivation to examine our lives, abandon our old ways, and *change*. So yes, such an attitude is *cruel*, for it invites additional misfortune upon ourselves and others.

It would be the height of cruelty to dismiss that which is occurring in the world today as mere *happenstance*. Great Torah luminaries of past generations, such as the Chofetz Chaim and Rabbi Elchanan Wasserman, told us that we are entering the final stages of history — a period in time called *"Ikvesa DiMeshicha"* — Footsteps of the Messiah. Our Torah foretells four exiles through which our people would suffer: Egypt, Babylonia — Persian-Mede Empires, Greece, and Rome — (the exile in which we presently find ourselves, for it was the Romans who exiled us when they destroyed the Second Temple).

In *Pirkei d'Rabbi Eliezer*, an early Midrashic work, it is written that, before the coming of Messiah, we will have to contend with a fifth source of tribulation that will come from Yishmael — the Arabs — who will inflict terrible suffering on the world and on our people. This teaching is reaffirmed by Rabbi Chaim Vital, the illustrious disciple of the Arizal, who wrote that, before the final curtain falls upon the stage of history, Yishmael will inflict torture on our people in ways the world has never before seen.

One need not have great powers of discernment to recognize the painful veracity of these predictions. Consider only the suicide bombers, the decapitations, the highjackings, the missiles, the rockets, and the constant, senseless, brutal acts of terror.

We are the generation that has been destined to witness the fulfillment of the prophecy given to Hagar (*Genesis* 16:11-13). "Behold, you will conceive and give birth to a son, and you shall name him Ishmael... and he shall be a wild ass of a man; with his hand against everyone and everyone's hand against him, and over all his brethren shall he dwell...."

The long arm of Ishmael's terror has indeed reached every part of the world.

There is yet another amazing prophecy in the *Yalkut Shemoni* — a Medieval/Midrashic compilation, that eerily foretells the events of today and should give us all pause: Rabbi Yitzchok said, "The year in which *Melech Hamashiach* will be revealed, all the nations of the world will be provoking each other. The King of Persia [Iran], will provoke the King of Arabia [Saudi Arabia]. The King of Arabia will go to Edom [the leader of the Christian nations — the President of the United States] to take counsel, and the King of Persia (Ahmadinejad), will threaten to destroy the entire world.

"The nations of the world will be outraged and panic. They will fall on their faces and experience pains like birth pangs. Israel, too, will be outraged and in a state of panic, ask, 'Where do we go?'

"But say unto them, 'My children, do not fear. The time of your redemption has come.... And this last redemption shall be different from the first that was followed by further bondage and pain. After this last redemption, you will not experience any further pain or subjugation" (*Yalkut Shemoni, Isaiah* 59).

The Klausenberger Rebbe, *z"tl*, referring to this teaching, said, "Remember these words. They are perhaps not understood now, but in time, they *will* be, and will be a source of strength to our people."

Had you heard these prophecies centuries ago, when they were written, you might have laughed and scoffed — even if you read them as recently as 1970, you would have been hard put to believe it, for of all the Moslem countries, the Shah's Iran was probably the friendliest. But today, the impossible has become possible, and events are unfolding so rapidly that we have difficulty absorbing their impact. So how are we to understand it all?

The *Yalkut* compares our suffering to *birth pangs*. But birth pangs are deceptive; when the contractions begin, it's easy to ignore them since they are mild and occur between long intervals. As the birth becomes imminent however, the contractions intensify and the pain becomes more intense. And just when it appears that the woman can no longer endure the pain, the baby is born and new life enters the world. It is these labor pains to which we are witness today. How long will the labor last? It's anyone's guess, but one thing is certain — please G-d, the birth is sure to take place. In the interim, however, we may very well ask, "Is it possible to ease the suffering? Is it possible to protect ourselves from these painful contractions?" For that too, our sages have an answer: "Let he who wishes to be spared the birth pangs of Messiah, occupy himself with Torah and *gemilus chasidim* (acts of loving-kindness) and let him be scrupulous about *Seudah Sh'lishis* — the third Sabbath meal."

The first two recommendations — Torah and *gemilus chasadim* — are self-explanatory and do not require much elaboration, for he who is committed to Torah and *mitzvos* and to reaching out with loving kindness, must, of necessity, become a better, more spiritual person. But eating a third Sabbath meal is not as readily comprehensible.

We are enjoined to have three *seudos* — meals — on the Sabbath — Sabbath eve (Friday night), Sabbath noon (following prayer in the synagogue) and the third *seudah* — meal — in the late afternoon as the Sabbath Queen prepares to depart. Through these three meals, we honor the three Patriarchs, the three sections of our Scriptures (Torah, Prophets, and the Writings), and we recall the three Sabbath meals of manna that G-d provided us during our sojourn in the wilderness (*Exodus* 16:25).

This final Sabbath *seudah* is called *Shalosh Seudos,* which, translated literally, means "Three Meals," rather than *Seudah S'hlishis* — the third meal. Our Sages explain that the reason for this is that all three Sabbath *seudos* are embodied in this one.

This third meal presents a most auspicious time for prayer. And to this very day, when I close my eyes, I can hear the sweet voices of my revered father and my beloved husband, of blessed memory, leading their congregants in singing Psalm 23, the psalm that is traditionally chanted at the *Shalosh Seudos.*

"The L-rd is my Shepherd, I shall not want...." The task of the shepherd is a lowly and lonely one. Day in and day out, he is destined to wander from place to place, seeking pasture for his flock, and yet, David did not hesitate to refer to G-d as a Shepherd, for he perceived that G-d's love is so total, so encompassing, that when it comes to caring for His children, nothing is beneath Him. What a magnificent and fortifying thought — for no matter where life takes us, even if we have to walk in the treacherous valley overshadowed by death, we need not fear, for G-d, our Shepherd, will always be there to lead us to greener pastures, even if, at first, we do not recognize that the pasture is green.

Still, it is difficult to comprehend how the mere eating of a third meal, singing Psalm 23, and discussing Words of Torah could have such awesome power that they can actually protect us from the suffering that will accompany the birth pangs. But there is a profound lesson at the root of this teaching. The first two Sabbath *seudos* are eaten when we are hungry, but after a festive noontime *seudah*, we are hardly in the mood for yet another meal. So, it is not to satiate our hunger that we gather around the *Shalosh Seudos* table. Rather, it is to celebrate the Sabbath and sing her praises, and that is why the Third Meal encompasses them all. *The Third Meal is symbolic of the conversion of the physical to the spiritual*, and *ultimately, that is our purpose — to become spiritual beings and to free ourselves from the shackles of materialism* — and that is something that our generation, obsessed with materialism and the pursuit of pleasure, has yet to learn.

You might, of course, wonder, "Why must we experience birth pangs in order for Messiah to come? Why can't he just announce his presence?" But the Messianic period will be very much like *Shalosh Seudos*, when we sit around the table — not to satiate our physical hunger nor to glory in our material achievements, but *to celebrate our spiritual attainments*.

In order for that to happen, we will have to divest ourselves of all the icons that we hold dear. Therefore, our hallowed institutions, the bastions of strength in which we placed our trust, will have to fall away. It is that painful disintegration to which we are witness today. From the corporate world to government, to religious institutions, to science and medicine, they have all failed us. And worse, we no longer feel safe or secure in our daily lives. Terrorists and suicide bombers have become a reality of our existence, and no army or police force is capable of shielding us from them. Shorn of all our defenses, we stand vulnerable and terrified, and wonder what life is all about as we see our idols crumble before our very eyes.

How long will these birth pangs last? Until we recognize the simple truth — that "*we can rely on no one but our Heavenly Father.*" So let us sound the shofar, awaken ourselves from our lethargy, and heed the voice of our Father calling us.

But even as we do so, let us not despair.

There is an amazing *Midrash* that recalls the story of three great Biblical figures: Reuven, Aaron, and Boaz, about whom the Sages said, had they only known that the Torah would record their deeds, they would have done even more.

How can we understand such puzzling teachings? How can it be that such spiritual giants would have needed the additional incentive of being inscribed in the Torah to conduct themselves more nobly? It has often occurred to me that there is a deep lesson to be gleaned from this Midrash that could be a great source of spiritual strength to all of us in these troubled times.

When Reuven discovered that the pit into which his brother Joseph had been cast was empty, he was overcome by inconsolable grief and cried out, "The lad is gone! And I? — Where can I go?" (*Genesis* 37:30). But had Reuven known that Joseph was on his way to Egypt to prepare the path for the family of Jacob, a path that would eventually lead the nation to Sinai, he would have rejoiced!

When Aaron went to greet Moses who was returning to the Auschwitz of Egypt, his heart fell, for he feared for the life of his younger brother. Had he only known that Moses was coming to redeem the nation, he would have greeted him with an orchestra!

Had Boaz, from whose fields Ruth gleaned, known that she would one day become his wife and the great-grandmother of King David, he would have rejoiced and made her a magnificent, festive meal.

Had they *only known what the Torah had mapped out for them*, their hearts would have been filled with elation rather than trepidation.

Similarly, all our journeys, be they personal or national, are guided by G-d. There is an ultimate goal — a destination to which we will all arrive. It is not for naught that we are launched on our paths. Our struggles are not in vain. So when our journeys become difficult, when our hearts tremble with fear, let us recall Reuven, Aaron, and Boaz. Let us remember that we have not witnessed the end yet — and *the end will be good*. That which we are experiencing are birth pangs. Let us hold fast, for very soon, we will see blessed new life that will make all our sacrifices and suffering worthwhile.

14

He Has Not Forgotten Us

Through the pages of this book, I have tried to address the many tests with which life confronts us. There remains however, one very painful and difficult test that we have not yet fully explored — the Holocaust. True, time and again, I have stated that we mortals have no way of comprehending why, for it is only in retrospect — sometimes not even in our own lifetime — that people can hope to gain a glimmer of understanding. Nevertheless, I have also quoted the teachings of our sages, *"Hafoch bah, v'hafoch bah, d'kula bah"* — "Turn the pages, turn the pages, everything is to be found therein," meaning that we need only search the pages of our Torah for illumination. Surely, therefore, the Holocaust must pass this scrutiny as well. But allow me one caveat — illumination does not mean that we will uncover absolute, definitive answers, but it does mean that we can shed some light on the darkness and find direction and understanding.

Still, you might protest, is it really necessary to focus on the Holocaust now? Don't we have enough to contend with just dealing with today? Are we not now confronted with our own possible Holocaust? Just consider the global escalation of terrorism and anti-Semitism — Ahmadinejad and Nasrallah's openly avowed plans to wipe Israel off the map. So why go back? Why not leave yesterday for history books and museums?

George Santayana said: "Those who cannot remember the past are condemned to repeat it." We, the Jewish people, have a different take on this concept. "The lives of our forefathers are signposts for their progeny" is the teaching of our sages, meaning that, by studying their lives, we can uncover the roadmap to guide us through our own challenges and dilemmas. G-d did not recount the stories of our patriarchs and matriarchs to entertain us with Bible stories, but rather, to teach us how to live our own lives and respond to our own struggles. So let us attempt to find some precedent in the Torah for the Holocaust, even if such a search evokes intense emotions.

Rabbi Yitzchok Dovid Grossman, founder and dean of Migdal Ohr, a youth village in Israel, visited our Hineni Young Leadership Torah Class in Manhattan. He related a remarkable incident that he heard from Moti Dotan, an Israeli who heads the Regional Council of the Galil. Moti went to Germany with other community leaders for a conference. At the conclusion of one of the sessions, he was approached by Dieter Hertzig, a member of the German Bundestag (parliament). Hertzig's father had died just a few weeks earlier, and on his death bed he confessed to his son that during World War Two, he had been a member of Hitler's Luftwaffe and had flown many missions, during which he had destroyed many synagogues.

He was curious to see the results of his work, so he decided to visit one of the synagogues that he had bombed. He surveyed the ruins and there, lying on the ground, in the midst of the rubble, he found a scroll made of parchment. He examined it, and decided that the sturdy material would make an excellent folder to preserve his identity papers, so he took a knife and cut a piece from the scroll. It was only much later that he learned that the scroll was something very holy to the Jews — a Torah. And now that he was dying, he told his son that he wanted to make amends by supplying evidence to refute the claims of all Holocaust deniers and show proof positive that the Holocaust really did occur. He beseeched his son to hand over the folder containing his identity card to the first Jew he met and ask him to transmit it to a rabbi in Israel who, he felt confident, would know what to do with it.

Upon his return to Israel, Moti decided to give the folder made from the Torah scroll to Rabbi Grossman. When the rabbi read the passages cut from the Torah, he began to tremble. The terrifying words were from the *Book of Deuteronomy*, the portion known as the "*Tochachah*" — the chapter of rebuke that foretells the terrible calamities that will befall us if we abandon G-d's Torah. Does this not allude to a Holocaust?

Can anyone attribute this to mere coincidence? That Nazi could have cut a piece from any part of the scroll. Why were his hands led to just these passages, and why did it come to the fore at a time when the Jewish people were once again threatened by global anti-Semitism and another tyrant who threatens to, G-d forbid, wipe out the Jewish people? As Rabbi Grossman read the chilling words on the parchment, everyone sat glued to their seats in awed silence.

"... in the siege and distress that your enemy will distress you in your cities. If you will not be careful to perform all the words of this Torah that are written in this Book to fear this honored and awesome Name: *HaShem*, your G-d, then *HaShem* will make extraordinary your blows and the blows of your offspring — great and fateful blows and evil and fateful illnesses. He will bring back upon you all the sufferings of Egypt, of which you were terrified, and they will cleave to you. Even any illness and any blow that is not written in this Book of the Torah, *HaShem* will bring upon you until you are destroyed. You will be left few in number, instead of having been like the stars of heaven in abundance, for you will not have hearkened to the voice of *HaShem*, your G-d" (*Deuteronomy* 28:57-62).

The English translation of any passage from the Torah is, at best, lacking. For example, where it states that "the blows that will be visited upon us will be extraordinary" — the Hebrew word used is "*hi-flo*," which comes from the word "*pella*" — miraculous. In English, this word has a positive connotation, and would thus be inappropriate in this context. But what the Torah is trying to impress upon us is that these catastrophes will be of a magnitude that mankind has never before experienced, something that is so horrifying that it is out of the realm of human experience.

Never before in the annals of mankind were there factories of death in which the lives of millions were snuffed out in minutes, where the skin of the victims was fashioned into lampshades, their bones ground into fertilizer, and their fat converted into soap. No generation has ever before experienced such satanic evil. I read and re-read the passages, and I was struck by the Torah's reference to our Egyptian bondage: "And G-d will bring back upon you all the suffering of Egypt...." What is the connecting link between our Egyptian bondage and the Holocaust?

What is there about our Egyptian exile that serves as a precursor to all future exiles and persecutions? And what are the instructive "signposts" — teachings — that our forefathers in Egypt left us? Let us attempt to review our Egyptian experience — how we got there; how we survived, and how we went forth to seal our Divine Covenant at Sinai.

Jacob's beloved son, Joseph, the victim of sibling rivalry and hatred, was sold into Egyptian bondage. After much travail and suffering, he became the viceroy of Egypt — the most powerful position in the land, second only to Pharaoh. For twenty-two years, Jacob had been led to believe that his precious son had been devoured by a wild beast. Then suddenly, miraculously, news reached him that "*od Yosef chai*" — "Joseph still lives" and is the viceroy of the most powerful country in the ancient world.

Often, when studying these passages, I tried to conjure up the emotions that "*Zeide Yaakov*" must have felt when the astounding news reached him. I invite you, the reader, to think about it as well. Imagine that you were "*Zeide Yaakov*," living in a *shtetl*, and for twenty-two years had been under the impression that your son had been killed, and then, one day you discover that he is not only alive, but has become the Vice-President or the Secretary of State of the United States of America. Then, you further discover that, prior to being elevated to this exalted position, he was the servant of immoral idol worshipers. And more — he also spent twelve years in prison, where he was exposed to the most degenerate criminals in the land. Now if you had heard all this, what thoughts would have run through your mind? What feelings would you have had in your heart? Yes — of course you would have praised G-d for His wondrous miracles, but then, when the dust settled, and you absorbed the full import of this information, your heart would be filled with terrifying thoughts.

"Is he still a Jew? Does he still believe in G-d? Is he still moral? Does he still keep *Shabbos*? Is he still keeping kosher? Whom did he marry? What about his children?" And your initially undiluted joy is now overshadowed by terrible fear and trepidation.

The Torah relates that Joseph sent wagons for his elderly father's safe journey. Our sages teach that those wagons had a second purpose. They were also to assure the patriarch that Joseph hadn't forgotten the last Torah lesson that they had studied together prior to his abduction so many years ago. But if you were "*Zeide Yaakov*," would those wagons have quelled the anxiety in your heart? Despite its coded message, would your heart still not throb with trepidation? So it was with mixed feelings of joy and fear that Jacob embarked on his journey to reunite with his beloved, long-lost son.

Joseph's reverence for his father was of such magnitude that when the news reached him that Jacob had crossed the border into Egypt, Joseph himself harnessed his chariot and rode to greet him. You can well imagine that, if Joseph went forth, all of Egypt followed — the nobility, the military, and many ordinary Egyptians. The great moment arrived for father and son to be united, and the eyes of all Egypt were focused on them.

What do you think were the first words they exchanged? What would you have said if you were Jacob or Joseph?

The Torah text itself is mute on the subject, but Rashi, the great Biblical commentator, fills in the gap and explains that Jacob chose this specific moment of their meeting to recite "the *Shema*."

Can you imagine arriving at JFK to meet your long-lost son, and just as he comes running toward you, you begin reciting the *Shema*, which prohibits you from speaking, embracing, or kissing. Couldn't the patriarch have waited a few minutes before starting to pray? Couldn't he have first greeted his son?

Our Sages teach that, when a holy, righteous person is elevated by an exalted moment of love, when his heart is bursting with joy, he harnesses his emotions to offer thanks to G-d. Thus, Jacob's recitation of the *Shema* was a proclamation of G-d's Oneness and sovereignty. It has often occurred to me, that, at that sublime moment, when Jacob's heart overflowed with exultation, he may also have been testing the tensile strength of his son's faith to determine what impact those twenty-two years of Egyptian exile had upon him. Would Joseph be embarrassed in the presence of this great entourage? Would he whisper, "Dad, this is Egypt, you can't be so Jewish in public — please wait until we get to the palace where there will be a private room in which to daven — but please, Dad, not here!"

Joseph not only passed the test, but he surpassed it. The Torah relates that he fell upon his father's neck and wept profusely (*Genesis* 46:29). We know that the neck is a metaphor for the Holy Temple, for even as the neck connects the physical (the body) with the spiritual (the head), the Temple connects us with G-d. Thus, Joseph also converted this moment of supreme joy to the service of G-d and wept, for he foresaw the pain of G-d and the suffering that would befall the Jewish people with the destruction of the Holy Temples.

The exchange between father and son, however, did not end there. But again, what do you think Joseph's first words were to his elderly father who had just made an arduous journey across a blistering, hot desert? And better still, what would you have said? You might perhaps have told your father how desperately you had missed him and assured him of your love and your continued fidelity to the commandments, or you might have told him that you had made provisions for his every need and that he would lack for nothing. But Joseph did not offer such comforting words. Instead, he made an astounding statement: He told his father and his brethren that he would have to introduce them to Pharaoh, who most certainly would ask what their occupation was — to which they should respond that they were a family of shepherds, and had been for generations. And then, Joseph went on to explain his reasoning: To the Egyptians, shepherds were an abomination, and therefore, Pharaoh would be happy to settle them in Goshen, far from the Egyptians themselves (*Genesis* 46: 31-34).

To say the least, Joseph's words are puzzling. Why would he wish to portray his family in such a negative light? Why would he wish to alienate them from Pharaoh and the Egyptian populace?

Joseph, who had survived in Egypt for twenty-two years as a lone Jew, had become an expert in preserving Jewish life in exile. He knew that if he were to protect his people from disappearing, he would have to settle them in their own community where they could adhere to their own traditions without being threatened by assimilation. But for that to happen, Pharaoh would have to see the wisdom of keeping Jews apart from the mainstream and designate Goshen a "Jewish city." Thus, Joseph laid down one of the first principles of Jewish survival — a strong Jewish community, and the formula worked throughout *Zeide Yaakov's* life. The Jewish people flourished and prospered, but while they became a vital part of Egypt, they remained in their own community — a nation apart, living by the laws of G-d. All this came to a dramatic halt with the death of the patriarch. This change is related in the Torah in so subtle a manner that the casual student would probably not even pick it up.

Every Torah portion is separated from the next by at least a nine-letter space. But the last portion of *Genesis, Vayechi* (*Genesis* 47:28-50:26), in which Jacob's demise is announced, is not separated from the previous portion (*Vayigash*), and is therefore known as "*Stuma*" — closed. Rashi explains that, "with the death of the patriarch, the eyes and hearts of the Jewish people closed — shut down due to the anguish of the bondage."

But that teaching is truly problematic, for the bondage did not commence until almost eighty years later, when the last of Jacob's sons died. Moreover, how can a nation's eyes and heart be closed — blind to the torture and suffering of enslavement? As a survivor of the Holocaust, I can testify that our affliction was constantly before us. We couldn't escape it for even a second. The torment enveloped us by day and by night. So how is it possible that our forefathers were blind to their bondage? What is the deeper meaning of this teaching?

Our Sages explain that one of the reasons why spaces are left between sections is to invite us to meditate upon the preceding verses. But the very fact that there is no break between these two portions indicates that the children of Jacob did not fully grasp the import of the last words of *Vayigash*, "Israel settled in the land of Egypt, in the land of Goshen and were fruitful and acquired property." The Hebrew word for "acquired property" — "*vaye'achazu*," — means much more than simply buying real estate. It connotes taking possession of the land, becoming part of the culture and assimilating. That assimilation was the first step toward bondage, and it was to that that our forefathers were blind.

Now we can understand why our Torah teaches us that our bondage commenced with the death of our *Zeide Yaakov*, for, as long as he was alive, our people stayed in their own environment, in their unique Jewish community, but after his demise, they "took possession of the land" and bought homes and real estate throughout the country. The *Book of Exodus* opens with this new reality. "The children of Israel were fruitful and multiplied. They prospered very, very much and the land became filled with them" (*Exodus* 1:7). Jews became a vital force in every segment of Egyptian society. Their presence was visible everywhere, and our Sages explain that this included whatever form of entertainment was popular in Egypt in those days. This acculturation — assimilation — was paralleled by a total change in government — "a new Pharaoh arose over Egypt who did not know Joseph" (*Exodus* 1:8). But how could that be? Can the president of the United States claim that he doesn't know who preceded him? Can the new Pharaoh not have known Joseph?

Once again, our sages shed illumination. Pharaoh did not want to know Joseph. He abolished the laws that Joseph enacted, denied Egypt's indebtedness to Joseph and his family and accused them of exploitation and sabotage. Overnight, Pharaoh demonized the Jewish genius and benevolence that had transformed a famine-plagued, bankrupt Egypt into a great, prosperous empire. Overnight, he accused Jews, who were his most loyal subjects, of being a fifth column that threatened the very survival of Egyptian civilization. He levied special taxes on them and commanded that they build cities for the welfare of the state; he cast them into slave labor camps and broke their bodies under the weight of excruciating labor, and he crushed their spirit with meaningless, futile tasks. And to assure their disappearance from Planet Earth, he ordered that every male child be killed at birth (*Exodus* 1:10-17).

Does it sound familiar? Do you recognize 20th-century Europe? Do you see parallels to the Holocaust?

I was born in Hungary, in the city of Szeged, a cosmopolitan cultural metropolis, with concert halls and universities. Szeged boasted one of the largest, most beautiful Neolog (Hungarian name for *Reform*) Temples in the world. The great majority of the Jewish population was assimilated — Hungarians first and Jews second, or not at all.

My father, of blessed memory, a man of great vision and love, settled in Szeged to try to salvage Jewish lives. It was a daring, revolutionary move. In those days, outreach was virtually unknown, and there was little communication between the religious and the rapidly growing assimilated population.

In pre-Holocaust Europe, it seemed possible for Jews to shed their Judaism and fully integrate into secular society. I remember the pitiful cry of one of the grande dames of our city who, in impeccable German (the language of the intelligentsia), protested to a Nazi guard, *"Bitte schoen, Ich bin nicht kein Jude"* — "Please, I'm not a Jew!" But the Nazis shoved her into the cattle car just the same. As far as Hitler was concerned, if you had any trace of Jewish blood, even if you had converted, your fate was sealed.

Such stories were repeated throughout Europe, but perhaps nowhere was it more tragic than in Germany, where Jews had sacrificed so much for the Fatherland. In vain did they display their medals, their Iron Crosses, which testified to their loyalty and valor in World .. In vain did they point to the contributions they had made to development and prosperity of their country. — "There was a new king in Germany who did not know Joseph."

The tragedy of our bondage in ancient Egypt commenced when the protective walls of Goshen crumbled, and thousands of years later, in Europe, the story was replayed, when, at the advent of the Jewish Enlightenment — the Haskalah Movement — in the 19th century, the walls of the ghettos fell, and many of our people melted into secular society. In 1880, a prominent German Jewish leader, Abraham Geiger, declared "It's time to bury Jerusalem — Berlin is our new Jerusalem."

This assimilation, which commenced in Germany, spread like wildfire from Western to Eastern Europe, although in the early 20th century, in countries such as Poland, Russia, and Lithuania, it took on a somewhat different form. Communism, Socialism, the Bundists and a host of other secular Jewish movements, all of which rejected G-d and our Torah, became the ideology of many. Painful stories of Jews mocking and attacking their own observant brethren and their own religion were all too commonplace. Admittedly, there were many great spiritual giants — holy sages — as well as multitudes of ordinary pious people who, at great sacrifice, clung to the Torah, but unfortunately, they could not overcome the wave of assimilation that swept over Europe.

We are a nation that can be likened to passengers on a boat. Should one individual drill a hole under his seat, in vain would he protest that that is his right, and is no one's business but his own — for once the hole is drilled, the water will gush in and the boat will sink. At Sinai, our nation stood "as one man with one heart" and in unison, we proclaimed "*Na'aseh V'Nishma*" — we shall do and we shall hear," rather than "*I* shall do and *I* shall hear." At Sinai, "all of Israel became responsible for one another."

And do not think that the Torah sages were silent in the face of this assimilation. Giants like the Meshech Chochmah, Rabbi Meir Simcha HaKohen of Dvinsk, Lithuania, sounded the alarm and warned that, because Berlin was proclaimed to be the "new Jerusalem," it would be from Berlin, G-d forbid, that tragedy would spill forth. But his warning fell on deaf ears, as did the words of such other great Torah sages as the Chofetz Chaim and Rabbi Elchanan Wasserman.

The covenant that G-d sealed with us is eternal. It is our destiny to be His witnesses — "…This nation I have created so that they might sing My praise" (*Isaiah* 43:21). Should we attempt to escape our mission, however, there will be those who will remind us of our calling.

"And that which enters your minds — it shall not be. As for what you say, 'Let us be like the nations, like the families of the land…. As I live, — the Word of the L-rd, *HaShem, Elokim* — surely, I will rule over you with a strong hand and an outstretched arm and with an outpouring of fury" (*Ezekiel* 20:32). That is one of the fundamental laws of our Jewish survival.

Even as a father never gives up on his children, G-d swore never to give up on us. The Hebrew name used for G-d in these passages — a combination of *HaShem*, which represents His mercy, and *Elokim*, which represents His justice, conveys both love and justice, teaching us that it is out of love for us that G-d sometimes punishes.

Our Sages teach that our forefathers in Egypt merited redemption because they retained three attributes — they did not alter their Jewish names, their mode of dress, or their language. These basic values were sadly missing among our assimilated brethren in Europe. It was so common among German Jews to have only secular names that one of the infamous Nuremberg Laws mandated that every Jewish female and male assume a Jewish name in addition to their secular ones (*Sarah* for females and *Israel* for males).

But perhaps the level of assimilation can be best understood through a documentary on the Holocaust. In an interview, a survivor related that when one of the Czech transports arrived in Auschwitz, they deluded themselves into believing that their group would be treated differently from the "*Ost Juden*" ("Eastern Jews," as the Germans referred derogatorily to Polish Jewry). But to the Nazis, a Jew was a Jew and the day soon came when this Czech transport was taken to the gas chambers. The man reported that when the people realized their fate, they panicked, and then they broke into spontaneous song. Listening to him, I was convinced that he would go on to say that the song they sang was "*Shema Yisrael*" or "*Ani Ma'Amin*" —"I Believe" — the hymn sung by the faithful as they were taken to their deaths. But, to my shock, this man revealed that they sang a different song — a song that had no roots in our faith — the Czech National Anthem. They sang that song because, in the last moments of their lives they felt a need to give voice to their spirit and they knew no other song. Can there be anything more tragic than to be killed because you are a Jew, and yet not know what it means to be a Jew?

It is with a heavy heart that I relate this story. It is not my intention, G-d forbid, to cast aspersions on their holy memories or on their martyrdom, and we dare not judge them, but I tell this story so that we may learn from the past and not repeat the mistakes of yesterday.

If, G-d forbid, our generation were called upon to sing a song of faith, what song would we sing? And more, how many of our brethren today know their Jewish names? Our names are not simply names — they symbolize our roots, our identity, our connection with our people, our faith. And I haven't even touched on the other two attributes that rendered our ancestors worthy of redemption — the retention of their Jewish dress and their unique Jewish language. Jewish dress is not reflected only by the *tallis* and *yarmulke*, but by modest, dignified clothing for women as well as men. And language means not only prayer and knowledge of the holy tongue, but refraining from speaking lashon hara — gossip — and using hurtful words. I invite you to determine for yourself how our generation is faring in these areas. How different is our generation from those who preceded us? Have we become wiser? Have we learned from our past?

The parchment that the Nazi cut from the Torah scroll referred to "the suffering of Egypt" that will be visited upon us if we abandon G-d's covenant. But what exactly constitutes that suffering? What was the nature of the malady that plagued Egypt? Could it be a spiritual blockage — Pharaoh's hardened heart? As plague after plague descended upon Egypt, Pharaoh continued to remain obdurate — blind and deaf to the call of G-d.

Can there be a disease more devastating than that? If suffering does not result in greater sensitivity, in the realization that we must re-examine our lives and make changes, then there can be no cure and all our pain will have been to no avail.

Suffering can be punitive or therapeutic, healing or destructive — the choice is ours to make. Will we allow the disease of Egypt to continue to plague us? Will we remain indifferent to G-d's imperatives — or will we emerge stronger and better, fortified by our new-found understanding of the purpose of our lives?

So allow me to ask once again — What have we learned from the mistakes of the past? How different are we from those who preceded us? Does the malady of Egypt still plague us?

I know that there are many committed Jews among us, but there were many in pre-Holocaust Europe as well, and that, unfortunately, did not change the reality of the multitudes who assimilated, nor does it change it today.

I write all this with deep pain, for, as a survivor, I know that the greatest, the most righteous, including my own saintly grandparents, aunts, uncles, and cousins, were killed sanctifying the Name of G-d. "They were swifter than eagles and stronger than lions to fulfill the will of their Creator." They were holy people whose kindness had no measure, whose goodness knew no bounds, and whose love of G-d and His people was deeper than the sea. May G-d remember them for good with the righteous of our people.

During the summer months, I often lead groups on a heritage tour of Europe. On one such occasion, we visited Terezienstadt, the infamous concentration camp in Czechoslovakia, and were shown a hidden synagogue that had been built by its doomed inmates. Inscribed on the walls were words from our morning prayers, words that cried out and pierced our hearts.

"Look down from the Heavens and see — we have become an object of scorn and derision among nations... we are regarded as sheep being led to the slaughter to be killed, destroyed, beaten, and humiliated. But despite all this, we have not forgotten Your Name. We beg You not to forget us!"

And despite everything, G-d has not forgotten us and will never forget us. That is His promise engraved in His Torah for all eternity. "... for *HaShem*, your G-d, is a merciful G-d. He will not abandon you nor destroy you, and He will not forget the covenant of your forefathers that He swore to them" (*Deuteronomy* 4:31).

No, G-d did not forget us, and if anyone should know this, it is I.

In February, 2005, I received a call from the White House. Yad V'Shem, the Holocaust Memorial Museum in Jerusalem, had just completed a new wing, and heads of state and other dignitaries were invited to participate in the dedication ceremony. President Bush was unable to attend, and appointed a delegation of seven people to represent him. I was invited to be one of them. I was deeply honored. It was a very moving and inspirational experience.

On our return trip to Andrews Air Force Base in Washington, Fred Zeidman, Chairman of the United States Holocaust Memorial Commission, approached me and said, "Rebbetzin, do you know where you are?"

I looked at him in puzzlement, not quite understanding the meaning of his question.

"Just take a look," he said, pointing to the map on the wall on which our route back to the States was being charted.

I gazed at the map and saw that we were at that moment flying over Germany. "Think about it, Rebbetzin," Fred said. "You, a child of the Holocaust, a survivor of Bergen-Belsen, are flying over Germany in the plane of the President of the United States, and you are coming from Jerusalem!"

For a moment, I choked up and had to swallow hard before I could speak. "Fred," I said, "I think about it every day. When I was a little girl standing for roll call in Bergen-Belsen, with shaven head, dressed in rags, and covered with lice, I didn't think that I would survive, never mind fly over Germany in the plane of the President of the United States coming from Jerusalem!"

But that is our Jewish history. Even as I flew over Germany, we shall fly over all our enemies. G-d does not forget us.

15

When the Tests Are Miracles

The Talmud relates that after the destruction of our Holy Temple, Rabbi Akiva and the Sages of Israel were walking on the streets of Jerusalem. As they came to the Temple Mount, they beheld a devastating sight. There, where the Sanctuary had once stood in majesty and splendor, where the Holy of Holies had been, were only ruins, and wild foxes were roaming about.

The Sages broke down and wept.

"Woe is us," they wailed, "that we have seen this with our own eyes."

But Rabbi Akiva did not weep. Instead, he smiled.

"How can you smile at such a time?" his colleagues asked, shocked.

"I smile," Rabbi Akiva answered, "because today I have seen the fulfillment of prophecy, for the same prophet who foretold the destruction also foretold that the Temple shall be rebuilt. The same prophet who prophesied our exile, also prophesied that we shall return to Jerusalem in joy. And so I smile, for now that the first part of our prophecy has come to pass, the second part will surely come to be."

"Akiva," the Sages declared, "you have comforted us."

That smile of Rabbi Akiva kept our people going throughout the centuries, and even in the darkest moments, we knew that G-d did not forget us.

From the ashes of Auschwitz we rose like a phoenix, and, by the grace of G-d, reinvented ourselves as a nation. We rebuilt the Torah academies that were once the pride and glory of European Jewry and raised a new generation of sons and daughters to live by the Law of G-d.

After almost two thousand years, we returned to our ancient land, and we, the dry bones of the Holocaust, were joined by Jews from the four corners of the world. They came from the most remote places — places where we were unaware that Jews even existed — the sick, the lame, the battered, the downtrodden, the poor, and the broken-hearted — they all came. And also the strong, the wise, the learned, the successful, the idealistic. Together, we formed a mighty company and were witness to the beginning of the fulfillment of the prophetic ingathering of the exiles.

"Fear not, My people, Israel, for I am with you.

"I will bring your seed from the east and gather them from the west, and I will say to the north, 'give up,' and to the south, 'Keep not back, bring My sons from afar and My daughters from the ends of the earth" (*Isaiah* 43:5-6).

At the genesis of our history, the Land of Israel was a paradise on earth, and we lovingly tilled her soil. When we were taken into exile, G-d made a promise that the land would revert to a wasteland and await our homecoming. Many nations tried to settle her, to rebuild her ruins, and bring forth her fruit, but the land would not yield to any of them and stubbornly remained a desert of thistles and stones. Throughout the long, painful centuries of our exile, we were denied the right to own land and all but forgot how to work the soil, and yet, when we returned, overnight, we converted that desert into a garden; planted orchards, vineyards, and forests; built highways and cities; and were witness to the miracle of a dormant land come to life again.

"I will restore the fortune of My people, Israel, and they shall rebuild the ruined cities and inhabit them. They shall plant vineyards and drink the wine and they shall plant gardens and eat the fruit" (*Amos* 9:14).

During our infancy as a nation we defeated mighty kingdoms and were led in battle by valorous men like Joshua and David, but during our long torturous exile, we became fair game, to be reviled, attacked, and killed, and were denied the right to defend ourselves. And yet overnight, we, the battered remnant of the Holocaust, who had long forgotten how to fight, enlisted a powerful army and triumphed over more than one hundred million Arabs who had sworn to drive us into the sea. The awesomeness of it all should have given us pause, should have made us realize that G-d did not forget us, but even as we were blind to the wake-up calls of suffering, *we were even more blind to the wake-up calls of blessings and victory.*

In days of darkness, there are always those who turn to G-d, but in times of prosperity and success, it is easy to take G-d's blessings for granted. It is easy to become arrogant, easy to declare G-d's miracles "ordinary events," easy to delude ourselves into believing that "my strength and my might did all this" (*Deuteronomy* 8:17).

Time and again throughout this book, I have pointed out that nothing that occurs in life is a random event, that that which we would term *coincidence* is also part of G-d's master plan. There are times, however, when the hand of G-d is hidden, but there are other moments when it is easier to discern His providence. Such was the time of the Six Day War. Not since Biblical times did we see miracles such as those we witnessed during that period. The combined forces of the Arab nations united to annihilate Israel. But it wasn't only the Arabs — former Nazi officers who had fled Germany at the end of WW II were ensconced in Cairo and Damascus and only too willing to share their Holocaust expertise. Russia not only encouraged and supported the Arabs, but provided them with the most sophisticated weaponry, as well as "advisors" to train them. Those were the days of the Cold War and the Communist countries eagerly supplied the Arabs with all the arms they needed. DeGaulle of France openly endorsed the Arabs and refused to deliver planes that Israel had paid for; England mouthed empty platitudes (they had already done their damage by training and equipping the crack Jordanian Arab Legion). The U.S. was mired in the war in Vietnam and President Lyndon Johnson told Abba Eban, the Israeli Foreign Minister, to practice restraint, while the State Department advised that U.S. involvement be limited to the framework of the UN. In short, the entire world was arrayed against Israel, and the Arabs were armed to the teeth.

Conventional wisdom saw Israel's defeat as a foregone conclusion. How could tiny Israel, overwhelmingly outnumbered, surrounded by enemies, prevail when no nation in the entire world was willing to help her. Once again, there was silence as the world readied itself for another Holocaust. But *we, the Jewish people, were not silent*, and in an unprecedented moment of unity turned to G-d in prayer and supplication.

I recall those days vividly. I remember how Jews who never went to synagogue, even on the High Holy Days, came to pray, and this held true not only for our community, but for Jews throughout the world. And more, we, the nation that had always been splintered, polarized, and divided, put aside our differences and became one in our love for Israel. Lines formed in front of every Israeli embassy, volunteers by the thousands offered their resources, their strength, their very lives.

In Israel itself, the nation responded above and beyond the call of duty. Debts were suspended and disputes were forgiven. Most adults were at the front. Youngsters took over the running of the social services and those who were in distant lands returned home to do battle for their country.

And then, the miracle occurred. In six lightning days, Israel vanquished all her foes and saw her enemies flee before her. The stories of the many miracles that took place in those days are legion and have yet to be recorded in the annals of history.

My brother-in-law, Rabbi Amram HaLevi Jungreis, of blessed memory, a great Torah scholar, who, prior to his appointment as a rabbi in Israel, was the Chief Rabbi of Budapest, wrote a letter to us during that time that I shall never forget.

In his congregation was a Yemenite family with eight sons, and all eight volunteered to fight. Their mother, beside herself with worry, consulted a sage and begged him to advise her where she might best pray for the safe return of her children.

"At which grave should I knock? Whom should I awaken from slumber? Who will be the righteous messenger to carry my plea to G-d's throne?" she begged to know.

The sage pondered her question, and then instructed her not to pray at any grave, but to go home and await her children.

"Know, my dear woman," he told her, "the graves of the holy souls are *all empty*. G-d has sent them forth to lead your sons, to watch over them and assure their safe homecoming."

When the war began on June 5, 1967, the miracles quickly unfolded. The Israeli Air Force went forth on a hazardous mission. The Egyptians had prepared hundreds of missiles for their attack on Israel, but before their planes could take off or their missiles could be launched, Israel destroyed the combined air power of Egypt, Jordan, Syria, and Iraq! Israel, with her outdated French Super Mystere fighters, destroyed the most sophisticated Russian MIGs on the ground.

Many tried to explain the Israel Air Force's success rationally: "The Israelis flew below the Egyptian radar" — "Egyptian intelligence reports on the advancing Israeli aircraft never reached the Egyptian Commander in Chief" — "The night before Israel attacked, there was a big bash for the Egyptian brass, and early the next morning, the Egyptians met with a distinguished Iraqi delegation, so when Israel struck, the Egyptian High Command was not at its post," and so on.

But miracles do not mean that G-d has to overturn the laws of nature or create something that never before existed. On the contrary, miracles are part of G-d's architectural plan. On the sixth day, as G-d was about to complete His creation, He added supernatural events, *making miracles part of nature*. Nature itself is a miracle in which G-d's hand is constantly manifest. The very fact that Egyptian radar did not detect the Israeli planes, that intelligence reports failed to reach the proper ears, that commanding officers were busy partying on the night prior to the attack and were again diverted the following morning by a high level meeting with Iraqis, were all *coincidences that were not coincidences, but miracles of G-d.*

I have often had discussions with people who insisted that the miracle of the splitting of the Reed Sea was not a miracle at all, but *low* tide. Instead of arguing, I would tell them that, if the tide was

Life Is a Test

low at the precise moment that the Jewish people had to cross, and suddenly rose again when the Egyptians entered the sea, that was miracle enough for me!

Call it what you will, but all the well-laid plans of the Arabs, the Russians, and their hate-mongering supporters, were foiled. As in days of yore, when Pharaoh and his host drowned in the sea while Israel went forth to the Promised Land, so too, Nasser, the modern Pharaoh, and his cohorts drowned and the Jewish people went forth to reclaim their ancient land.

When G-d's miracles are hidden in natural events, when we are far removed from spirituality, miracles can be dismissed as "luck," "coincidence," or just smart moves made by clever people.

As generations move farther away from that awesome spiritual moment when G-d spoke at Sinai, they also become less spiritual, less capable of believing in His involvement in their daily lives. But, as I said earlier, nature itself is no less miraculous than the supernatural. This concept is reinforced throughout our Torah and prayers. For example, in the second blessing of *Shemoneh Esrei*, the Silent Meditation, in which we praise G-d for bringing souls back to life, we also pronounce the blessing for rain, teaching us that one is no more difficult for G-d than the other.

There is a famous story in the Talmud about Rabbi Chanina's daughter, who was heartbroken when she discovered that she had mistakenly bought vinegar rather than oil for the Sabbath lamps.

"Don't worry, my daughter," the Rabbi assured her. "The same G-d Who decrees that oil should burn, can command that vinegar should do so as well." Hence the popular Yiddish saying, "If G-d wills it, a broom can shoot, but if not, even the most powerful weapon is of no avail."

A close study of the Torah will reveal that supernatural miracles are always couched in the natural: G-d feeds us manna in the desert, but He sandwiches the manna between two layers of dew so that their freshness appears natural. Prior to his death, G-d tells Moses to ascend to the mountain so that he may behold the entire land of Israel and the future history of our people.

But why? Why did Moses have to ascend to the mountain top to see all that? After all, it wasn't the height of the mountain that granted him vision. Nevertheless, the Almighty wished for Moses to ascend, thus clothing the supernatural in the natural.

And even the oft-quoted miracle of the splitting of the Reed Sea — this, too, was presented in the framework of the natural. The Torah tells us that an east wind blew the entire night prior to the onset of that miracle. Now surely, G-d could have split the sea without the east wind blowing. Nevertheless, G-d wanted us to understand that nature is equally miraculous.

Once we were exiled from our Holy Land, however, the equation changed. G-d's miracles became hidden, and the Purim story is a prime example of that. At first glance, there is nothing miraculous about the events that unfold in the Megillah. Everything could be attributed to natural causes, and to add to the enigma, G-d's Name is not even mentioned in the Megillah. Yet we know that the story of Purim is a miracle of colossal dimensions, so much so that our Sages declared it a holiday for all eternity, when we proclaim G-d's *miracles* with rejoicing, gratitude, and thanksgiving.

If, however, someone wishes to take the path of the agnostic, he can remain blind to G-d's role in history and deny that there is anything miraculous in that which unfolds before his very eyes. The choice is his or hers to make. Thus, if you wish, you can see the miracles inherent in the survival of the Jewish people — the ingathering of the exiles, the redemption of the soil, Israel's stunning victories in battle — or you can choose to ignore them all and declare them to be "ordinary events."

Having said all this, I must point out that our fate as Jews is not contingent on miracles, but on *commitment* — Torah study, service and sacrifice. Whether we see G-d's beneficence or feel the sting of His rod, our loyalty remains constant.

If so, you might ask, what is the purpose of miracles? There are two popular words in the Hebrew language for miracles, *"nes"* and *"os."* Literally translated, *"nes"* means a *"banner"* and *"os"* means a *"sign."* Miracles serve as banners and signs through which G-d's Holy Name is glorified and sanctified — banners and signs that inspire people to sing His praises. And that was accomplished above and beyond all expectations during the Six Day War. The banners flew high, and we all saw the signs. There was a great Jewish spiritual awakening throughout the world — even if, shortly afterward, we reverted to our old ways. *But those signs are there even if we have lost sight of them,* and it is that which I would like to recall for us and for future generations in this, my concluding chapter.

Bearing all this in mind, let us review some highlights of those six lightning days.

In the desert, the Egyptians had positioned more than eight hundred of the most powerful Soviet-made tanks, while the Israelis had outdated World War II-era tanks, trucks, and station wagons.

The Israeli tanks advanced across the Sinai during the night, but halted when they reached a minefield and lost one of their armored troop carriers. At dawn, they came upon a whole brigade of Soviet tanks behind which were large self-propelled guns — a formidable, frightening sight. How could the Israelis possibly overcome them? But incredibly, the tanks facing them in the desert did not make a move — the Egyptians, fleeing for their lives, had abandoned them. As a matter of fact, they ran so quickly, that they left the desert littered with countless boots. Captured Egyptians, questioned as to why they ran, responded that they saw *mysterious Biblical figures walking in the desert.*

Delusions, coincidence, or miracles? You decide.

Another general in the armored corps reported that when his men confronted the Soviet T34 tanks, they were overcome by fear. The Israeli tanks were no match for these behemoths. But then they noticed that an auxiliary gas tank was attached to every tank — standard procedure during maneuvers to insure that they would not run out of fuel. For some inexplicable reason, the enemy had failed to remove those containers of gas. The Israeli gunners aimed for these gas tanks, and as each was hit, the tank went up in flames.

Coincidence that the Egyptians abandoned their armor? Coincidence that they fled in terror? Coincidence that they left their spare fuel containers attached to the tanks? Or miracles? Again, the choice is yours.

In the north, Israel had to confront Syria, whose forces were also equipped by the Russians. The Syrians presented a formidable challenge. For over nineteen years, Israeli citizens in the valley below, had been sitting ducks for their bullets and Katyusha rockets. The Syrians had the high ground, the Golan Heights. Looking down on Israel from the vantage of their well-fortified mountain bunkers, the Syrians were confident of their invincibility. They could attack without fear of retaliation. Furthermore, their Russian "advisors" taught the Syrians to buttress their positions by planting thousands of mines.

The Syrians had the most advanced military hardware as well as an unlimited supply of Katyusha rockets and T55 tanks equipped for night battle.

To this very day, if you visit the Golan heights and see what our soldiers had to overcome, the sheer impossibility of penetrating their fortifications and ascending the mined, twisting paths, must make you realize that Israel's victory was nothing less than the Hand of G-d.

The liberation of Judea and Samaria, known as the West Bank, was equally miraculous. When Israeli soldiers arrived in Nablus, the

Biblical city of Shechem where Joseph is buried, they took it without a shot being fired. As they entered the city, the Arabs greeted them with smiles and applause. Only later did they discover the reason for this unusual welcome. The residents mistook the Israelis for Iraqi replacements. By the time they realized that they were Israelis, the city had been taken. Coincidence or miracle? Call it what you wish — it's the Hand of G-d.

But nothing can compare to the miracle of Jerusalem. In order, however, for us to fully perceive the awesomeness of that miracle, some history is in order.

As a little girl in Hungary, I knew very little of world geography. I had never heard of Paris, New York, or London, but I knew all about Jerusalem. The very words evoked a song in my soul and joy in my heart. It is written that Jerusalem received her name from the Almighty G-d Himself. It is comprised of two words: *yira,* to see, and *shalem,* which means peace, complete. When the patriarch Abraham ascended to Mount Moriah with his son Isaac, and perceived its sanctity, he proclaimed, "This is the place where G-d was seen!" And indeed, in Jerusalem you can feel and see holiness — you can feel G-d. It is like no other city. Throughout our long and painful exile, we never forgot her, but sang the immortal words of David, "If I forget you O Jerusalem, let my right hand forget its cunning...."

And Jerusalem, the Holy City, never forgot us, her children, but waited in solitude for our return.

In the early fifties, I made my first trip to Israel. I went to study and to teach newly arrived immigrants from Yemen. In those days, Jerusalem was a divided city. To see the Holy Wall in the Old City, we had to climb the tower of the YMCA building located opposite the King David Hotel, and there, armed with a pair of binoculars, we were able to catch a glimpse. The Old City was occupied by the Jordanian army, which savagely destroyed many of the gravesites on the Mount of Olives and used the monuments to pave roads and build latrines. Officially, Jordan had agreed that Jews would have the right to pray at the Wall, the only remnant of our ancient Temple, but they never kept that promise and defiled that holy site with refuse and the dung of donkeys.

Of all the Arab armies, Jordan's Arab Legion was the best trained and fiercest. Moreover, the border with Jordan was the most difficult to defend, so it was no surprise that, when King Hussein's army first attacked, the Israeli military was convinced that the shots were just tokens to accommodate Nasser, and that Hussein would not risk war. But Jordan kept pounding away, its artillery and bullets raining upon Jerusalem. Still, Israel requested the UN Truce Supervision Office to convey to Jordan assurances of peace. But it was all to no avail, and Israel had no choice but to open a second front. The Jordanians possessed hundreds of Patton tanks, and tens of thousands of Legionnaires, powerful warriors, equipped with the most sophisticated weapons, who were prepared to fight to the end. The battles were fierce and savage, made all the more complicated by orders given to Israeli paratroopers to avoid damaging the many sites in the Old City. Many brave young men were injured or lost their lives — the sacrifice was great, but so were the miracles.

The Holy City was not prepared for battle. There were hardly any bomb shelters to protect the civilian population. Shells fell and did not explode, and many that fell and did explode caused no injury. A shell landed on Shaarei Tzedek Hospital's baby nursery. Fearing the worst, nurses rushed in to save the infants, but miraculously, they were all unharmed. A shell penetrated the roof of the Mirrer Yeshivah but did not explode.

Over the centuries, Jerusalem was ravaged and sacked many times, but G-d made a promise that the Wall, the remnant of the Holy Temple, would stand eternally and bear witness to the homecoming of our people. And now, almost two thousand years later, the moment had come. I have read countless reports from journalists and soldiers who participated in the battle for Jerusalem, and all their stories had one focus — "the Wall."

Moshe Amirav, a paratrooper, describes the first minutes at the Wall: "Forward! Forward! Hurriedly, we pushed our way through the Magreb Gate, and suddenly we stopped, thunderstruck. There it was, before our eyes! Gray and massive, silent and restrained. The Western Wall!

"Slowly, slowly, I began to approach the Wall in fear and trembling, like a pious cantor going to the lectern to lead the prayers. I approached it as the messenger of my father and my grandfather, of my great-grandfather and of all the generations in all the exiles who had never merited seeing it — and so they had sent me to represent them. Somebody recited the festive blessing, 'Blessed are You, Oh L-rd our G-d, King of the Universe, Who has kept us alive and maintained us and brought us to this time.' I put my hand on the stones and wept, but the tears that started to flow were not my tears. They were the tears of all Israel, tears of hope and prayer, tears of Hasidic tunes, tears of Jewish dances, tears that scorched and burned the heavy gray stone."

And who can forget the photograph of our soldiers standing in awe — just looking up at the Wall? And who can forget the report of the IDF radio announcer: "…Suddenly, we recognized the familiar voice of the commander of the paratroops brigade, Colonel Mordechai 'Motta' Gur, giving orders to the battalion commanders to occupy the Old City: 'Attention, all battalion commanders! We are sitting on the mountain range that looks down on the Old City, and are about to enter it. The Old City of Jerusalem that all generations have been dreaming about and striving toward. We will be the first to enter it.'

"With us on the roof," the announcer continued, "was General Shlomo Goren, at that time, the Chief Rabbi of the Israeli Army. Rabbi Goren informed Gur over the walkie talkie that he was on his way to meet him so as to be among the first to enter the Old City. As far as I remember, we were the only ones in the whole area running without helmets or weapons. Goren was armed only with a *shofar* and a prayer book and we carried only a tape recorder and a knapsack filled with batteries and rolls of recording tape.

"We ran, while trying to stay as close as we could to the Old City Wall to our right, but exposed to the sniper fire coming from the Mount of Olives on our left. As we ran, we passed two lines of paratroopers who were progressing carefully toward the Lions Gate. Goren was determined to get to the head of the line as quickly as possible. At the top of the street leading to the Lions Gate, we passed a still-smoking Jordanian bus. We stopped only at the Gate itself, which was blocked by an Israeli Sherman tank that had gotten stuck in the entrance. We climbed over the tank and entered into the Old City.

"Now the excitement reached its peak. Goren did not stop blowing the *shofar* and reciting prayers. His enthusiasm infected the soldiers, and from every direction came cries of 'Amen!'"

The *shofar* was sounded in Jerusalem and its call reached Jewish hearts in the four corners of the world. The effect was magical. Our people became spiritually rejuvenated. Even those who had never believed, those who were hardened agnostics, felt something in their hearts. The Wall called them, and despite themselves, they felt a need to respond, to touch its stones, to place a note with a prayer in its crevices, to pour out their hearts and cry.

My husband and I made a decision. We knew that no matter what, we too had to be there, and so we took our four small children and traveled to Jerusalem. The city was congested with people

— there wasn't a hotel room to be had. For a moment, I panicked, but then my husband reminded me of the teaching of our Talmud: In Jerusalem, no one ever complained of discomfort, in the City of G-d, every man had a place, everyone was welcome.

It was Friday, *Erev Shabbos*, when we arrived, and there was no time to lose — the Queen Sabbath was quickly approaching and the entire city was readying herself for the arrival of the royal guest. Everywhere, stores were closing and public transportation was coming to a halt. As the siren was sounded, a stillness descended on the Holy City.

Suddenly, scores of people spilled into the streets. They came from every direction: young and old, men and women, Israelis and tourists, students and soldiers, pious Chassidim in long black coats and westernized Jews in business suits. They spoke in many tongues, espoused many ideas, and wondrously, they all merged into one. All of them were rushing, running to the same place, to the Wall.

We too, melted into the crowd. We didn't know our way, but we followed the others. My heart beat faster and I clutched my children's hands. I saw tears in my husband's eyes. We were in Jerusalem.

We made our way through the dark alleyways. My son tugged at my sleeve. "Eema," he asked, "how did our soldiers do it? How did they liberate the city? How did they get through these gates, these alleys?"

"Jerusalem's time has come," I answered, "and G-d Himself opened the gates."

Then suddenly, without warning, the Wall was before us, more majestic than I could ever have imagined. We could not speak; there were only tears. For two thousand years we had waited for this moment. Our ancestors had prayed for this day. What would they not have given to stand here, even for a fleeting second, and yet they were denied the privilege. How strange that our generation, which was unworthy and wanting in faith, was the one to stand here in the presence of sanctity.

I looked up at the Heavens and searched for my grandfather. Surely the angels had gathered his ashes from Auschwitz and brought them as an offering to this very spot.

"*Zeide, Zeide,*" I cried into the night, "please walk with me, for here I cannot stand alone."

All around us, people were praying and our voices became one with theirs. I poured out my soul. I looked up at the greenery sprouting from the crevices. Strange, I thought to myself, how these little branches grow without being watered. But then I saw the people around me and I understood from whence the branches received their nourishment. They were watered by the tears of a nation that had been waiting for two thousand years.

Walking back to our hotel we met a young soldier who had been among those who liberated Jerusalem. He told us about his best friend who had fallen on the Temple Mount on the very spot where once, long ago, the Altar had stood.

"I ran to my friend," he told us. "I tried to help him, but it was too late. I broke down and wept, and as I cried, I heard an eerie sound. It was the braying of a donkey echoing in the night. The donkey actually seemed to sob with me, crying in pain as if imploring to be allowed to carry Messiah into the Holy City."

Never before in the annals of mankind did a war last only six days.

Coincidence? *Or was the seventh day begging to come? — The seventh day that is all Sabbath, the day that is Messiah.*

For a very brief moment, it appeared as if our people might just understand and be prepared to respond to this awesome challenge. But all too soon, the magic of the moment evaporated, and once again, *we failed the test.*

We reverted to our old ways — we congratulated ourselves on our success and came to take all those miracles for granted. *Those of us who lived it have forgotten, and those who were not yet born were never touched by it.*

The fundamental law of Jewish survival stipulates that we cannot assimilate or become "like all the other nations of the world." This law holds true not only in the countries of our exile, *but in Israel as well.* G-d did not bring us back to our ancient land so that we might become like all the other nations and convert Jerusalem into New York, Paris, or London.

Just consider the tragedy that has befallen us. To live in the Land of the Patriarchs and yet spurn their legacy; to speak Hebrew impeccably, and yet not know how to pray; to live in the Land of G-d, and yet lack faith in Him.

We have failed the test.

But even if we failed the test, even if we forgot G-d, He does not forget us. His covenant and love are eternal and He will continue to call us. If we are blind to His miracles, He will find other ways to awaken us. So it is that since those heady days of the Six Day War, we have suffered many painful wake-up calls, but sadly, we have remained impervious to all. Nevertheless, G-d continues to call.

Many of us have heard the call, many are committed and live genuine Torah Jewish lives, but there are still so, so many who have yet to hear the call.

As we enter the final stages of our history, we have a choice — to stand straight and tall, to embrace with open arms and loving hearts our G-d-given covenant and sing His praise, or to continue to be blind and obdurate and delude ourselves into believing that we can live our lives without Him. But even as we stumble through the darkness, He will be holding our hand. He will not let go. He will not forget us. He will not forsake us. So let us return to Him with willing hearts, with love. *Let us pass our test.*

Epilogue

A Personal Note

*I*t's time to say goodbye, and that's always difficult. There is so much more that I would have liked to impart, so much more that I would have liked to share with you.

We have a teaching, "Words that emanate from the heart will enter another's heart." I wrote this book from my heart, and I hope and pray that you have accepted it as such — a gift of love.

Whenever I am invited to speak in a foreign country, I always try to set aside at least one day to visit the gravesites of the holy sages buried there. This became a formidable challenge when I visited Russia and the Ukraine, for the distances are vast and travel can be complicated and hazardous. Nevertheless, I was determined to pray at as many gravesites as possible. We started out at the crack of dawn, but even so, by the time we arrived at our last stop, Berditchev, the home of the *tzaddik*, the saintly Rabbi Levi Yitzchok (1740-1810), it was almost midnight. Despite the late hour, Rabbi and Rebbetzin Shlomo Breuer, who at the behest of the Skverer Rebbe re-established a synagogue there, welcomed us in the true tradition of our Father Abraham. A beautifully set table with a delicious, hot, home-made meal awaited us, which, I must say, we deeply appreciated after a long, tiring day of travel. By the time Rabbi Breuer showed us the way to the *ohel* (the tomb built over the Rebbe's grave), it was way past midnight, an eerie but powerful time to pray at a grave. The "Berditchiver" as Rabbi Levi Yitzchok was called, was renowned for his unconditional love and devotion to every Jew. His loyalty was such that he didn't hesitate to take on G-d Himself to champion their cause. He authored many beautiful Yiddish prayers that reflect the heart, the soul and the yearnings of our people. One of them, *"G-t fun Avrohom,"* he wrote especially for women. It is said every Saturday night as the Sabbath departs, and is a plea for a good, blessed week. To this day, many women, including myself, recite it, and it can be found in every ArtScroll prayer book.

I was especially anxious to pray at the grave of the *tzaddik*, because on every front, our people were beset by terrible problems and we needed the Rebbe to intercede on our behalf, to act as our emissary and present our case to *HaShem*. As if the Berditchever had anticipated our visit, on the wall of the *ohel*, we found a Yiddish prayer that he had composed — a prayer that spoke to us and said it all. I started to read it aloud, but then had to stop because my tears were choking me. I committed the words to memory, and I am pleased to share them with you.

"*Ribbonoh Shel Olam* — Almighty G-d — Let us make a *deal*. I will give You all our sins — sins of negligence, sins of spite and rebelliousness, sins encompassing all possible transgressions — and if You will ask me what You must give me in return for all this, *Oy! Tateh Zeese*, Oy! my sweet Father, I will tell You: You will give us *forgiveness!* — *forgiveness* that is total and complete, *forgiveness* that will repair all damages, *forgiveness* that will wipe the slate clean and enable Your children to start life anew. *Oy! Tateh Zeese.*"

I have recounted all this because, as I have said throughout this book, *life is a test*, and tests are often very difficult. To each person, his/her test is the most challenging, the most painful, the most overwhelming. More often than not, we fail our tests and give up on ourselves. But we should never throw in the towel. The Berdichever Rebbe showed us the way. He taught us that it's actually possible to "cut a deal" with G-d and *start life anew*, for G-d is not an impersonal Supreme Being, He is *Tateh Zeese* — our *sweet Father*, Who wants us to pass our tests, Who wants us to fulfill the purpose for which He created us and walk in honor and dignity on the road of life. Lovingly, He pleads with us. "Make an opening *the size of the eye of a needle, and I will open for you a doorway the size of a banquet hall.*" We need only indicate to G-d that we want to change — that we want to come closer to Him, that we want to improve ourselves — and He will do the rest.

There are no barriers between ourselves and G-d. There is no act or deed that could consign us to doom. *The only wall that exists between ourselves and our "sweet Father" is the one that we ourselves build in our hearts and minds.* If we will it, each and every one of us has the ability to make a difference in our personal and in our nation's destiny. We need only call out to G-d and He will walk us through all our tests, from the most trivial to the most difficult. So never despair — never give up. Be assured that G-d knows you better than you know yourself, and He will never challenge you with tests that are beyond you.

Finally, I would like to close with my own plea to G-d. Not too long ago, my brothers and I were reminiscing about our Holocaust experiences, and we agreed that the one word that stood out most in our minds from those years was "*Schnell.*" The Nazi were constantly yelling, "*Schnell! Schnell!*" — "*Quickly! quickly!*" — *Quickly,* we had to depart from our homes; *quickly,* we had to climb into the cattle cars; *quickly,* we had to march from the railroad station to Bergen Belsen, *quickly,* we had to ready ourselves for roll call every morning, and *schnell! schnell! quickly,* they shoved our people into the gas chambers.

Oy! Tateh Zeese, if it was so urgent for those evil ones to *quickly* bring about our demise, then surely, Almighty G-d, our *Tateh Zeese,* it should be even more urgent for *You to bring us, Schnell! Schnell!* — *Quickly! Quickly!* our redemption speedily in our own day.

We, Your children, are very tired — two thousand years is a very long time.

With love of Torah and Israel,

Esther Jungreis

Rebbetzin Esther Jungreis

may be reached at:

The Hineni Heritage Center

232 West End Avenue

New York, NY 10023

Telephone: 212-496-1660

Fax: 212-496-1908

E-mail: hineni@hineni.org